ERIC

Bibliographical note:

this facsimile has been made from a copy in the
Beinecke Library of Yale University
(Ip.F243.858E)

ERIC, OR LITTLE BY LITTLE.

ERIC

OR

LITTLE BY LITTLE

A TALE OF ROSLYN SCHOOL.

BY

FREDERIC W. FARRAR,

FELLOW OF TRINITY COLLEGE, CAMBRIDGE.

'Tis one thing to be tempted, Escalus,
Another thing to fall.
Measure for Measure, Act ii. Scene 1

EDINBURGH:

ADAM AND CHARLES BLACK, NORTH BRIDGE.

MDCCCLVIII.

PRINTED BY R. AND R. CLARK, EDINBURGH.

TO

THE RIGHT REVEREND

THE LORD BISHOP OF CALCUTTA,

THIS STORY OF SCHOOL LIFE

IS

AFFECTIONATELY DEDICATED

IN

GRATEFUL MEMORY OF THE PAST.

PREFACE.

———◆———

THIS tale was written during the few leisure hours of a profession in which " ne otium quidem otiosum est," and I am well aware that it is not free from literary and artistic faults. But as these faults are not the result of carelessness, and still less of that indifference which looks lightly on the publication of a book, I would earnestly deprecate that severe criticism which magnifies a trivial inaccuracy into a grave error, and a solecism into something like a crime. In all humility I claim for the story a higher merit than that of style,— the merit of truthfulness. If the pictures here painted are not always such as it would have been most pleasant to contemplate, they owe the darker shades of their colouring not to fancy, but to life. To the best of my belief, the things here dealt with are not theories, but realities; not imaginations, but facts.

Even had the book been anonymous, as was originally intended, it would have been necessary to state distinctly that no place of education can be identified with Roslyn. The scenery, indeed, with which it is surrounded, may be recognised by many; but I hope that such readers will let their discovery end there. If not, they will be doing great injustice to a school of which the arrangements *entirely* differ from those herein described, and of which, as of the valued friends connected with it, I have no wish to speak except in terms of cordial eulogy and sincere recommendation.

F. W. F.

CONTENTS.

PART I.

PART II.

PART 1.

CHAPTER I.

CHILDHOOD.

"Ah dear delights, that o'er my soul
On memory's wing like shadows fly!
Ah flowers that Joy from Eden stole,
While Innocence stood laughing by."—COLERIDGE.

"HURRAH! hurrah! hurrah!" cried a young boy, as he capered vigorously about, and clapped his hands, "Papa and mamma will be home in a week now, and then we shall stay here a little time, and *then*, and *then*, I shall go to school."

The last words were enunciated with immense importance, as he stopped his impromptu dance before the chair where his sober cousin Fanny was patiently working at her crochet; but she did not look so much affected by the announcement as the boy seemed to demand, so he again exclaimed, "And then, Miss Fanny, I shall go to school."

"Well, Eric," said Fanny, raising her matter-of-

fact quiet face from her endless work, " I doubt, dear,
whether you will talk of it with quite as much joy a
year hence."

" O ay, Fanny, that's just like you to say so;
you're always talking and prophesying ; but never
mind, I'm going to school, so, hurrah! hurrah! hurrah!"
and he again began his capering,—jumping over the
chairs, trying to vault the tables, singing and dancing
with an exuberance of delight, till, catching a sudden
sight of his little spaniel Flo, he sprang through the
open window into the garden, and disappeared behind
the trees of the shrubbery; but Fanny still heard his
clear, ringing, silvery laughter, as he continued his
games in the summer air.

She looked up from her work after he had gone,
and sighed.   In spite of the sunshine and balm of the
bright weather, a sense of heaviness and foreboding
oppressed her.   Everything looked smiling and beautiful, and there was an almost irresistible contagion in
the mirth of her young cousin, but still she could not
help feeling sad.   It was not merely that she would
have to part with Eric, " but that bright boy," thought
Fanny, " what will become of him?   I have heard
strange things of schools ; oh, if he should be spoilt and
ruined, what misery it would be.   Those baby lips, that
pure young heart, a year may work sad change in their
words and thoughts!"   She sighed again, and her eyes
glistened as she raised them upwards, and breathed a
silent prayer.

She loved the boy dearly, and had taught him from his earliest years. In most things she found him an apt pupil. Truthful, ingenuous, quick, he would acquire almost without effort any subject that interested him. and a word was often enough to bring the impetuous blood to his cheeks, in a flush of pride or indignation. He required the gentlest teaching, and had received it, while his mind seemed cast in such a mould of stainless honour, that he avoided most of the faults to which children are prone. But he was far from blameless. He was proud to a fault; he well knew that few of his fellows had gifts like his, either of mind or person, and his fair face often shewed a clear impression of his own superiority. His passion, too, was imperious, and though it always met with prompt correction, his cousin had latterly found it difficult to subdue. She felt, in a word, that he was outgrowing her rule. Beyond a certain age no boy of spirit can be safely guided by a woman's hand alone.

Eric Williams was now twelve years old. His father was a civilian in India, and was returning on furlough to England, after a long absence. Eric had been born in India, but had been sent to England by his parents at an early age, in charge of a lady friend of his mother. The parting, which had been agony to his father and mother, he was too young to feel; indeed the moment itself passed by without his being conscious of it. They took him on board the ship, and, after a time, gave him a hammer and some nails to play with.

These had always been to him a supreme delight, and while he hammered away, Mr. and Mrs. Williams, denying themselves, for the child's sake, even one more tearful embrace, went ashore in the boat and left him. It was not till the ship sailed that he was told he would not see them again for a long, long time.   Poor child, his tears and cries were wild when he first understood it; but the sorrows of four years old are very transient, and before a week was over, little Eric felt almost reconciled to his position, and had become the universal pet and plaything of every one on board, from Captain Broadland down to the cabin boy, with whom he very soon struck up an acquaintance.   Yet twice a day at least, he would shed a tear, as he lisped his little prayer, kneeling at Mrs. Munro's knee, and asked God " to bless his dear dear father and mother, and make him a good boy."

When Eric arrived in England, he was intrusted to the care of a widowed aunt, whose daughter, Fanny, had the main charge of his early teaching.   At first, the wayward little Indian seemed likely to form no accession to the quiet household, but he soon became its brightest ornament and pride.   Everything was in his favour at the pleasant home of Mrs. Trevor.   He was treated with motherly kindness and tenderness, yet firmly checked when he went wrong.   From the first he had a well-spring of strength against temptation, in the long letters which every mail brought from his parents; and all his childish affections were entwined round the fancied image of a brother born since he had left India. In his bed-room there hung a cherub's head, drawn in pencil by his mother, and this picture was inextricably identified in his imagination with his " little brother Vernon." He loved it dearly, and whenever he went astray, nothing weighed on his mind so strongly as the thought, that if he were naughty he would teach little Vernon to be naughty too when he came home.

And Nature also—wisest, gentlest, holiest of teachers —was with him in his childhood. Fairholm Cottage, where his aunt lived, was situated in the beautiful Vale of Ayrton, and a clear stream ran through the valley at the bottom of Mrs. Trevor's orchard. Eric loved this stream, and was always happy as he roamed by its side, or over the low green hills and scattered dingles, which lent unusual loveliness to every winding of its waters. He was allowed to go about a good deal by himself, and it did him good. He grew up fearless, and self-dependent, and never felt the want of amusement. The garden and orchard supplied him a theatre for endless games and romps, sometimes with no other companion than his cousin and his dog, and sometimes with the few children of his own age whom he knew in the hamlet. Very soon he forgot all about India; it only hung like a distant golden haze on the horizon of his memory. When asked if he remembered it, he would say thoughtfully, that in dreams and at some other times, he saw a little child, with long curly hair,

running about in a little garden, near a great river, in
a place where the air was very bright. But whether
the little boy was himself or his brother Vernon, whom
he had never seen, he couldn't quite tell.

But above all, it was happy for Eric that his training was religious and enlightened. With Mrs. Trevor
and her daughter, religion was not a system but a habit
—not a theory, but a continued act of life. All was
simple, sweet, and unaffected about their charity and
their devotions. They loved God, and they did all the
good they could to those around them. The floating
gossip and ill-nature of the little village never affected
them; it melted away insensibly in the presence of
their cultivated minds; and so friendship with them
was a bond of union among all, and from the vicar to
the dairyman every one loved and respected them, asked
their counsel, and sought their sympathy.

They called themselves by no sectarian name, nor
could they have told to what " party " they belonged.
They troubled themselves with no theories of education,
but mingled gentle nurture with " wholesome neglect."
There was nothing exotic or constrained in the growth
of Eric's character. He was not one of your angelically
good children at all, and knew none of the phrases of
which infant prodigies are supposed to be so fond. He
had not been taught any distinction between " Sunday
books " and " week-day books," but no book had been
put in his way that was not healthy and genuine in
tone. He had not been told that he might use his

Noah's ark on Sunday, because it was "a Sunday play-thing," while all other toys were on that day forbidden. Of these things the Trevors thought little; they only saw that no child could be happy in enforced idleness or constrained employment; and so Eric grew up to love Sunday quite as well as any other day in the week, though, unlike your angelic children, he never professed to like it better. But to be truthful, to be honest, to be kind, to be brave, these had been taught him, and he never *quite* forgot the lesson; nor amid the sorrows of after life did he ever quite lose the sense—learnt at dear quiet Fairholm—of a present loving God, of a tender and long-suffering Father.

As yet he could be hardly said to know what school was. He had been sent indeed to Mr. Lawley's grammar school for the last half-year, and had learned a few declensions in his Latin grammar. But as Mr. Lawley allowed his upper class to hear the little boys their lessons, Eric had managed to get on pretty much as he liked. Only *once* in the entire half-year had he said a lesson to the dreadful master himself, and of course it was a ruinous failure, involving some tremendous pulls of Eric's hair, and making him tremble like a leaf. Several things combined to make Mr. Lawley dreadful to his imagination. Ever since he was quite little, he remembered hearing the howls which proceeded from the "Latin school" as he passed by, whilst some luckless youngster was getting caned; and the reverend peda-gogue was notoriously passionate. Then, again, he

spoke so indistinctly with his deep, gruff voice, that
Eric never could and never did syllable a word he said,
and this kept him in a perpetual terror.   Once Mr.
Lawley had told him to go out, and see what time it
was by the church clock.   Only hearing that he was
to do something, too frightened to ask what it was, and
feeling sure that even if he did, he should not understand what the master said, Eric ran out, went straight
to Mr. Lawley's house, and after having managed by
strenuous jumps to touch the knocker, informed the
servant "that Mr. Lawley wanted his man."

"What man?" said the maid-servant, "the young
man? or the butler? or is it the clerk?"

Here was a puzzler! all Eric knew was that he was
in the habit of sending sometimes for one or other of
these functionaries; but he was in for it, so with a
faltering voice he said "the young man" at hazard,
and went back to the Latin school.

"Why have you been so long?" roared Mr. Lawley, as he timidly entered.   Fear entirely prevented
Eric from hearing what was said, so he answered at
random, "He's coming, sir."   The master seeing by
his scared look that something was wrong, waited to
see what would turn up.

Soon after, in walked "the young man," and coming
to the astonished Mr. Lawley, bowed, scraped, and said,
"Master Williams said you sent for me, sir."

"A mistake," growled the schoolmaster, turning on
Eric a look which nearly petrified him; he quite ex-

pected a book at his head, or at best a great whack of the cane; but Mr. Lawley had naturally a kind heart, soured as it was, and pitying perhaps the child's white face, he contented himself with the effects of his look.

The simple truth was, that poor Mr. Lawley was a little wrong in the head. A scholar and a gentleman, early misfortunes and an imprudent marriage had driven him to the mastership of the little country grammar school; and here the perpetual annoyance caused to his refined mind by the coarseness of clumsy or spiteful boys, had gradually unhinged his intellect. Often did he tell the boys "that it was an easier life by far to break stones by the roadside than to teach them;" and at last his eccentricities became too obvious to be any longer overlooked.

The dénouement of his history was a tragic one, and had come a few days before the time when our narrative opens. It was a common practice among the Latin-school boys, as I suppose among all boys, to amuse themselves by putting a heavy book on the top of a door left partially ajar, and to cry out " Crown him " as the first luckless youngster who happened to come in received the book thundering on his head. One day, just as the trap had been adroitly laid, Mr. Lawley walked in unexpectedly. The moment he entered the school-room, down came an Ainsworth's Dictionary on the top of his hat, and the boy, concealed behind the door, unconscious of who the victim was, enunciated with mock gravity, " Crown him! three cheers."

It took Mr. Lawley a second to raise from his eye-brows the battered hat, and recover from his confusion; the next instant he was springing after the boy who had caused the mishap, and who, knowing the effects of the master's fury, fled with precipitation. In one minute the offender was caught, and Mr. Lawley's heavy hand fell recklessly on his ears and back, until he screamed with terror. At last by a tremendous writhe, wrenching himself free, he darted towards the door, and Mr. Lawley, too exhausted to pursue, snatched his large gold watch out of his fob, and hurled it at the boy's retreating figure. The watch flew through the air;—crash! it had missed its aim, and, striking the wall above the lintel, fell smashed into a thousand shivers.

The sound, the violence of the action, the sight of the broken watch, which was the gift of a cherished friend, instantly woke the master to his senses. The whole school had seen it; they sate there pale and breathless with excitement and awe. The poor man could bear it no longer. He flung himself into his chair, hid his face with his hands, and burst into hysterical tears. It was the outbreak of feelings long pent up. In that instant all his life passed before him—its hopes, its failures, its miseries, its madness. "Yes!" he thought, "I am mad."

Raising his head, he cried wildly, "Boys, go, I am mad!" and sank again into his former position, rocking himself to and fro. One by one the boys stole out, and he was left alone. The end is soon told. Forced to leave Ayrton, he had no means of earning his daily bread; and the weight of this new anxiety hastening the crisis, the handsome, proud scholar became an inmate of the Brerely Lunatic Asylum. A few years afterwards, Eric heard that he was dead. Poor broken human heart! may he rest in peace.

Such was Eric's first school and schoolmaster. But although he learnt little there, and gained no experience of the character of others or of his own, yet there was one point about Ayrton Latin School, which he never regretted. It was the mixture there of all classes. On those benches gentlemen's sons sat side by side with plebeians, and no harm, but only good, seemed to come from the intercourse. The neighbouring gentry, most of whom had begun their education there, were drawn into closer and kindlier union with their neighbours and dependants, from the fact of having been their associates in the days of their boyhood. Many a time afterwards, when Eric, as he passed down the streets, interchanged friendly greetings with some young glazier or tradesman whom he remembered at school, he felt glad that thus early he had learnt practically to despise the accidental and nominal differences which separate man from man.

CHAPTER II.

A NEW HOME.

"Life hath its May, and all is joyous then;
  The woods are vocal, and the flowers breathe odour,
  The very breeze hath mirth in't."—OLD PLAY.

AT last the longed-for yet dreaded day approached, and a letter informed the Trevors that Mr. and Mrs. Williams would arrive at Southampton on July 5th, and would probably reach Ayrton the evening after. They particularly requested that no one should come to meet them on their landing. "We shall reach Southampton," wrote Mrs. Trevor, "tired, pale, and travel-stained, and had much rather see you first at dear Fairholm, where we shall be spared the painful constraint of a meeting in public. So please expect our arrival at about seven in the evening."

Poor Eric! although he had been longing for the time ever since the news came, yet now he was too agitated to enjoy. Exertion and expectation made him restless, and he could settle down to nothing all day, every hour of which hung most heavily on his hands.

At last the afternoon wore away, and a soft summer evening filled the sky with its gorgeous calm. Far off they caught the sound of wheels; a carriage dashed up to the door, and the next moment Eric sprang into his mother's arms.

" O mother, mother ! "

" My own darling, darling boy ! "

And as the pale sweet face of the mother met the bright and rosy child-face, each of them was wet with a rush of ineffable tears. In another moment Eric had been folded to his father's heart, and locked in the arms of " little brother Vernon." Who shall describe the emotions of those few moments ? they did not seem like earthly moments; they seemed to belong not to time, but to eternity.

The first evening of such a scene is too excited to be happy. The little party at Fairholm retired early, and Eric was soon fast asleep with his arm round his new-found brother's neck.

Quiet steps entered the little room, and noiselessly the father and mother sat down by the bedside of their children. Earth could have shewn no scene more perfect in its beauty than that which met their eyes. The pure moonlight flooded the little room, and shewed distinctly the forms and countenances of the sleepers, whose soft regular breathing was the only sound that broke the stillness of the July night. The small shining flower-like faces, with their fair hair—the trustful loving arms folded round each brother's neck—the

closed lids and parted lips made an exquisite picture,
and one never to be forgotten. Side by side, without
a word, the parents knelt down, and with eyes wet
with tears of joyfulness, poured out their hearts in
passionate prayer for their young and beloved boys.

Very happily the next month glided away; a
new life seemed opened to Eric in the world of rich
affections which had unfolded itself before him. His
parents—above all, his mother—were everything that
he had longed for; and Vernon more than fulfilled to
his loving heart the ideal of his childish fancy. He
was never tired of playing with and patronising his
little brother, and their rambles by stream and hill
made those days appear the happiest he had ever spent.
Every evening (for he had not yet laid aside the habits
of childhood) he said his prayers by his mother's
knee, and at the end of one long summer's day, when
prayers were finished, and full of life and happiness he
lay down to sleep, "O mother," he said, "I am so
happy—I like to say my prayers when you are here."

"Yes, my boy, and God loves to hear them."

"Aren't there some who never say prayers, mother?"

"Very many, love, I fear."

"How unhappy they must be! *I* shall *always*
love to say my prayers."

"Ah, Eric, God grant that you may."

And the fond mother hoped he always would. But
these words often came back to Eric's mind in later
and less happy days—days when that gentle hand

could no longer rest lovingly on his head—when those mild blue eyes were dim with tears, and the fair boy, changed in heart and life, often flung himself down with an unreproaching conscience to prayerless sleep.

It had been settled that in another week Eric was to go to school in the Isle of Roslyn. Mr. Williams had hired a small house in the town of Ellan, and intended to stay there for his year of furlough, at the end of which period Vernon was to be left at Fairholm, and Eric in the house of the head-master of the school. Eric enjoyed the prospect of all things, and he hardly fancied that Paradise itself could be happier than a life at the seaside with his father and mother and Vernon, combined with the commencement of schoolboy dignity. When the time for the voyage came, his first glimpse of the sea, and the sensation of sailing over it with only a few planks between him and the deep waters, struck him silent with admiring wonder. It was a cloudless day; the line of blue sky melted into the line of blue wave, and the air was filled with sunlight. At evening they landed, and the coach took them to Ellan. On the way Eric saw for the first time the strength of the hills, so that when they reached the town and took possession of their cottage, he was dumb with the inrush of new and marvellous impressions.

Next morning he was awake early, and jumping out of bed, so as not to disturb the sleeping Vernon, he drew up the window-blind, and gently opened the window. A very beautiful scene burst on him, one

destined to be long mingled with all his most vivid
reminiscences. Not twenty yards below the garden,
in front of the house, lay Ellan Bay, at that moment
rippling with golden laughter in the fresh breeze of
sunrise. On either side of the bay was a bold headland,
the one stretching out in a series of broken crags, the
other terminating in a huge mass of rock, called from
its shape the Stack. To the right lay the town, with
its grey old castle, and the mountain stream running
through it into the sea; to the left, high above the
beach, rose the crumbling fragment of a picturesque
fort, behind which towered the lofty buildings of Roslyn
School. Eric learnt the whole landscape by heart, and
thought himself a most happy boy to come to such a
place. He fancied that he should be never tired of
looking at the sea, and could not take his eyes off the
great buoy that rolled about in the centre of the bay,
and flashed in the sunlight at every move. He turned
round full of hope and spirits, and, after watching for a
few moments the beautiful face of his sleeping brother,
he awoke him with a boisterous kiss.

That day Eric was to have his first interview with
Dr. Rowlands. The school had already reopened, and
one of the boys in his college cap passed by the window
while they were breakfasting. He looked very happy
and engaging, and was humming a tune as he strolled
along. Eric started up and gazed after him with the
most intense curiosity. At that moment the unconscious schoolboy was to him the most interesting person

in the whole world, and he couldn't realize the fact that, before the day was over, he would be a Roslyn boy himself. He very much wondered what sort of a fellow the boy was, and whether he should ever recognise him again, and make his acquaintance. Yes, Eric, the thread of that boy's destiny is twined a good deal with yours; his name is Montagu, as you will know very soon.

At nine o'clock Mr. Williams started towards the school with his son. The walk led them by the seaside, over the sands, and past the ruin, at the foot of which the waves broke at high tide. At any other time Eric would have been overflowing with life and wonder at the murmur of the ripples, the sight of the ships passing by the rock-bound bay, and the numberless little shells, with their bright colours and sculptured shapes, which lay about the beach. But now his mind was too full of a single sensation, and when, after crossing a green playground, they stood by the headmaster's door, his heart fluttered, and it required all his energy to keep down the nervous trembling which shook him.

Mr. Williams gave his card, and they were shewn into Dr. Rowlands' study. He was a kind-looking gentlemanly man, and when he turned to address Eric, after a few minutes' conversation with his father, the boy felt instantly reassured by the pleasant sincerity and frank courtesy of his manner. A short examination shewed that Eric's attainments were very slight as yet, and he was to be put in the lowest form of all, under the superintendence of the Rev. Henry Gordon. Dr. Rowlands wrote a short note in pencil, and giving it to Eric, directed the servant to shew him to Mr. Gordon's school-room.

The bell had just done ringing when they had started for the school, so that Eric knew that all the boys would be by this time assembled at their work, and that he should have to go alone into the middle of them. As he walked after the servant through the long corridors and up the broad stairs, he longed to make friends with him, so as, if possible, to feel less lonely. But he had only time to get out, "I say, what sort of a fellow is Mr. Gordon ?"

" Terrible strict, Sir, I hear," said the man, touching his cap with a comic expression, which didn't at all tend to enliven the future pupil. "That's the door," he continued, "and you'll have to give him the Doctor's note;" and, pointing to a door at the end of the passage, he walked off.

Eric stopped irresolutely. The man had disappeared, and he was by himself in the great silent building. Afraid of the sound of his own footsteps, he ran along the passage, and knocked timidly. He heard a low, a very low murmur in the room, but there was no answer. He knocked again a little louder; still no notice; then, overdoing it in his fright, he gave a very loud tap indeed.

" Come in," said a voice, which to the new boy

sounded awful; but he opened the door, and entered. As he came in every head was quickly raised, he heard a whisper of "New fellow," and the crimson flooded his face, as he felt himself the cynosure of some forty intensely-inquisitive pairs of eyes.

He found himself in a high airy room, with three large windows opening towards the sea. At one end was the master's throne, and facing it, all down the room, were desks and benches, along which the boys were sitting at work. Every one knows how very confusing it is to enter a strange room full of strange people, and especially when you enter it from a darker passage. Eric felt dazzled, and not seeing the regular route to the master's desk, went towards it between two of the benches. As these were at no great distance from each other, he stumbled against several legs on his way, and felt pretty sure that they were put out on purpose to trip him, especially by one boy, who, pretending to be much hurt, drew up his leg, and began rubbing it, ejaculating *sotto voce*, "awkward little fool."

In this very clumsy way he at last reached the desk, and presented his missive. The master's eye was on him, but all Eric had time to observe was, that he looked rather stern, and had in his hand a book which he seemed to be studying with the deepest interest. He glanced first at the note, and then looked full at the boy, as though determined to read his character at a glance.

"Williams, I suppose?"

"Yes, Sir," said Eric, very low, still painfully conscious that all the boys were looking at him, as well as the master.

"Very well, Williams, you are placed in the lowest form—the fourth. I hope you will work well. At present they are learning their Cæsar. Go and sit next to that boy," pointing towards the lower end of the room; "he will shew you the lesson, and let you look over his book. Barker, let Williams look over you!"

Eric went and sat down at the end of a bench by the boy indicated. He was a rough-looking fellow, with a shock head of black hair, and a very dogged look. Eric secretly thought that he was n't a very nice-looking specimen of Roslyn school. However, he sate by him, and glanced at the Cæsar which the boy shoved about a quarter of an inch in his direction. But Barker did n't seem inclined to make any farther advances, and presently Eric asked in a whisper,

"What's the lesson?"

The boy glanced at him, but took no further notice.

Eric repeated, "I say, what's the lesson?"

Instead of answering, Barker stared at him, and grunted,

"What's your name?"

"Eric—I mean Williams."

"Then why don't you say what you mean?"

Eric moved his foot impatiently at this ungracious reception; but as he seemed to have no redress, he pulled the Cæsar nearer towards him.

"Drop that; 'tisn't yours."

Mr. Gordon heard a whisper, and glanced that way. "Silence!" he said, and Barker pretended to be deep in his work, while Eric, resigning himself to his fate, looked about him.

He had plenty to occupy his attention in the faces round him. He furtively examined Mr. Gordon, as he bent over his high desk, writing, but couldn't make out the physiognomy. There had been something reserved and imperious in the master's manner, yet he thought he should not dislike him on the whole. With the countenances of his future schoolfellows he was not altogether pleased, but there were one or two which thoroughly attracted him. One boy, whose side face was turned towards him as he sat on the bench in front, took his fancy particularly, so, tired of doing nothing, he plucked up courage, and leaning forward whispered, "Do lend me your Cæsar for a few minutes." The boy at once handed it to him with a pleasant smile, and as the lesson was marked, Eric had time to hurry over a few sentences, when Mr. Gordon's sonorous voice exclaimed,

"Fourth form, come up!"

Some twenty of the boys went up, and stood in a large semicircle round the desk. Eric of course was placed last, and the lesson commenced.

"Russell, begin," said the master; and immediately the boy who had handed Eric his Cæsar, began reading a few sentences, and construed them very

creditably, only losing a place or two.   He had a frank
open face, bright intelligent fearless eyes, and a very
taking voice and manner.   Eric listened admiringly,
and felt sure he should like him.

Barker was put on next.   He bungled through
the Latin in a grating irresolute sort of way, with
several false quantities, for each of which the next boy
took him up.   Then he began to construe ;—a frightful
confusion of nominatives without verbs, accusatives
translated as ablatives, and perfects turned into pre-
positions ensued, and after a hopeless flounder, during
which Mr. Gordon left him entirely to himself, Barker
came to a full stop ; his catastrophe was so ludicrous,
that Eric could not help joining in the general titter.
Barker scowled.

"As usual, Barker," said the master, with a curl of
the lip.   "Hold out your hand!"

Barker did so, looking sullen defiance, and the cane
immediately descended on his open palm.   Six similar
cuts followed, during which the form looked on, not
without terror ; and Barker, squeezing his hands tight
together, went back to his seat.

"Williams, translate the piece in which Barker has
just failed!"

Eric did as he was bid, and got through it pretty
well.   He had now quite recovered his ordinary bearing, and spoke out clearly and without nervousness.
He afterwards won several places by answering questions, and at the end of the lesson was marked about half-

way up the form. The boys' numbers were then taken down in the weekly register, and they went back to their seats.

On his desk Eric found a torn bit of paper, on which was clumsily scrawled, " I 'll teach you to grin when I 'm turned, you young brute."

The paper seemed to fascinate his eyes. He stared at it fixedly, and augured ominously of Barker's intentions, since that worthy obviously alluded to his having smiled in form, and chose to interpret it as an intentional provocation. He felt that he was in for it, and that Barker meant to pick a quarrel with him. This puzzled and annoyed him, and he felt very sad to have found an enemy already.

While he was looking at the paper, the great school-clock struck twelve ; and the captain of the form getting up, threw open the folding-doors of the school-room.

" You may go," said Mr. Gordon ; and leaving his seat disappeared by a door at the further end of the room.

Instantly there was a rush for caps, and the boys poured out in a confused and noisy stream, while at the same moment the other school-rooms disgorged their inmates. Eric naturally went out among the last ; but just as he was going to take his cap, Barker seized it, and flung it with a whoop to the end of the passage, where it was trampled on by a number of the boys as they ran out.

Eric, gulping down his fury with a great effort,

turned to his opponent, and said coolly, " Is that what you always do to new fellows ?"

" Yes, you bumptious young owl, it is, and that too;" and a tolerably smart slap on the face followed—leaving a red mark on a cheek already aflame with anger and indignation,—" should you like a little more ?"

He was hurt, both mind and body, but was too proud to cry. " What's that for ?" he said, with flashing eyes.

" For your conceit in laughing at me when I was caned."

Eric stamped. " I did nothing of the kind, and you know it as well as I do."

" What ? I'm a liar, am I ? O we shall take this kind of thing out of you, you young cub, take that ;" and a heavier blow followed.

" You brutal cowardly bully," shouted Eric ; and in another moment he would have sprung upon him. It was lucky for him that he did not, for Barker was three years older than he, and very powerful. Such an attack would have been most unfortunate for him in every way. But at this instant some boys hearing the quarrel ran up, and Russell among them.

" Hallo Barker," said one, " what's up ?"

" Why, I'm teaching this new fry to be less bumptious, that's all."

" Shame!" said Russell, as he saw the mark on Eric's cheek ; " what a fellow you are, Barker. Why couldn't you leave him alone for his first day, at any rate ?"

" What's that to you? I'll kick you too, if you say much."

" Cavè, cavè !" whispered half a dozen voices, and instantly the knot of boys dispersed in every direction, as Mr. Gordon was seen approaching. He had caught a glimpse of the scene without understanding it, and seeing the new boy's red and angry face, he only said, as he passed by, " What, Williams ! fighting already? Take care."

This was the cruellest cut of all. " So," thought Eric, " a nice beginning! it seems both boys and masters are against me ;" and very disconsolately he walked to pick up his cap.

The boys were all dispersed in the play-ground at different games, and as he went home he was stopped perpetually, and had to answer the usual questions, " What's your name ? Are you a boarder or a day scholar ? What form are you in ?" Eric expected all this, and it therefore did not annoy him. Under any other circumstances, he would have answered cheerfully and frankly enough ; but now he felt miserable at his morning's rencontre, and his answers were short and sheepish, his only desire being to get away as soon as possible. It was an additional vexation to feel sure that his manner did not make a favourable impression.

Before he had got out of the play-ground, Russell ran up to him. " I'm afraid you won't like this, or think much of us, Williams," he said. " But never mind. It'll only last a day or two, and the fellows are not so bad as they seem; except that Barker. I'm sorry you've come across him, but it can't be helped."

It was the first kind word he had had since the morning, and after his troubles kindness melted him. He felt half inclined to cry, and for a few moments could say nothing in reply to Russell's soothing words. But the boy's friendliness went far to comfort him, and at last, shaking hands with him, he said—

"Do let me speak to you sometimes, while I am a new boy, Russell."

"O yes," said Russell, laughing, "as much as ever you like. And as Barker hates me pretty much as he seems inclined to hate you, we are in the same box. Good bye."

So Eric left the field, and wandered home, like Calchas in the Iliad, "sorrowful by the side of the sounding sea." Already the purple mantle had fallen from his ideal of schoolboy life. He got home later than they expected, and found his parents waiting for him. It was rather disappointing to them to see his face so melancholy, when they expected him to be full of animation and pleasure. Mrs. Williams drew her own conclusions from the red mark on his cheek, as well as the traces of tears welling to his eyes; but, like a wise mother, she asked nothing, and left the boy to tell his own story,—which in time he did, omitting all the painful part, speaking enthusiastically of Russell, and only admitting that he had been a little teased.

CHAPTER III.

BULLYING.

" **Give to the morn of life its natural blessedness.**"—WORDSWORTH.

HY is it that new boys are almost invariably ill-treated? I have often fancied that there must be in boyhood a pseudo-instinctive cruelty, a sort of " wild trick of the ancestral savage," which no amount of civilization can entirely repress. Certain it is, that to most boys the first term is a trying ordeal. They are being tested and weighed. Their place in the general estimation is not yet fixed, and the slightest circumstances are seized upon to settle the category under which the boy is to be classed. A few apparently trivial accidents of his first few weeks at school often decide his position in the general regard for the remainder of his boyhood. And yet these are *not* accidents; they are the slight indications which give an unerring proof of the general tendencies of his character and training. Hence much of the apparent cruelty with which new boys are treated is not exactly intentional. At first of course, as they can have no

friends worth speaking of, there are always plenty of
coarse and brutal minds that take a pleasure in their
torment, particularly if they at once recognise any
innate superiority to themselves. Of this class was
Barker. He hated Eric at first sight, simply because
his feeble mind could only realise one idea about him,
and that was the new boy's striking contrast with his
own imperfections. Hence he left no means untried to
vent on Eric his low and mean jealousy. He shewed
undisguised pleasure when he fell in form, and signs of
disgust when he rose; he fomented every little source
of disapproval or quarrelling which happened to arise
against him; he never looked at him without a frown
or a sneer; he waited for him to kick and annoy him
as he came out of, or went in to, the school-room. In
fact, he did his very best to make the boy's life miserable, and the occupation of hating him seemed in some
measure to fill up the vacuity of an ill-conditioned and
degraded mind.

Hatred is a most mysterious and painful phenomenon
to the unhappy person who is the object of it, and more
especially if he have incurred it by no one assignable
reason. To Eric it was peculiarly painful; he was
utterly unprepared for it. In his bright joyous life at
Fairholm, in the little he saw of the boys at the Latin
school, he had met with nothing but kindness and
caresses, and the generous nobleness of his character
had seemed to claim them as a natural element. " And
now, why," he asked impatiently, " should this bull-

dog sort of fellow have set his whole aim to annoy, vex, and hurt me ? " Incapable himself of so mean a spirit of jealousy at superior excellence, he could not make it out ; but such was the fact, and the very mysteriousness of it made it more intolerable to bear.

But it must be admitted that he made matters worse by his own bursts of passion. His was not the temper to turn the other cheek ; but, brave and spirited as he was, he felt how utterly hopeless would be any attempt on his part to repel force by force. He would have tried some slight conciliation, but it was really impossible with such a boy as his enemy. Barker never gave him even so much as an indifferent look, much less a civil word. Eric loathed him, and the only good and happy part of the matter to his own mind was, that conscientiously his only desire was to get rid of him and be left alone, while he never cherished a particle of revenge.

While every day Eric was getting on better in form, and winning himself a very good position with the other boys, who liked his frankness, his mirth, his spirit, and cleverness, he felt this feud with Barker like a dark background to all his enjoyment. He even had to manœuvre daily how to escape him, and violent scenes were of constant occurrence between them. Eric could not, and would not, brook his bullying with silence. His resentment was loud and stinging, and, Ishmaelite as Barker was, even *his* phlegmatic tem-

perament took fire when Eric shouted his fierce
and uncompromising retorts in the hearing of the
others.

Meanwhile Eric was on the best of terms with the
rest of the form, and such of the other boys as he knew,
although, at first, his position as a home-boarder prevented his knowing many.   Besides Russell, there were
three whom he liked best, and respected most—Duncan,
Montagu, and Owen.   They were very different boys, but
all of them had qualities, which well deserved his esteem.
Duncan was the most boyish of boys, intensely full of
fun, good nature, and vigour; with fair abilities, he
never got on well, because he could not be still for two
minutes, and even, if in some fit of sudden ambition, he
got up high in the form, he was sure to be put to the
bottom again before the day was over, for trifling or
talking.   But out of school he was the soul of every
game; whatever *he* took up was sure to be done pleasantly, and no party of amusement was ever planned
without endeavouring to secure him as one of the number.

Montagu's chief merit was, that he was such a
thorough little gentleman; "such a jolly little fellow"
every one said of him.   Without being clever or athletic,
he managed to do very fairly both at work and at the
games, and while he was too exclusive to make many
intimate friends, everybody liked walking about or
talking with him.   Even Barker, blackguard as he was,
seemed to be a little uneasy when confronted with
Montagu's naturally noble and chivalrous bearing.   In

nearly all respects his influence was thoroughly good, and few boys were more generally popular.

Owen, again, was a very different boy. His merit was a ceaseless diligence, in which it was doubtful whether ambition or conscientiousness had the greatest share. Reserved and thoughtful, unfitted for or indifferent to most games, he was anything but a favourite with the rest, and Eric rather respected than liked him. When he first came, he had been one of the most natural butts for Barker's craving ill-nature, and for a time he had been tremendously bullied. But gradually his mental superiority asserted itself. He took everything without tears and without passion, and this diminished the pleasure of annoying him. One day when Barker had given him an unprovoked kick, he quietly said,

"Barker, next time you do that, I'll tell Mr. Gordon."

"Sneak! do it if you dare." And he kicked him again; but the moment after he was sorry for it, for there was a dark look in Owen's eyes, as he turned instantly into the door of the master's room, and laid a formal complaint against Barker for bullying.

Mr. Gordon didn't like "telling," and he said so to Owen, without reserve. An ordinary boy would have broken into a flood of explanations and palliations, but Owen simply bowed, and said nothing. "He stood there for justice," and he had counted the cost. Strong-minded, and clear-headed, he calculated correctly that the momentary dislike of his schoolfellows, with whom he well knew that he never could be popular, would be less unbearable than Barker's villainous insults. The consequence was that Barker was caned soundly, although, with some injustice, Mr. Gordon made no attempt to conceal that he did it unwillingly.

Of course the fellows were very indignant with Owen for sneaking, as they called it, and for a week or two he had the keen mortification of seeing " Owen is a sneak," written up all about the walls. But he was too proud or too cold to make any defence till called upon, and bore it in silence. Barker vowed eternal vengeance, and the very day after, had seized Owen with the avowed intention of "half murdering him." But before he could once strike him, Owen said in the most chill tone, " Barker, if you touch me, I shall go straight to Dr. Rowlands." The bully well knew that Owen never broke his word, but he could not govern his rage, and first giving Owen a violent shake, he proceeded to thrash him without limit or remorse.

Pale but unmoved, Owen got away, and walked straight to Dr. Rowlands' door. The thing was unheard of, and the boys were amazed at his temerity, for the doctor was to all their imaginations a regular *Deus ex machinâ*. That afternoon, again, Barker was publicly caned, with the threat that the next offence would be followed by instant and public expulsion. This punishment he particularly dreaded, because he was intended for the army, and he well knew that it

might ruin his prospects. The consequence was, that
Owen never suffered from him again, although he daily
received a shower of oaths and curses, which he passed
over with silent contempt.

My dear boy-reader, don't suppose that I want
you to imitate Owen in this matter. I despise a boy
who " tells " as much as you do, and it is a far better
and braver thing to bear bullying with such a mixture
of spirit and good humour, as in time to disarm it.
But Owen was a peculiar boy, and remember he had *no*
redress. He bore for a time, until he felt that he *must*
have the justice and defence, without which it would
have been impossible for him to continue at Roslyn
school.

But why, you ask, didn't he tell the monitors?
Unfortunately at Roslyn the monitorial system was not
established. Although it was a school of 250 boys, the
sixth form, with all their privileges, had no prerogative
of authority. They hadn't the least right to interfere,
because no such power had been delegated to them,
and therefore they felt themselves merely on a par with
the rest, except for such eminence as their intellectual
superiority gave them. The consequence was, that
any interference from them would have been of a simply
individual nature, and was exerted very rarely. It
would have done Owen no more good to tell a sixth-
form boy, than to tell any other boy; and as he was
not a favourite, he was not likely to find any champion
to fight his battles or maintain his just rights.

All this had happened before Eric's time, and he heard it from his best friend Russell. His heart clave to that boy. They became friends at once by a kind of electric sympathy; the first glance of each at the other's face prepared the friendship, and every day of acquaintance more firmly cemented it. Eric could not have had a better friend; not so clever as himself, not so diligent as Owen, not so athletic as Duncan, or so fascinating as Montagu, Russell combined the best qualities of them all. And, above all, he acted invariably from the highest principle; he presented that noblest of all noble spectacles—one so rare that many think it impossible—the spectacle of an honourable, pure-hearted, happy boy, who, as his early years speed by, is ever growing in wisdom, and stature, and favour with God and man.

" Did that brute Barker ever bully you as he bullies me ? " said Eric, one day, as he walked on the sea-shore with his friend.

" Yes," said Russell; " I slept in his dormitory when I first came, and he has often made me so wretched that I have flung myself on my knees at night in pretence of prayer, but really to get a little quiet time to cry like a child."

" And when was it he left off at last ? "

" Why, you know, Upton in the fifth is my cousin, and very fond of me ; he heard of it, though I didn't say anything about it, and told Barker that if ever he caught him at it, he would thrash him within an inch of his life; and that frightened him for one thing. Besides, Duncan, Montagu, and other friends of mine began to cut him in consequence, so he thought it best to leave off."

" How is it, Russell, that fellows stand by and let him do it? "

" You see, Williams," said Russell, " Barker is an enormously strong fellow, and that makes the younger chaps, whom he fags, look up to him as a great hero. And there isn't one in our part of the school who can thrash him. Besides, people never do interfere you know—at least not often. I remember once seeing a street-row in London, at which twenty people stood by, and let a drunken beast of a husband strike his wife without ever stirring to defend her."

" Well," sighed Eric, " I hope my day of deliverance will come soon, for I can't stand it much longer, and ' tell ' I won't, whatever Owen may do."

Eric's deliverance came very soon. It was afternoon; the boys were playing at different games in the green playground, and he was waiting for his turn at rounders. At this moment Barker lounged up, and calmly snatching off Eric's cap, shied it over Dr. Rowlands' garden wall. " There, go and fetch that."

" You blackguard!" said Eric, standing irresolutely for a few minutes; and then with tears in his eyes began to climb the wall. It was not very high, but boys were peremptorily forbidden to get over it under any circumstances, and Eric broke the rule not without trepidation. However, he dropped down on one of Mrs. Rowlands' flower-beds, got his cap in a hurry, and clambered back undiscovered.

He thought this would have satisfied his tormentor for one day; but Barker was in a mischievous mood, so he again came up to Eric, and calling out, " Who'll have a game at football?" again snatched the cap, and gave it a kick; Eric tried to recover it, but every time he came up Barker gave it a fresh kick, and finally kicked it into a puddle.

Eric stood still, trembling with rage, while his eyes lightened scorn and indignation. " You hulking, stupid, cowardly bully"—here Barker seized him, and every word brought a tremendous blow on the head, but blind with passion Eric went on—" you despicable bully, I won't touch that cap again, you shall pick it up yourself. Duncan, Russell, here! do help me against this intolerable brute."

Several boys ran up, but they were all weaker than Barker, who besides was now in a towering fury, and kicked Eric unmercifully.

" Leave him alone," shouted Duncan, " or by heaven I'll get you a sound thrashing from some fellow."

" I won't; mind your own business," growled Barker, shaking himself free from Duncan's hand.

" Barker, I'll never speak to you again from this day," said Montagu, turning on his heel with a look of withering contempt.

" What do I care? puppy, you want taking down

too," was the reply, and some more kicks at Eric followed.

"Barker, I won't stand this any longer," said Russell; and seizing him by the arm, he dealt him a swinging blow on the face.

The bully stood in amazement, and dropped Eric, who fell on the turf nearly fainting, and bleeding at the nose. But now Russell's turn came, and in a moment Barker, who was twice his weight, had tripped him up,—when he found himself collared in an iron grasp.

There had been an unobserved spectator of the whole scene, in the person of Mr. Williams himself, and it was his strong hand that now griped Barker's shoulder. He was greatly respected by the boys, who all knew his tall handsome figure by sight, and he frequently stood a quiet and pleased observer of their games. The boys in the playground came crowding round, and Barker in vain struggled to escape. Mr. Williams held him firmly, and said in a calm voice, "I have just seen you treat one of your schoolfellows with the grossest violence. It makes me blush for you, Roslyn boys," he continued, turning to the group that surrounded him, "that you can stand by unmoved, and see such things done. You know that you despise any one who tells a master, yet you allow this bullying to go on, and that, too, without any provocation. Now, mark; it makes no difference that the boy hurt is my own son; I would have punished this scoundrel whoever it had been, and I shall punish him now." With these words

he lifted the riding-whip which he happened to be carrying, and gave Barker one of the most satisfactory
castigations he had ever undergone; the boys declared
that Dr. Rowlands' "swishings" were nothing to it. Mr.
Williams saw that the offender was a tough subject, and
determined that he should not soon forget the punishment
he then received. He had never heard from Eric how
this boy had been treating him, but he had heard it
from Russell, and now he had seen one of the worst
specimens of it with his own eyes. He therefore
belaboured him till his sullen obstinacy gave way to a
roar for mercy, and promises never so to offend again.

At this crisis he flung the boy from him with a
"phew" of disgust, and said, "I give nothing for your
word; but if ever you do bully in this way again, and I
see or hear of it, your present punishment shall be a trifle
to what I shall then administer. At present, thank me
for not informing your master." So saying, he made
Barker pick up the cap, and, turning away, walked
home with Eric leaning on his arm.

Barker, too, carried himself off with the best grace
he could; but it certainly didn't mend matters when
he heard numbers of fellows, even little boys, say
openly, "I'm so glad; serves you right."

From that day Eric was never troubled with personal violence from Barker or any other boy. But
rancour smouldered deep in the mind of the baffled
tyrant, and, as we shall see hereafter, there are subtler
means of making an enemy wretched than striking or
kicking him.

CHAPTER IV.

CRIBBING.

" Et nos ergo manum ferulæ subduximus."—Juv. i. 15.

T must not be thought that Eric's year as a home-boarder was made up of dark experiences. Roslyn had a very bright as well as a dark side, and Eric enjoyed it "to the finger-tips." School-life, like all other life, is an April day of shower and sunshine. Its joys may be more childish, its sorrows more trifling than those of after years;—but they are more keenly felt.

And yet, although we know it to be a mere delusion, we all idealise and idolise our childhood. The memory of it makes pleasant purple in the distance, and as we look back on the sunlight of its blue far-off hills, we forget how steep we sometimes found them.

After Barker's discomfiture, which took place some three weeks after his arrival, Eric liked the school more and more, and got liked by it more and more. This might have been easily foreseen, for he was the type of a thoroughly boyish mind in its more genial and honourable characteristics, and his round of acquain-

tances daily increased. Among others, a few of the
sixth, who were also day-scholars, began to notice and
walk home with him. He looked on them as great
heroes, and their condescension much increased his
dignity both in his own estimation and that of his
equals.

Now, too, he began to ask some of his most intimate acquaintances to spend an evening with him sometimes at home. This was a pleasure much coveted, for
no boy ever saw Mrs. Williams without loving her, and
they felt themselves humanised by the friendly interest
of a lady who reminded every boy of his own mother.
Vernon, too, now a lively and active child of nine, was a
great pet among them, so that every one liked Eric
who "knew him at home." A boy generally shews
his best side at home; the softening shadows of a
mother's tender influence play over him, and tone down
the roughnesses of boyish character. Duncan, Montagu, and Owen were special favourites in the home
circle, and Mrs. Williams felt truly glad that her son
had singled out friends who seemed, on the whole, so
desirable. But Montagu and Russell were the most
frequent visitors, and the latter became almost like one
of the family; he won so much on all their hearts that
Mrs. Williams was not surprised when Eric confided to
her one day that he loved Russell almost as well as he
loved Vernon.

As Christmas approached, the boys began to take
a lively interest in the half-year's prizes, and Eric was

particularly eager about them. He had improved wonderfully, and as both his father and mother prevented him from being idle, even had he been so inclined, he had soon shewn that he was one of the best in the form. Two prizes were given half-yearly to each remove; one for "marks" indicating the boy who had generally been highest throughout the half-year, and the other for the best proofs of proficiency in a special examination. It was commonly thought in the form that Owen would get the first of these prizes, and Eric the other; and towards the approach of the examination, he threw his whole energy into the desire to win. The desire was not selfish. Some ambition was of course natural; but he longed for the prize chiefly for the delight which he knew his success would cause at Fairholm, and still more to his own family.

During the last week, an untoward circumstance happened, which, while it increased his popularity, diminished a good deal (as he thought) his chance of success. The fourth form were learning a Homer lesson, and Barker, totally unable to do it by his own resources, was trying to borrow a crib. Eric, much to their mutual disgust, still sat next to him in school, and would have helped him if he had chosen to ask; but he never did choose, nor did Eric care to volunteer. The consequence was, that unless he could borrow a crib, he was invariably turned, and he was now particularly anxious to get one, because the time was nearly up.

There was a certain idle, good-natured boy, named
Llewellyn, who had " cribs" to every book they did, and
who, with a pernicious *bonhommie*, lent them promis-
cuously to the rest, all of whom were only too glad to
avail themselves of the help, except the few at the top
of the form, who found it a slovenly way of learning
the lesson, which was sure to get them into -worse
difficulties than an honest attempt to master the meaning for themselves.   Llewellyn sat at the farther end of
the form in front, so Barker scribbled in the fly-leaf of
his book, " Please send us your Homer crib," and got
the book passed on to Llewellyn, who immediately shoved
his crib in Barker's direction.   The only danger of the
transaction being noticed, was when the book was
being handed from one bench to another, and as Eric
unluckily had an end seat, he had got into trouble more
than once.

On this occasion, just as Graham, the last boy on
the form in front, handed Eric the crib, Mr. Gordon
happened to look up, and Eric, very naturally anxious
to screen another from trouble, popped the book under
his own Homer.

" Williams, what are you doing?"

" Nothing, Sir," said Eric, looking up innocently.

" Bring me that book under your Homer."

Eric blushed, hesitated—but at last, amid a dead
silence, took up the book.   Mr. Gordon looked at it
for a minute, let it fall on the ground, and then, with
an unnecessary affectation of disgust, took it up with

the tongs, and dropped it into the fire. There was a titter round the room.

" Silence," thundered the master; " this is no matter for laughing. So sir, *this* is the way you get up to the top of the form? "

" I wasn't using it, sir, " said Eric.

" Not using it! Why, I saw you put it, open, under your Homer."

" It isn't mine, sir."

" Then whose is it?" Mr. Gordon looked at the fly-leaf, but of course no name was there; in those days it was dangerous to write one's name in a translation.

Eric was silent.

" Under the circumstances, Williams, I must punish you," said Mr. Gordon. " Of course I am *bound* to believe you, but the circumstances are very suspicious. You had no business with such a book at all. Hold out your hand."

As yet, Eric had never been caned. It would have been easy for him in this case to clear himself without mentioning names, but (very rightly) he thought it unmanly to clamour about being punished, and he felt nettled at Mr. Gordon's merely official belief of his word. He knew that he had his faults, but certainly want of honour was not among them. Indeed, there were only three boys out of the twenty in the form, who did not resort to modes of unfairness far worse than the use of cribs, and those three were Russell,

Owen, and himself; even Duncan, even Montagu, inured to it by custom, were not ashamed to read their lesson off a concealed book, or copy a date from a furtive piece of paper. They would have been ashamed of it before they came to Roslyn school, but the commonness of the habit had now made them blind or indifferent to its meanness. It was peculiarly bad in the fourth form, because the master treated them with implicit confidence, and being scrupulously honourable himself was unsuspicious of others. He was therefore extremely indignant at this apparent discovery of an attempt to overreach him in a boy so promising and so much of a favourite as Eric Williams.

"Hold out your hand," he repeated.

Eric did so, and the cane tingled sharply across his palm. He could bear the pain well enough, but he was keenly alive to the disgrace ; he, a boy at the head of his form, to be caned in this way by a man who didn't understand him, and unjustly too! He mustered up an indifferent air, closed his lips tight, and determined to give no further signs. The defiance of his look made Mr. Gordon angry, and he inflicted in succession five hard cuts on either hand, each one of which was more excruciating than the last.

"Now, go to your seat."

Eric did go to his seat, with all his bad passions roused, and he walked in a jaunty and defiant kind of way that made the master really grieve at the disgrace into which he had fallen. But he instantly became a hero with the form, who unanimously called him a great brick for not telling, and admired him immensely for bearing up without crying under so severe a punishment. The punishment *was* most severe, and for some weeks after, there were dark weals visible across Eric's palm, which rendered the use of his hands painful.

" Poor Williams," said Duncan, as they went out of school, " how very plucky of you not to cry."

> "Vengeance deep brooding o'er the *cane*,
> Had locked the source of softer woe ;
> And burning pride, and high disdain,
> Forbade the gentler tear to flow,"

said Eric, with a smile.

But he only bore up till he got home, and there, while he was telling his father the occurrence, he burst into a storm of passionate tears, mingled with the fiercest invectives against Mr. Gordon for his injustice.

" Never mind, Eric," said his father ; " only take care that you never get a punishment *justly*, and I shall always be as proud of you as I am now. And don't cherish this resentment, my boy ; it will only do you harm. Try to forgive and forget."

" But, Papa, Mr. Gordon is so hasty. I have indeed been rather a favourite of his, yet now he shews that he has no confidence in me. It is a great shame that he shouldn't believe my word. I don't mind the pain ; but I shan't like him any more, and I'm sure, now I shan't get the examination prize."

" You don't mean, Eric, that he will be influenced by partiality in the matter?"

" No, Papa, not exactly; at least I dare say he won't *intend* to be. But it is unlucky to be on bad terms with a master, and I know I shan't work so well."

On the whole, the boy was right in thinking this incident a misfortune. Although he had nothing particular for which to blame himself, yet the affair had increased his pride, while it lowered his self-respect; and he had an indistinct consciousness that the popularity in his form would do him as much harm as the change of feeling in his master. He grew careless and dis-spirited, nor was it till in the very heat of the final competition, that he felt his energies fully revived.

Half the form were as eager about the examination as the other half were indifferent; but none were more eager than Eric. He was much hindered by Barker's unceasing attempt to copy his papers surreptitiously; and very much disgusted at the shameless way in which many of the boys " cribbed " from books, and from each other, or used torn leaves concealed in their sleeves, or dates written on their wristbands, and on their nails. He saw how easily much of this might have been prevented; but Mr. Gordon was fresh at his work, and had not yet learnt the practical lesson, that to trust young boys to any great extent, is really to increase their temptations. He *did* learn the lesson afterwards, and then almost entirely suppressed the practice, partly by increased vigilance, and partly by forbidding *any* book to be brought into the room during the time of examination. But meanwhile, much evil had been done by the habitual abuse of his former confidence.

I shall not linger over the examination. At its close, the day before the breaking-up, the list was posted on the door of the great school-room, and most boys made an impetuous rush to see the result. But Eric was too nervous to be present at the hour when this was usually done, and he had asked Russell to bring him the news.

He was walking up and down the garden, counting the number of steps he took, counting the number of shrubs along each path, and devising every sort of means to beguile the time, when he heard hasty steps, and Russell burst in at the back gate, breathless with haste, and bright with excitement.

" Hurrah ! old fellow," he cried, seizing both Eric's hands ; " I never felt so glad in my life ;" and he shook his friend's arms up and down, laughing joyously.

" Well ! tell me," said Eric.

" First, $\left\{\begin{array}{l}\text{Owen}\\\text{Williams}\end{array}\right\}$ Æquales," said he ; " you've got head remove you see, in spite of your forebodings, as I always said you would; and I congratulate you with all my heart."

" No ? " said Eric, " have I really ?—you're not joking ? Oh ! hurrah !—I must rush in and tell them ;" and he bounded off.

In a second he was back at Russell's side. "What a selfish animal I am! Where are you placed, Russell?"

"Oh! magnificent; I'm third;—far higher than I expected."

"I'm so glad," said Eric. "Come in with me and tell them. I'm head remove, mother," he shouted, springing into the parlour where his father and mother sat.

In the lively joy that this announcement excited, Russell stood by for the moment unheeded; and when Eric took him by the hand to tell them that he was third, he hung his head, and a tear was in his eye.

"Poor boy! I'm afraid you're disappointed," said Mrs. Williams kindly, drawing him to her side.

"Oh no, no! it's not *that*," said Russell, hastily as he lifted his swimming eyes towards her face.

"Are you hurt, Russell?" asked Eric, surprised.

"Oh! no; don't ask me; I am only foolish to-day;" and with a burst of sorrow he flung his arms round Mrs. Williams' neck. She folded him to her heart, and kissed him tenderly; and when his sobs would let him speak, he whispered to her in a low tone, "It is but a year since I became an orphan."

"Dearest child," she said, "look on me as a mother; I love you very dearly for your own sake as well as Eric's."

Gradually he grew calmer. They made him stay to dinner and spend the rest of the day there, and by the evening he had recovered all his usual sprightliness. Towards sunset he and Eric went for a stroll down the bay, and talked over the term and the examination.

They sat down on a green bank just beyond the beach, and watched the tide come in, while the sea-distance was crimson with the glory of evening. The beauty and the murmur filled them with a quiet happiness, not untinged with the melancholy thought of parting the next day.

At last Eric broke the silence. " Russell, let me always call you Edwin, and call me Eric."

" Very gladly, Eric. Your coming here has made me so happy." And the two boys squeezed each other's hands, and looked into each other's faces, and silently promised that they would be loving friends for ever.

CHAPTER V.

THE SECOND TERM.

"Take us the foxes, the little foxes that spoil our vines; for our vines have tender grapes."—CANT. ii. 15.

THE second term at school is generally the great test of the strength of a boy's principles and resolutions. During the first term the novelty, the loneliness, the dread of unknown punishments, the respect for authorities, the desire to measure himself with his companions—all tend to keep him right and diligent. But many of these incentives are removed after the first brush of novelty, and many a lad who has given good promise at first, turns out, after a short probation, idle, or vicious, or indifferent.

But there was little comparative danger for Eric, so long as he continued to be a home boarder, which was for another half-year. On the contrary, he was anxious to support in his new remove the prestige of having been head boy; and as he still continued under Mr. Gordon, he really wished to turn over a new leaf in his conduct towards him, and recover, if possible, his lost esteem.

His popularity was a fatal snare. He enjoyed and was very proud of it, and was half inclined to be angry with Russell for not fully sharing his feelings; but Russell had a far larger experience of school life than his new friend, and dreaded with all his heart lest "he should follow a multitude to do evil."

The "cribbing," which had astonished and pained Eric at first, was more flagrant than even in the Upper Fourth, and assumed a chronic form. In all the repetition lessons one of the boys used to write out in a large hand the passage to be learnt by heart, and dexterously pin it to the front of Mr. Gordon's desk. There any boy who chose could read it off with little danger of detection, and, as before, the only boys who refused to avail themselves of this trickery were Eric, Russell, and Owen.

Eric did *not* yield to it; never once did he suffer his eyes to glance at the paper when his turn to repeat came round. But although this was the case, he never spoke against the practice to the other boys, even when he lost places by it. Nay more, he would laugh when any one told him how he had escaped " skewing" (*i. e.* being turned) by reading it off; and he even went so far as to allow them to suppose that he wouldn't himself object to take advantage of the master's unsuspicious confidence.

" I say, Williams," said Duncan, one morning as they strolled into the school-yard, " do you know your Rep.? "

" No," said Eric, " not very well; I haven't given more than ten minutes to it."

" Oh, well, never mind it now; come and have a game at racquets? Russell and Montagu have taken the court."

" But I shall skew."

" Oh no, you needn't, you know. I'll take care to pin it up on the desk near you."

" Well, I don't much care. At any rate I'll chance it." And off the boys ran to the racquet-court, Eric intending to occupy the last quarter of an hour before school-time in learning his lesson. Russell and he stood the other two, and they were very well matched. They had finished two splendid games, and each side had been victorious in turn, when Duncan, in the highest spirits shouted, " Now, Russell, for the con-queror."

" Get some one else in my place," said Russell; " I don't know my Rep., and must cut and learn it."

" O bother the Rep.," said Montagu; " somebody's sure to write it out in school, and old Gordon 'll never see."

" You forget, Montagu, I never condescend to that."

" O ay, I forgot. Well, after all, you're quite right; I only wish I was as good."

" What a capital fellow he is," continued Montagu, leaning on his racquet and looking after him, as Russell left the court; " but I say, Williams, you're not going too, are you?"

" I think I must, I don't know half my lesson."

" O no! don't go; there's Llewellyn; he'll take Russell's place, and we *must* have the conquering game."

Again Eric yielded; and when the clock struck, he ran into school, hot, vexed with himself, and certain to break down, just as Russell strolled in, whispering, " I've had lots of time to get up the Horace, and know it pat."

Still he clung to the little thistledown of hope that he should have plenty of time to cram it before the form were called up. But another temptation waited him. No sooner was he seated than Graham whispered, " Williams, it's your turn to write out the Horace ; I did last time, you know."

Poor Eric. He was reaping the fruits of his desire to keep up popularity, by never denying his complicity in the general cheating. Everybody seemed to assume now that *he* at any rate didn't think much of it, and he had never claimed his real right up to that time of asserting his innocence. But this was a step farther than he had ever gone before. He drew back—

" My *turn*, what do you mean?"

" Why, you know as well as I do that we all write it out by turns."

" Do you mean to say Owen or Russell ever wrote it out?"

" Of course not; you wouldn't expect the saints to be guilty of such a thing, would you?"

" I'd rather not, Graham," he said, getting very red.

" Well, that *is* cowardly," answered Graham angrily; " then I suppose I must do it myself."

" Here, I'll do it," said Eric suddenly; " shy us the paper."

His conscience smote him bitterly. In his silly dread of giving offence, he was doing what he heartily despised, and he felt most uncomfortable.

" There," he said, pushing the paper from him in a pet; " I've written it, and I'll have nothing more to do with it."

Just as he finished, they were called up, and Barker, taking the paper, succeeded in pinning it as usual on the front of the desk. Eric had never seen it done so carelessly and clumsily before, and firmly believed, what was indeed a fact, that Barker had done it badly on purpose, in the hope that it might be discovered, and so Eric be got once more into a scrape. He was in an agony of apprehension, and when put on, was totally unable to say a word of his Rep. But low as he had fallen, he would not cheat like the rest; he kept his eyes resolutely turned away from the guilty paper, and even refused to repeat the words which were prompted in his ear by the boys on each side. Mr. Gordon, after waiting a moment, said—

" Why, Sir, you know nothing about it; you can't have looked at it. Go to the bottom, and write it out five times."

"*Write it out*," thought Eric; "this is retribution, I suppose;" and, covered with shame and vexation, he took his place below the malicious Barker at the bottom of the form.

It happened that during the lesson the fire began to smoke, and Mr. Gordon told Owen to open the window for a moment. No sooner was this done than the mischievous whiff of sea air which entered the room began to trifle and coquet with the pendulous half sheet pinned in front of the desk, causing thereby an unwonted little pattering crepitation. In alarm, Duncan thoughtlessly pulled out the pin, and immediately the paper floated gracefully over Russell's head, as he sat at the top of the form, and, after one or two gyrations, fluttered down in the centre of the room.

"Bring me that piece of paper," said Mr. Gordon, full of vague suspicion.

Several boys moved uneasily, and Eric looked nervously round.

"Did you hear? fetch me that half sheet of paper."

A boy picked it up, and handed it to him. He held it for a full minute in his hands without a word, while vexation, deep disgust, and rising anger struggled in his countenance. At last, he suddenly turned full on Eric, whose writing he recognised, and broke out,

"So, Sir! a second time caught in gross deceit. I should not have thought it possible. Your face and manners belie you. You have lost my confidence for ever. I *despise* you."

"Indeed, Sir," said the penitent Eric, "I never meant ——"

"Silence—you are detected, as cheats always will be. I shall report you to Dr. Rowlands."

The next boy was put on, and broke down. The same with the next, and the next, and the next; Montagu, Graham, Llewellyn, Duncan, Barker, all hopeless failures; only two boys had said it right—Russell and Owen.

Mr. Gordon's face grew blacker and blacker. The deep undisguised pain which the discovery caused him was swallowed up in unbounded indignation. "False-hearted, dishonourable boys," he exclaimed, "henceforth my treatment of you shall be very different. The whole form, except Russell and Owen, shall have an extra lesson every half-holiday; not one of the rest of you will I trust again. I took you for gentlemen. I was mistaken. Go." And so saying, he waved them to their seats with imperious disdain.

They went, looking sheepish and ashamed. Eric, deeply vexed, kept twisting and untwisting a bit of paper, without raising his eyes, and even Barker thoroughly repented his short-sighted treachery; the rest were silent and miserable.

At twelve o'clock two boys lingered in the room to speak to Mr. Gordon; they were Eric Williams and Edwin Russell, but they were full of very different feelings.

Eric stepped to the desk first. Mr. Gordon looked up.

"You! Williams, I wonder that you have the audacity to speak to me. Go — I have nothing to say to you!"

"But sir, I want to tell you that——"

"Your guilt is only too clear, Williams. You will hear more of this. Go, I tell you."

Eric's passion overcame him; he stamped furiously on the ground, and burst out, "I *will* speak, sir; you have been unjust to me for a long time, but I will *not* be ——"

Mr. Gordon's cane fell sharply across the boy's back; he stopped, glared for a moment, and then saying, "Very well, sir! I shall tell Dr. Rowlands that you strike before you hear me," he angrily left the room, and slammed the door violently behind him.

Before Mr. Gordon had time to recover from his astonishment, Russell stood by him.

"Well, my boy," said the master, softening in a moment, and laying his hand gently on Russell's head, "what have you to say? You cannot tell how I rejoice, amid the deep sorrow that this has caused me, to find that *you* at least are uncontaminated. But I *knew*, Edwin, that I could trust you."

"O sir, I come to speak for Eric—for Williams." Mr. Gordon's brow darkened again, and the storm gathered, as he interrupted vehemently, "Not a word, Russell; not a word. This is the *second* time that he has wilfully deceived me; and this time he has involved others too in his base deceit."

" Indeed, sir, you wrong him. I can't think how
he came to write the paper, but I *know* that he did
not and would not use it. Didn't you see yourself, sir,
how he turned his head quite another way when he
broke down."

" It is very kind of you, Edwin, to defend him ;"
said Mr. Gordon coldly, " but at present, at any rate, I
must not hear you. Leave me ; I feel very sad, and
must have time to think over this disgraceful affair."

Russell went away disconsolate, and met his friend
striding up and down the passage, waiting for Dr. Rowlands to come out of the library.

" O Eric," he said, " how came you to write that
paper ?"

" Why, Russell, I did feel very much ashamed, and
I would have explained it, and said so ; but that Gordon
spites me so. It is such a shame ; I don't feel now as
if I cared one bit."

" I am sorry you don't get on with him ; but remember you have given him in this case good cause to
suspect. You never crib, Eric, I know, but I can't
help being sorry that you wrote the paper."

" But then Graham asked me to do it, and called
me cowardly because I refused at first."

" Ah, Eric," said Russell, " they will ask you to do
worse things if you yield so easily. I wouldn't say
anything to Dr. Rowlands about it, if I were you."

Eric took the advice, and, full of mortification, went
home. He gave his father a true and manly account of

the whole occurrence, and that afternoon Mr. Williams wrote a note of apology and explanation to Mr. Gordon. Next time the form went up, Mr. Gordon said, in his most freezing tone, " Williams, at present I shall take no further notice of your offence beyond including you in the extra lesson every half-holiday."

From that day forward Eric felt that he was marked and suspected, and the feeling worked on him with the worst effects. He grew more careless in work, and more trifling and indifferent in manner. Several boys now beat him whom he had easily surpassed before, and his energies were for a time entirely directed to keeping that supremacy in the games which he had won by his activity and strength.

It was a Sunday afternoon, toward the end of the summer term, and the boys were sauntering about in the green playground, or lying on the banks reading and chatting. Eric was with a little knot of his chief friends, enjoying the sea breeze as they sat on the grass. At last the bell of the school chapel began to ring, and they went in to the afternoon service. Eric usually sat with Duncan and Llewellyn, immediately behind the benches allotted to chance visitors. The bench in front of them happened on this afternoon to be occupied by some rather odd people, viz., an old man with long white hair, and two ladies remarkably stout, who were dressed with much juvenility, although past middle age. Their appearance immediately attracted notice, and no sooner had they taken their seats than Duncan and

Llewellyn began to titter. The ladies' bonnets, which were of white, trimmed with long green leaves and flowers, just peered over the top of the boys' pew, and excited much amusement. But Eric had not yet learnt to disregard the solemnity of the place, and the sacred act in which they were engaged. He tried to look away, and attend to the service, and for a time he partially succeeded, although, seated as he was between the two triflers, who were perpetually telegraphing to each other their jokes, he found it a difficult task, and secretly he began to be much tickled.

At last the sermon commenced, and Llewellyn, who had imprisoned a grasshopper in a paper cage, suddenly let it hop out. The first hop took it to the top of the pew; the second perched it on the shoulder of the stoutest lady. Duncan and Llewellyn tittered louder, and even Eric could not resist a smile. But when the lady, feeling some irritation on her shoulder, raised her hand, and the grasshopper took a frightened leap into the centre of the green foliage which enwreathed her bonnet, none of the three could stand it, and they burst into fits of laughter, which they tried in vain to conceal by bending down their heads and cramming their handkerchiefs into their mouths. Eric, having once given way, enjoyed the joke uncontrollably, and the lady made matters worse by her uneasy attempts to dislodge the unknown intruder, and discover the cause of the tittering, which she could not help hearing. At last all three began to laugh so violently that several heads

were turned in their direction, and Dr. Rowlands' stern
eye caught sight of their levity. He stopped short in
his sermon, and for one instant transfixed them with
his indignant glance. Quiet was instantly restored,
and alarm reduced them to the most perfect order,
although the grasshopper still sat imperturbable among
the artificial flowers. Meanwhile the stout lady had
discovered that for some unknown reason she had been
causing considerable amusement, and, attributing it to
intentional ridicule, looked round, justly hurt. Eric,
with real shame, observed the deep vexation of her
manner, and bitterly repented his share in the transaction.

Next morning Dr. Rowlands, in full academicals,
sailed into the fourth-form room. His entrance was
the signal for every boy to rise, and after a word or
two to Mr. Gordon, he motioned them to be seated.
Eric's heart sank within him.

"Williams, Duncan, and Llewellyn, stand out!"
said the Doctor. The boys, with downcast eyes and
burning cheeks, stood before him.

"I was sorry to notice," said he, "your shameful
conduct in chapel yesterday afternoon. As far as I
could observe, you were making yourselves merry in
that sacred place with the personal defects of others.
The lessons you receive here must be futile indeed if
they do not teach you the duty of reverence to God,
and courtesy to man. It gives me special pain,
Williams, to have observed that you, too, a boy high in

your remove, were guilty of this most culpable levity. You will all come to me at twelve o'clock in the library."

At twelve o'clock they each received a flogging. The pain inflicted was not great, and Duncan and Llewellyn, who had got into similar trouble before, cared very little for it, and went out laughing to tell the number of swishes they had received, to a little crowd of boys who were lingering outside the library door. But not so Eric. It was his *first* flogging, and he felt it deeply. To his proud spirit the disgrace was intolerable. At that moment he hated Dr. Rowlands, he hated Mr. Gordon, he hated his schoolfellows, he hated everybody. He had been flogged; the thought haunted him; he, Eric Williams, had been forced to receive this most degrading corporal punishment. He pushed fiercely through the knot of boys, and strode as quick as he could along the playground, angry and impenitent.

At the gate Russell met him. Eric felt the meeting inopportune; he was ashamed to meet his friend, ashamed to speak to him, envious of him, and jealous of his better reputation. He wanted to pass him by without notice, but Russell would not suffer this. He came up to him and took his arm affectionately. The slightest allusion to his late disgrace would have made Eric flame out into passion; but Russell was too kind to allude to it then. He talked as if nothing had happened, and tried to turn his friend's thoughts to more pleasant subjects. Eric appreciated his kindness, but he was still sullen and fretful, and it was not until they parted that his better feelings won the day. But when Russell said to him " Good bye, Eric," it was too much for him, and seizing Edwin's hand, he wrung it hard, and tears rushed to his eyes.

" Dear, good Edwin! how I wish I was like you. If all my friends were like you, I should never get into these troubles."

" Nay, Eric," said Russell, " you may be far better than I. You have far better gifts, if you will only do yourself justice."

They parted by Mr. Williams' door, and Russell walked home sad and thoughtful; but Eric, barely answering his brother's greeting, rushed up to his room, and, flinging himself on his bed, sobbed like a child at the remembrance of his disgrace. They were not refreshing tears; he felt something hard at his heart, and, as he prayed neither for help nor forgiveness, it was pride and rebellion, not penitence, that made him miserable.

CHAPTER VI.

HOME AFFECTIONS.

" Keep the spell of home affection
Still alive in every heart;
May its power, with mild direction,'
Draw our love from self apart,
Till thy children
Feel that thou their Father art.".

SCHOOL HYMN.

"HAVE caught such a lot of pretty sea ane-
mones, Eric," said little Vernon Williams, as
his brother strolled in after morning school;
" I wish you would come and look at them."

" O, I can't come now, Verny; I am going
out to play cricket with some fellows directly."

" But it won't take you a minute; do come."

" What a little bore you are. Where are the
things?"

" O, never mind, Eric, if you don't want to look at
them," said Vernon, hurt at his brother's rough manner.

" First you ask me to look, and then say ' never
mind,' " said Eric impatiently; " here, shew me them."

The little boy brought a large saucer, round which

the crimson sea-flowers were waving their long tentacula in the salt water.

"Oh, ay; very pretty indeed. But I must be off to cricket."

Vernon looked up at his brother sadly.

"You aren't so kind to me, Eric, as you used to be."

"What nonsense! and all because I don't admire those nasty red-jelly things, which one may see on the shore by thousands any day. What a little goose you are, Vernon."

Vernon made no reply, but was putting away his sea-anèmones with a sigh, when in came Russell to fetch Eric to the cricket.

"Well Verny," he said "have you been getting those pretty sea-anemones? come here and shew me them. Ah, I declare you've got one of those famous white plumosa fellows among them. What a lucky little chap you are!"

Vernon was delighted.

"Mind you take care of them," said Russell. "Where did you find them?"

"I have been down the shore getting them."

"And have you had a pleasant morning?"

"Yes, Russell, thank you. Only it is rather dull being always by myself, and Eric never comes with me now."

"Naughty Eric," said Russell, playfully. "Never mind, Verny; you and I will cut him, and go by ourselves."

Eric had stood by during the conversation, and the contrast of Russell's unselfish kindness with his own harsh want of sympathy, struck him. He threw his arms round his brother's neck, and said, " We will both go with you, Verny, next half holiday."

" O, thank you, Eric," said his brother; and the two schoolboys ran out. But when the next half holiday came, warm and bright, with the promise of a good match that afternoon, Eric repented his promise, and left Russell to amuse his little brother, while he went off, as usual, to the playground.

There was one silent witness of scenes like these, who laid them up deeply in her heart. Mrs. Williams was not unobservant of the gradual but steady falling off in Eric's character, and the first thing she noticed was the blunting of his home affections. When they first came to Roslyn, the boy used constantly to join his father and mother in their walks; but now he went seldom or never; and even if he did go, he seemed ashamed, while with them, to meet any of his schoolfellows. The spirit of false independence was awake and growing in her darling son. The bright afternoons they had spent together on the sunny shore, or seeking for sea-flowers among the lonely rocks of the neighbouring headlands,— the walks at evening and sunset among the hills, and the sweet counsel they had together, when the boy's character opened like a flower in the light and warmth of his mother's love,—the long twilights when he would sit on a stool with his young head resting on her knees, and her loving hand among his fair hair,—all these things were becoming to Mrs. Williams memories, and nothing more.

It was the trial of her life, and very sad to bear ; the more so because they were soon to be parted, certainly for years, perhaps for ever. The time was drawing nearer and nearer ; it was now June, and Mr. Williams' term of furlough ended in two months. The holidays at Roslyn were the months of July and August, and towards their close Mr. and Mrs. Williams intended to leave Vernon at Fairholm, and start for India—sending back Eric by himself as a boarder in Dr. Rowlands' house.

After morning school, on fine days, the boys used to run straight down to the shore and bathe. A bright and joyous scene it was. They stripped off their clothes on the shingle that adjoined the beach, and then running along the sands, would swim out far into the bay till their heads looked like small dots glancing in the sunshine. This year Eric had learned to swim, and he enjoyed the bathing more than any other pleasure.

One day after they had dressed, Russell and he began to amuse themselves on the sea-shore. The little translucent pools left on the sands by the ebbing tide always swarm with life, and the two boys found great fun in hunting audacious little crabs, or catching the shrimps that shuffled about in the shallow water. At last Eric picked up a piece of wood which he found lying on the beach, and said, " What do you say to coming crabfishing, Edwin? this bit of stick will do capitally to thrust between the rocks in the holes where they lie?"

Russell agreed, and they started to the rocks of the Ness to seek a likely place for their purpose. The Ness was a mile off, but in the excitement of their pleasure they were oblivious of time.

The Williams', for the boys' convenience, usually dined at one, but on this day they waited half an hour for Eric. Since, however, he didn't appear, they dined without him, supposing that he was accidentally detained, and expecting him to come in every minute. But two o'clock came, and no Eric; half-past two, and no Eric; three, but still no Eric. Mrs. Williams became seriously alarmed, and even her husband grew uneasy.

Vernon was watching for his brother at the window, and seeing Duncan pass by, ran down to ask him " If he knew where Eric was?"

" No," said Duncan; " last time I saw him was on the shore. We bathed together, and I remember his clothes were lying by mine when I dressed. But I havn't seen him since. If you like we'll go and look for him. I daresay he's on the beach somewhere." .

But they found no traces of him there; and when they returned with this intelligence, his mother got so agitated that it required all her husband's firm gentleness to support her sinking spirits. There was enough to cause anxiety, for Vernon repeatedly ran out to ask the boys who were passing if they had seen his brother, and the answer always was, that they had left him bathing in the sea.

Meanwhile our young friends, having caught several crabs, suddenly noticed by the sun that it was getting late.

"Good gracious, Edwin," said Eric, pulling out his watch, "it's half-past three; what have we been thinking of? How frightened they'll be at home;" and running back as fast as they could, they reached the house at five o'clock, and rushed into the room.

"Eric, Eric," said Mrs. Williams faintly, "where have you been? has anything happened to you, my child?"

"No mother, nothing. I've only been crabfishing with Russell, and we forgot the time."

"Thoughtless boy," said his father, "your mother has been in an agony about you."

Eric saw her pale face and tearful eyes, and flung himself in her arms, and mother and son wept in a long embrace. "Only two months," whispered Mrs. Williams, "and we shall leave you, dear boy, perhaps for ever. O do not forget your love for us in the midst of new companions."

The end of term arrived; this time Eric came out eighth only instead of first, and, therefore, on the prize-day, was obliged to sit among the crowd of undistinguished boys. He saw that his parents were disappointed, and his own ambition was grievously

mortified. But he had full confidence in his own
powers, and made the strongest resolutions to work hard
the next half-year, when he had got out of "that
Gordon's" clutches.

The Williams' spent the holidays at Fairholm, and
now, indeed, in the prospect of losing them, Eric's
feelings to his parents came out in all their strength.
Most happily the days glided by, and the father and
mother used them wisely. All their gentle influence,
all their deep affection, were employed in leaving on the
boy's heart lasting impressions of godliness and truth.
He learnt to feel that their love would encircle him for
ever with its heavenly tenderness, and their pure prayers
rise for him night and day to the throne of God.

The day of parting came, and most bitter and
heart-rending it was. In the wildness of their passionate
sorrow, Eric and Vernon seemed to hear the sound of
everlasting farewells. It is God's mercy that ordains
how seldom young hearts have to endure such misery.

At length it was over. The last sound of wheels
had died away; and during those hours the hearts of
parents and children felt the bitterness of death. Mrs.
Trevor and Fanny, themselves filled with grief, still
used all their unselfish endeavours to comfort their dear
boys. Vernon, weary of crying, soon sank to sleep;
but not so Eric. He sat on a low stool, his face buried
in his hands, breaking the stillness every now and then
with his convulsive sobs.

" O Aunty," he cried, " do you think I shall ever

see them again? I have been so wicked, and so little grateful for all their love. O, I wish I had thought at Roslyn how soon I was to lose them."

"Yes, dearest," said Mrs. Trevor, "I have no doubt we shall all meet again soon. Your father is only going for five years, you know, and that will not seem very long. And then they will be writing continually to us, and we to them. Think, Eric, how gladdened their hearts will be to hear that you and Vernon are good boys, and getting on well."

"O, I *will* be a better boy, I *will* indeed," said Eric; "I mean to do great things, and they shall have nothing but good reports of me."

"God helping you, dear," said his aunt, pushing back his hair from his forehead, and kissing it softly; "without His help, Eric, we are all weak indeed."

She sighed. But how far deeper her sigh would have been had she known the future. Merciful is the darkness that shrouds it from human eyes!

CHAPTER VII.

" We were, fair queen,
Two lads that thought there was no more behind,
But such a day to-morrow as to-day,
And to be boy eternal."—WINTER'S TALE, I. 2.

THE holidays were over. Vernon was to have
a tutor at Fairholm, and Eric was to return
alone, and be received into Dr. Rowlands'
house.

As he went on board the steam-packet, he
saw numbers of the well-known faces on deck,
and merry voices greeted him.

" Hallo, Williams! here you are at last,"
said Duncan, seizing his hand. " How have you
enjoyed the holidays? It's so jolly to see you again."

" So you're coming as a boarder," said Montagu,
" and to our noble house, too. Mind you stick up for
it, old fellow. Come along, and let's watch whether
the boats are bringing any more fellows; we shall be
starting in a few minutes."

" Ha! there's Russell," said Eric, springing to the

gangway, and warmly shaking his friend's hand as he
came on board.

"Have your father and mother gone, Eric?" said
Russell, after a few minutes' talk.

"Yes," said Eric, turning away his head, and
hastily brushing his eyes. "They are on their way
back to India."

"I'm so sorry," said Russell; "I don't think any
one has ever been so kind to me as they were."

"And they loved you, Edwin, dearly, and told me,
almost the last thing, that they hoped we should always
be friends. Stop! they gave me something for you."
Eric opened his carpet-bag, and took out a little box
carefully wrapped up, which he gave to Russell. It
contained a pretty silver watch, and inside the case was
engraved—"Edwin Russell, from the mother of his
friend Eric."

The boy's eyes glistened with joyful surprise.
"How good they are," he said; "I shall write and
thank Mrs. Williams directly we get to Roslyn."

They had a fine bright voyage, and arrived that
night. Eric, as a new comer, was ushered at once into
Dr. Rowlands' drawing-room, where the head master
was sitting with his wife and children. His greeting
was dignified, but not unkindly; and, on saying "good
night," he gave Eric a few plain words of affectionate
advice.

At that moment Eric hardly cared for advice. He
was full of life and spirits, brave, bright, impetuous,

tingling with hope, in the flush and flower of boyhood.
He bounded down the stairs, and in another minute
entered the large room where all Dr. Rowlands' boarders
assembled, and where most of them lived, except the
few privileged sixth form, and other boys who had
" studies." A cheer greeted his entrance into the
room. By this time most of the Rowlandites knew
him, and were proud to have him among their number.
They knew that he was clever enough to get them
credit in the school, and, what was better still, that he
would be a capital accession of strength to the cricket
and football. Except Barker, there was not one who
had not a personal liking for him, and on this occasion
even Barker was gracious.

The room in which Eric found himself was large
and high. At one end was a huge fire-place, and there
was generally a throng of boys round the great iron
fender, where, in cold weather, a little boy could seldom
get. The large windows opened on the green playground ; and iron bars prevented any exit through them.
This large room, called " the boarders' room," was the
joint habitation of Eric and some thirty other boys ;
and at one side ran a range of shelves and drawers,
where they kept their books and private property.
There the younger Rowlandites breakfasted, dined, had
tea, and, for the most part, lived. Here, too, they had
to get through all such work as was not performed
under direct supervision. How many and what varied
scenes had not that room beheld ! had those dumb walls

any feeling, what worlds of life and experience they would have acquired! If against each boy's name, as it was rudely cut on the oak panels, could have been also cut the fate that had befallen him, the good that he had there learnt, the evil that he there had suffered—what *noble* histories would the records unfold of honour and success, of baffled temptations and hard-won triumphs; what *awful* histories of hopes blighted and habits learned, of wasted talents and ruined lives!

The routine of school-life was on this wise :—At half-past seven the boys came down to prayers, which were immediately followed by breakfast. At nine they went into school, where they continued, with little interruption, till twelve. At one they dined, and, except on half-holidays, went into school again from two till five. The lock-up bell rang at dusk; at six o'clock they had tea—which was a repetition of breakfast, with leave to add to it whatever else they liked—and immediately after sat down to " preparation," which lasted from seven till nine. During this time one of the masters was always in the room, who allowed them to read amusing books, or employ themselves in any other quiet way they liked, as soon as ever they had learnt their lessons for the following day. At nine Dr. Rowlands came in and read prayers, after which the boys were dismissed to bed.

The arrangement of the dormitories was peculiar. They were a suite of rooms, exactly the same size, each opening into the other ; six on each side of a lavatory,

which occupied the space between them, so that, when
all the doors were open, you could see from one end
of the whole range to the other. The only advantage
of this arrangement was, that one master walking
up and down could keep all the boys in order while
they were getting into bed. About a quarter of an
hour was allowed for this process, and then the master
went along the rooms putting out the lights. A few
of the "study-boys" were allowed to sit up till ten,
and their bedrooms were elsewhere. The consequence
was, that in these dormitories the boys felt perfectly
secure from any interruption. There were only two
ways by which a master could get at them ; one up the
great staircase, and through the lavatory ; the other by
a door at the extreme end of the range, which led into
Dr. Rowlands' house, but was generally kept locked.

In each dormitory slept four or five boys, distributed
by their order in the school list, so that, in all the dormitories, there were nearly sixty ; and of these a goodly
number were, on Eric's arrival, collected in the boarders'
room, the rest being in their studies, or in the class-
rooms which some were allowed to use in order to
prevent too great a crowd in the room below.

At nine o'clock the prayer-bell rang. Immediately
all the boarders took their seats for prayers, each with
an open Bible before him ; and when the school servants had also come in, Dr. Rowlands read a chapter,
and offered up an extempore prayer. While reading,
he generally interspersed a few pointed remarks or

graphic explanations, and Eric learnt much in this simple way. The prayer, though short, was always well suited to the occasion, and calculated to carry with it the attention of the worshippers.

Prayers over, the boys noisily dispersed to their bed-rooms, and Eric found himself placed in a room immediately to the right of the lavatory, occupied by Duncan, Graham, Llewellyn, and two other boys named Bull and Attlay, all in the same form with himself. They were all tired with their voyage, and the excitement of coming back to school, so that they did not talk much that night, and before long Eric was fast asleep, dreaming, dreaming, dreaming that he should have a very happy life at Roslyn school, and seeing himself win no end of distinctions, and make no end of new friends.

CHAPTER VIII.

" TAKING UP."

> " We are not worst at once ;—the course of evil
> Begins so slowly, and from such slight source,
> An infant's hand might stop the breach with clay :
> But let the stream grow wider, and Philosophy—
> Ay, and Religion too—may strive in vain
> To stem the headlong current !"—ANON.

WITH intense delight Eric heard it announced next morning, when the new school-list was read, that he had got his remove into the "Shell," as the form was called which intervened between the fourth and the fifth. Russell, Owen, and Montagu also got their removes with him, but his other friends were left for the present in the form below.

Mr. Rose, his new master, was in every respect a great contrast with Mr. Gordon. He was not so brilliant in his acquirements, nor so vigorous in his teaching, and therefore clever boys did not catch fire from him so much as from the fourth-form master. But he was a far truer and deeper Christian; and, with no less scrupulous a sense of honour and detestation of every form of moral obliquity, he never yielded to those storms of passionate indignation which Mr. Gordon found it impossible to control. Disappointed in early life, subjected to the deepest and most painful trials, Mr. Rose's fine character had come out like gold from the flame. He now lived in and for the boys alone, and his whole life was one long self-devotion to their service and interests. The boys felt this, and even the worst of them, in their worst moments, loved and honoured Mr. Rose. But he was not seeking for gratitude, which he neither expected nor required ; he asked no affection in return for his self-denials; he worked with a pure spirit of human and self-sacrificing love, happy beyond all payment if ever he were instrumental in saving one of his charge from evil, or turning one wanderer from the error of his ways.

He was an unmarried man, and therefore took no boarders himself, but lived in the school-buildings, and had the care of the boys in Dr. Rowlands' house.

Such was the master under whom Eric was now placed, and the boy was sadly afraid that an evil report would have reached his ears, and given him already an unfavourable impression. But he was soon happily undeceived. Mr. Rose at once addressed him with much kindness, and he felt that, however bad he had been before, he would now have an opportunity to turn over a new leaf, and begin again a career of hope. He worked admirably at first, and even beat, for the first week or two, his old competitors, Owen and Russell.

From the beginning, Mr. Rose took a deep interest in him. Few could look at the boy's bright blue eyes and noble face without doing so, and the more when they knew that his father and mother were thousands of miles away, leaving him alone in the midst of so many dangers. Often the master asked him, and Russell, and Owen, and Montagu, to supper with him in the library, which gave them the privilege of sitting up later than usual, and enjoying a more quiet and pleasant evening than was possible in the noisy rooms. Boys and master were soon quite at home with each other, and in this way Mr. Rose had an opportunity of instilling many a useful warning without the formality of regular discipline or stereotyped instruction.

Eric found the life of the "boarders' room" far rougher than he had expected. Work was out of the question there, except during the hours of preparation, and the long dark winter evenings were often dull enough. Sometimes, indeed, they would all join in some regular indoor boys' game like "baste the bear," or "high-cockolorum;" or they would have amusing "ghost-hunts," as they called them, after some dressed-up boy among the dark corridors and staircases. This was good enough fun, but at other times they got tired of games, and could not get them up, and then numbers of boys felt the idle time hang heavy on their hands. When this was the case, some of the worse sort, as might have been expected, would fill up their leisure with bullying or mischief.

For some time they had a form of diversion which disgusted and annoyed Eric exceedingly. On each of the long iron-bound deal tables were placed two or three tallow candles in tin candlesticks, and this was the only light the boys had. Of course, these candles often wanted snuffing, and as snuffers were sure to be thrown about and broken as soon as they were brought into the room, the only resource was to snuff them with the fingers, at which all the boys became great adepts from necessity. One evening Barker, having snuffed the candle, suddenly and slyly put the smouldering wick unnoticed on the head of a little quiet inoffensive fellow named Wright, who happened to be sitting next to him. It went on smouldering for some time without Wright's perceiving it, and at last Barker, highly delighted, exclaimed—

"I see a chimney," and laughed.

Four or five boys looked up, and very soon every one in the room had noticed the trick except little Wright himself, who unconsciously wrote on at the letter he was sending home.

Eric did not like this; but, not wishing to come across Barker again, said nothing, and affected not to have observed. But Russell said quietly, " There's something on your head, Wright," and the little boy putting up his hand, hastily brushed off the horrid wick.

" What a shame !" he said, as it fell on his letter, and made a smudge.

" Who told you to interfere ?" said Barker, turning

fiercely to Russell. Russell, as usual, took not the
slightest notice of him, and Barker, after a little more
bluster, repeated the trick on another boy. This time
Russell thought that every one might be on the look-
out for himself, and so went on with his work. But
when Barker again chanted maliciously—

"I see a chimney," every boy who happened to be
reading or writing, uneasily felt to discover whether this
time he were himself the victim or no; and so things
continued for half an hour.

Ridiculous and disgusting as this folly was, it became, when constantly repeated, very annoying. A
boy could not sit down to any quiet work without constant danger of having some one creep up behind him
and put the offensive fragment of smoking snuff on his
head; and neither Barker nor any of his little gang
of imitators seemed disposed to give up their low
mischief.

One night, when the usual exclamation was made,
Eric felt sure, from seeing several boys looking at him,
that this time some one had been treating him in the
same way. He indignantly shook his head, and sure
enough the bit of wick dropped off. Eric was furious,
and, springing up, he shouted—

"By Jove! I *won't* stand this any longer."

"You'll have to sit it then," said Barker.

"O, it was *you* who did it, was it? Then take
that;" and, seizing one of the tin candlesticks, Eric
hurled it at Barker's head. Barker dodged, but the

edge of it cut open his eyebrow as it whizzed by, and the blood flowed fast.

"I'll kill you for that," said Barker, leaping at Eric, and seizing him by the hair.

"You'll get killed yourself then, you brute," said Upton, Russell's cousin, a fifth-form boy, who had just come into the room—and he boxed his ears as a premonitory admonition. "But, I say, young un," continued he to Eric, "this kind of thing won't do, you know. You'll get into rows if you shy candlesticks at fellows' heads at that rate."

"He has been making the room intolerable for the last month by his filthy tricks," said Eric hotly; "some one must stop him, and I will somehow, if no one else does."

"It wasn't I who put the thing on your head, you passionate young fool," growled Barker.

"Who was it then? How was I to know? You began it."

"You shut up, Barker," said Upton; "I've heard of your ways before, and when I catch you at your tricks, I'll teach you a lesson. Come up to my study, Williams, if you like."

Upton was a fine sturdy fellow of eighteen, immensely popular in the school for his prowess and good looks. He hated bullying, and often interfered to protect little boys, who accordingly idolised him, and did anything he told them very willingly. He meant to do no harm, but he did great harm. He was full of misdirected impulses, and had a great notion of being manly, which he thought consisted in a fearless disregard of all school rules, and the performance of the wildest tricks. For this reason he was never very intimate with his cousin Russell, whom he liked very much, but who was too scrupulous and independent to please him. Eric, on the other hand, was just the boy to take his fancy, and to admire him in return ; his life, strength, and pluck, made him a ready pupil in all schemes of mischief, and Upton, who had often noticed him, would have been the first to shudder had he known how far his example went to undermine all Eric's lingering good resolutions, and ruin for ever the boy of whom he was so fond.

From this time Eric was much in Upton's study, and constantly by his side in the playground. In spite of their disparity in age and position in the school, they became sworn friends, though their friendship was broken every now and then by little quarrels, which united them all the more closely after they had not spoken to each other perhaps for a week.

" Your cousin Upton has ' taken up' Williams," said Montagu to Russell one afternoon, as he saw the two strolling together on the beach, with Eric's arm in Upton's.

" Yes, I am sorry for it."

" So am I. We shan't see so much of him now."

" O, that's not my only reason," answered Russell, who had a rare habit of always going straight to the point.

" You mean you don't like the ' taking-up ' system."

" No, Montagu; I used once to have fine theories about it. I used to fancy that a big fellow would do no end of good to one lower in the school, and that the two would stand to each other in the relation of knight to squire. You know what the young knights were taught, Monty—to keep their bodies under, and bring them into subjection; to love God, and speak the truth always. That sounds very grand and noble to me. But when a big fellow takes up a little one, *you* know pretty well that *those* are not the kind of lessons he teaches."

" No, Russell; you're quite right. Its bad for a fellow in every way. First of all, it keeps him in an unnatural sort of dependence; then ten to one it makes him conceited, and prevents his character from really coming out well. And besides, the young chap generally gets paid out in kicks and abuse from the jealousy and contempt of the rest; and if his protector happens to leave, or anything of that kind, woe betide him !"

" No fear for Eric in that line, though," said Russell; " he can hold his own pretty well against any one. And after all, he is a most jolly fellow. I don't think even Upton will spoil him; it's chiefly the soft self-indulgent fellows, who are all straw and no iron, who get spoilt by being ' taken up.' "

Russell was partly right. Eric learnt a great deal of harm from Upton, and the misapplied hero-worship led to bad results.   But he was too manly a little fellow, and had too much self-respect, to sink into the effeminate condition which usually grows on the young delectables who have the misfortune to be " taken up."

Nor did he in the least drop his old friends, except Owen.   A coolness grew up between the latter and Eric, not unmingled with a little mutual contempt. Eric sneered at Owen as a fellow who did nothing but grind all day long, and had no geniality in him ; while Owen pitied the love of popularity which so often led Eric into delinquencies, which he himself despised. Owen had, indeed, but few friends in the school; the only boy who knew him well enough to respect and like him thoroughly was Russell, who found in him the only one who took the same high ground with himself. But Russell loved the good in every one, and was loved by all in return, and Eric he loved most of all, while he oftened mourned over his increasing failures.

One day as the two were walking together in the green playground, Mr. Gordon passed by ; and as the boys touched their caps, he nodded and smiled pleasantly at Russell, but hardly noticed, and did not return Eric's salute.   He had begun to dislike the latter more and more, and had given him up altogether as one of the reprobates.

" What a surly devil that is," said Eric, when he had passed ; " did you see how he purposely cut me ?"

" A surly . . . . ?   Oh Eric, that's the first time I ever heard you swear."

Eric blushed. He hadn't meant the word to slip out in Russell's hearing, though similar expressions were common enough in his talk with other boys. But he didn't like to be reproved, even by Russell, and in the ready spirit of self-defence, he answered—

"Pooh, Edwin, you don't call that swearing, do you? You're so strict, so religious, you know. I love you for it, but then, there are none like you. Nobody thinks anything of swearing here."

Russell was silent.

"Besides, what can be the harm of it? it means nothing. I was thinking the other night, and I concluded that you and Owen are the only two fellows here who don't swear."

Russell still said nothing.

"And, after all, I didn't swear; I only called that fellow a surly devil."

"O, hush! Eric, hush!" said Russell sadly. "You wouldn't have said so half-a-year ago."

Eric knew what he meant. The image of his father and mother rose before him, as they sate far away in their lonely Indian home, thinking of him, praying for him, centering all their hopes in him. In him!—and he knew how many things he was daily doing and saying, which would cut them to the heart. He knew that all his moral consciousness was fast vanishing, and leaving him a bad and reckless boy.

In a moment, all this passed through his mind. He remembered how shocked he had been at swearing at first ; and even when it became too familiar to shock him, how he determined never to fall into the habit himself. Then he remembered how gradually it had become quite a graceful sound in his ears ; a sound of entire freedom and independence of moral restraint ; an open casting off, as it were, of all authority, so that he had begun to admire it, particularly in Duncan, and above all, in his new hero, Upton ; and he recollected how, at last, an oath had one day slipped out suddenly in his own words, and how strange it sounded to him, and how Upton smiled to hear it, though conscience had reproached him bitterly ; but now that he had done it once, it became less dreadful, and gradually grew common enough, till even conscience hardly reminded him that he was doing wrong.

He thought of all this, and hung his head. Pride struggled with him for a moment, but at length, he answered, " O Edwin, I fear I am getting utterly bad ; I wish I were more like you," he added, in a low sad tone.

" Dear Eric, I have no right to say it, full of faults as I am myself; but you will be so much happier, if you try not to yield to all the bad things round us. Remember, I know more of school than you."

The two boys strolled on silently. That night Eric knelt at his bedside, and prayed as he had not done for many a long day.

CHAPTER IX.

"In the twilight, in the evening, in the black and dark night."—
                                                    PROV. vii. 9.

T Roslyn, even in summer, the hour for going to bed was half-past nine. It was hardly likely that so many boys, overflowing with turbulent life, should lie down quietly, and get to sleep. They never dreamt of doing so. Very soon after the masters were gone, the sconces were often relighted, sometimes in separate dormitories, sometimes in all of them, and the boys amused themselves by reading novels or making a row. They would play various games about the bedrooms, vaulting or jumping over the beds, running races in sheets, getting through the windows, upon the roofs, to frighten the study-boys with sham ghosts, or playing the thousand other pranks which suggested themselves to the fertile imagination of fifteen. But the favourite amusement was a bolstering match. One room would challenge another, and, stripping the covers off their bolsters, would meet in mortal fray. A bolster well wielded,

E 2

especially when dexterously applied to the legs, is a
very efficient instrument to bring a boy to the ground;
but it doesn't hurt very much, even when the blows
fall on the head.   Hence these matches were excellent
trials of strength and temper, and were generally
accompanied with shouts of laughter, never ending
until one side was driven back to its own room.   Many
a long and tough struggle had Eric enjoyed, and his
prowess was now so universally acknowledged, that his
dormitory, No. 7, was a match for any other, and far
stronger in this warfare than most of the rest.   At
bolstering, Duncan was a perfect champion; his strength
and activity were marvellous, and his mirth uproarious.
Eric and Graham backed him up brilliantly; while
Llewellyn and Attlay, with sturdy vigour, supported the
skirmishers.   Bull, the sixth boy in No. 7, was the only
fainéant among them, though he did occasionally help
to keep off the smaller fry.

Happy would it have been for all of them if Bull
had never been placed in No. 7; happier still if he had
never come to Roslyn school.   Backward in work,
overflowing with vanity at his supposed good looks, of
mean disposition and feeble intellect, he was the very
worst specimen of a boy that Eric had ever seen.   Not
even Barker so deeply excited Eric's repulsion and contempt.   And yet, since the affair of Upton, Barker and
Eric were declared enemies, and, much to the satisfaction of the latter, never spoke to each other; but with
Bull—much as he inwardly loathed him—he was pro-

fessedly and apparently on good terms. His silly love of universal popularity made him accept and tolerate the society even of this worthless boy.

Any two boys talking to each other about Bull would probably profess to like him " well enough," but if they were honest, they would generally end by allowing their contempt.

" We've got a nice set in No. 7, haven't we?" said Duncan to Eric one day.

" Capital. Old Llewellyn's a stunner, and I like Attlay and Graham."

" Don't you like Bull then?"

" O yes; pretty well."

The two boys looked each other in the face, and then, like the confidential augurs, burst out laughing.

" You know you detest him," said Duncan.

" No, I don't. He never did me any harm that I know of."

" Hm!—well, *I* detest him."

" Well!" answered Eric, " on coming to think of it, so do I. And yet he's popular enough in the school. I wonder how that is."

" He's not *really* popular. I've often noticed that fellows pretty generally despise him, yet somehow don't like to say so."

" Why do you dislike him, Duncan?"

" I don't know. Why do you?"

" I don't know either."

Neither Eric nor Duncan meant this answer to be

false, and yet if they had taken the trouble to consider, they would have found out in their secret souls the reasons of their dislike.

Bull had been to school before, and of this school he often bragged as the acmé of desirability and wickedness. He was always telling boys what they did at " his old school," and he quite inflamed the minds of such as fell under his influence by marvellous tales of the wild and wilful things which he and his former school-fellows had done. Many and many a scheme of sin and mischief at Roslyn was suggested, planned, and carried out on the model of Bull's reminiscences of his previous life.

He had tasted more largely of the tree of the knowledge of evil than any other boy, and, strange to say, this was the secret why the general odium was never expressed. He claimed his guilty experience so often as a ground of superiority, that at last the claim was silently allowed. He spoke from the platform of more advanced iniquity, and the others listened first curiously, then eagerly to his words.

" Ye shall be as gods, knowing good and evil." Such was the temptation which assailed the other boys in dormitory No. 7; and Eric among the number. Bull was the tempter. Secretly, gradually, he dropped into their too willing ears the poison of his polluting acquirements.

In brief, Bull was cursed with a degraded and corrupting mind.

I hurry over a part of my subject inconceivably painful; I hurry over it, but if I am to perform my self-imposed duty of giving a true picture of what school life *sometimes* is, I must not pass it by altogether.

The first time that Eric heard indecent words in dormitory No. 7, he was shocked beyond bound or measure. Dark though it was, he felt himself blushing scarlet to the roots of his hair, and then growing pale again, while a hot dew was left upon his forehead. Bull was the speaker; but this time there was a silence, and the subject instantly dropped. The others felt that "a new boy" was in the room; they did not know how he would take it; they were unconsciously abashed.

Besides, though they had themselves joined in such conversation before, they did not love it, and on the contrary, felt ashamed of yielding to it.

Now, Eric, now or never! Life and death, ruin and salvation, corruption and purity, are perhaps in the balance together, and the scale of your destiny may hang on a single word of yours. Speak out, boy! Tell these fellows that unseemly words wound your conscience; tell them that they are ruinous, sinful, damnable; speak out and save yourself and the rest. Virtue is strong and beautiful, Eric, and vice is downcast in her awful presence. Lose your purity of heart, Eric, and you have lost a jewel which the whole world, if it were "one entire and perfect chrysolite," cannot replace.

Good spirits guard that young boy, and give him grace in this his hour of trial! Open his eyes that he may see the fiery horses and the fiery chariots of the angels who would defend him, and the dark array of spiritual foes who throng around his bed. Point a pitying finger to the yawning abyss of shame, ruin, and despair that even now perhaps is being cleft under his feet. Shew him the garlands of the present and the past, withering at the touch of the Erinnys in the future. In pity, in pity shew him the canker which he is introducing into the sap of the tree of life, which shall cause its root to be hereafter as bitterness, and its blossom to go up as dust.

But the sense of sin was on Eric's mind. How *could* he speak? was not his own language sometimes profane? How—how could he profess to reprove another boy on the ground of morality, when he himself said and did things less ruinous perhaps, but equally forbidden?

For half an hour, in an agony of struggle with himself, Eric lay silent. Since Bull's last words nobody had spoken. They were going to sleep. It was too late to speak now, Eric thought. The moment passed by for ever; Eric had listened without objection to foul words, and the irreparable harm was done.

How easy it would have been to speak! With the temptation, God had provided also a way to escape. Next time it came, it was far harder to resist, and it soon became, to men, impossible.

Ah Eric, Eric! how little we know the moments

which decide the destinies of life. We live on as usual. The day is a common day, the hour a common hour. We never thought twice about the change of intention, which by one of the accidents—(accidents!) —of life determined for good or for evil, for happiness or misery, the colour of our remaining years. The stroke of the pen was done in a moment which led unconsciously to our ruin; the word was uttered quite heedlessly, on which turned for ever the decision of our weal or woe.

Eric lay silent. The darkness was not broken by the flashing of an angel's wing, the stillness was not syllabled by the sound of an angel's voice; but to his dying day Eric never forgot the moments which passed, until, weary and self-reproachful, he fell asleep.

Next morning he awoke, restless and feverish. He at once remembered what had passed. Bull's words haunted him; he could not forget them; they burnt within him like the flame of a moral fever. He was moody and petulant, and for a time could hardly conceal his aversion to Bull. Ah Eric! moodiness and petulance cannot save you, but prayerfulness would; one word, Eric, at the throne of grace—one prayer before you go down among the boys, that God in his mercy would wash away, in the blood of his dear Son, your crimson stains, and keep your conscience and memory clean.

The boy knelt down for a few minutes, and repeated to himself a few formal words. Had he stayed longer on his knees, he might have given way to a

burst of penitence and supplication—but he heard Bull's
footstep, and getting up, he ran down stairs to breakfast; so Eric did not pray.

Conversations did not generally drop so suddenly
in dormitory No. 7. On the contrary, they generally
flashed along in the liveliest way, till some one said,
" Good night ;" and then the boys turned off to sleep.
Eric knew this, and instantly conjectured that it was
only a sort of respect for him, and ignorance of the
manner in which he would consider it, that prevented
Duncan and the rest from taking any further notice of
Bull's remark. It was therefore no good disburdening
his mind to any of them ; but he determined to speak
about the matter to Russell in their next walk.

They usually walked together on Sunday. Dr.
Rowlands had discontinued the odious and ridiculous
custom of the younger boys taking their exercise under
a master's inspection. Boys are not generally fond of
constitutionals, so that on the half-holidays they almost
entirely confined their open-air exercise to the regular
games, and many of them hardly left the play-ground
boundaries once a week. But on Sundays they often
went walks, each with his favourite friend or companion. When Eric first came as a boarder, he invariably went with Russell on Sunday, and many a pleasant
stroll they had taken together, sometimes accompanied by
Duncan, Montagu, or Owen. The latter, however, had
dropped even this intercourse with Eric, who for the last
few weeks had more often gone with his new friend Upton.

"Come a walk, boy," said Upton, as they left the dining-room.

"O excuse me to-day, Upton," said Eric, "I'm going with your cousin."

"Oh *very* well," said Upton, in high dudgeon, and, hoping to make Eric jealous, he went a walk with Graham, whom he had "taken up" before he knew Williams.

Russell was rather surprised when Eric came to him and said, "Come a stroll to Fort Island, Edwin—will you?"

"O yes," said Russell cheerfully; "why, we haven't seen each other for some time lately! I was beginning to fancy that you meant to drop me, Eric."

He spoke with a smile, and in a rallying tone, but Eric hung his head; for the charge was true. Proud of his popularity among all the school, and especially at his friendship with so leading a fellow as Upton, Eric had *not* seen much of his friend since their last conversation about swearing. Indeed, conscious of failure, he felt sometimes uneasy in Russell's company.

He faltered, and answered humbly, "I hope you will never drop *me*, Edwin, however bad I get? But I particularly want to speak to you to-day."

In an instant Russell had twined his arm in Eric's, as they turned towards Fort Island; and Eric, with an effort, was just going to begin, when they heard Montagu's voice calling after them—

F

"I say, you fellows, where are you off to? may I come with you?"

"O yes, Monty, do," said Russell. "It will be quite like old times; now that my cousin Horace has got hold of Eric, we have to sing ' When shall we three meet again?' "

Russell only spoke in fun; but, unintentionally, his words jarred in Eric's heart. He was silent, and answered in monosyllables, so the walk was provokingly dull. At last they reached Fort Island, and sate down by the ruined chapel looking on the sea.

"Why what's the row with you, old boy," said Montagu, playfully shaking Eric by the shoulder, "you're as silent as Zimmerman on Solitude, and as doleful as Harvey on the Tombs. I expect you've been going through a select course of Blair's Grave, Young's Night Thoughts, and Drelincourt on Death."

To his surprise Eric's head was still bent, and, at last, he heard a deep suppressed sigh.

"My dear child, what is the matter with you?" said Russell, affectionately taking his hand, "surely you're not offended at my nonsense?"

Eric had not liked to speak while Montagu was by, but now he gulped down his rising emotion, and briefly told them of Bull's vile words the night before. They listened in silence.

"I knew it must come, Eric," said Russell at last, "and I am so sorry you didn't speak at the time."

" Do the fellows ever talk in that way in either of your dormitories ? " asked Eric.

" No," said Russell.

" Very little," said Montagu.

A pause followed, during which all three plucked the grass and looked away.

" Let me tell you," said Russell solemnly ; " my father (he is dead now you know, Eric), when I was sent to school, warned me of this kind of thing. I had been brought up in utter ignorance of such coarse knowledge as is forced upon one here, and with my reminiscences of home, I could not bear even that much of it which was impossible to avoid. But the very first time such talk was begun in my dormitory I spoke out. What I said I don't know, but I felt as if I was trampling on a slimy poisonous adder, and, at any rate, I showed such pain and distress that the fellows dropped it at the time. Since then I have absolutely refused to stay in the room if ever such talk is begun. So it never is now, and I do think the fellows are very glad of it themselves."

" Well," said Montagu, " I don't profess to look on it from the religious ground you know, but I thought it blackguardly, and in bad taste, and said so. The fellow who began it, threatened to kick me for a conceited little fool, but he didn't ; and they hardly ever venture on that ground now."

" It is more than blackguardly, it is deadly," answered Russell ; " my father said it was the most fatal curse which could ever become rife in a public school."

"Why do masters never give us any help or advice on these matters?" asked Eric thoughtfully.

"In sermons they do.   Don't you remember Rowlands' sermon not two weeks ago on Kibroth-Hattaavah?   But I for one think them quite right not to speak to us privately on such subjects, unless we invite confidence.   Besides, they cannot know that any boys talk in this way.   After all, it is only a very few of the worst who ever do."

They got up and walked home, but from day to day Eric put off performing the duty which Russell had advised, viz.—a private request to Bull to abstain from his offensive communications, and an endeavour to enlist Duncan into his wishes.

One evening they were telling each other stories in No. 7.   Bull's turn came, and in his story the vile element again appeared.   For a while Eric said nothing, but as the strain grew worse, he made a faint remonstrance.

"Shut up there, Williams," said Attlay, " and don't spoil the story."

"Very well.   It's your own fault, and I shall shut my ears."

He did for a time, but a general laugh awoke him. He pretended to be asleep but he listened.   Iniquity of this kind was utterly new to him; his curiosity was awakened; he no longer feigned indifference, and the poison flowed deep into his veins. Before that evening was over, Eric Williams was " a god, knowing good and evil."

O young boys, if your eyes ever read these pages, pause and beware. The knowledge of evil is ruin, and the continuance in it hell. That little matter—that beginning of evil,—it will be like the snowflake detached by the breath of air from the mountain-top, which, as it rushes down, gains size, and strength, and impetus, till it has swollen to the mighty and irresistible avalanche that overwhelms garden, and field, and village, in a chaos of undistinguishable death.

Kibroth-Hattaavah! Many and many a young Englishman has perished there! Many and many a happy English boy, the jewel of his mother's heart,— brave, and beautiful, and strong,—lies buried there. Very pale their shadows rise before us—the shadows of our young brothers who have sinned and suffered. From the sea and the sod, from foreign graves and English churchyards, they start up and throng around us in the paleness of their fall. May every schoolboy who reads this page be warned by the waving of their wasted hands, from that burning marle of passion, where they found nothing but shame and ruin, polluted affections, and an early grave.

CHAPTER X.

Ἀσπασίη τρίλλιστος ἐπήλυθε νὺξ ἐρεβέννη.

HOM.

OR a few days after the Sunday walk narrated in the last chapter, Upton and Eric cut each other dead. Upton was angry at Eric's declining the honour of his company, and Eric was piqued at Upton's unreasonableness. In the " taking up" system, such quarrels were of frequent occurrence, and as the existence of a misunderstanding was generally indicated in this very public way, the variations of good will between such friends generally excited no little notice and amusement among the other boys. But both Upton and Eric were too sensible to carry their differences so far as others similarly circumstanced; each thoroughly enjoyed the other's company, and they generally seized an early opportunity for effecting a reconciliation, which united them more firmly than ever.

As soon as Eric had got over his little pique, he made the first advances, by writing a note to Upton, which he slipped under his study door, and which ran as follows :—

" Dear Horace—Don't let us quarrel about nothing. Silly fellow, why should you be angry with me because for once I wanted to go a walk with Russell, who, by the bye, is twice as good a fellow as you? I shall expect you to make it up directly after prayers.—Yours, if you are not silly, E. W."

The consequence was, that as they came out from prayers, Upton seized Eric's hand, and slapped him on the back, after which they had a good laugh over their own foolish fracas, and ran up stairs, chattering merrily.

" There's to be an awful lark in the dormitories to-night," said Eric; " the doctor's gone to a dinner-party, and we're going to have no end of fun."

" Are you? Well, if it gets amusing, come to my study and tell me, and I'll come and look on."

" Very well; depend upon it I'll come." And they parted at the foot of the study stairs.

It was Mr. Rose's night of duty. He walked slowly up and down the range of dormitories until every boy seemed ready to get into bed, and then he put out all the candles. So long as he was present, the boys observed the utmost quiet and decorum. All continued quite orderly until he had passed away through the lavatory, and one of the boys, following him as a scout, had seen the last glimmer of his candle disappear round the corner at the foot of the great staircase, and heard the library door close behind him.

After that, particularly as Dr. Rowlands was absent, the boys knew that they were safe from disturbance, and the occupants of No. 7 were the first to stir.

" Now for some fun," said Duncan, starting up, and by way of initiative pitching his pillow at Eric's head.

" I'll pay you out for that when I'm ready," said Eric, laughing; " but give us a match first."

Duncan produced some vestas, and no sooner had they lighted their candle, than several of the dormitory doors began to be thrown open, and one after another all requested a light, which Duncan and Eric conveyed to them in a sort of emulous lampadephoria, so that at length all the twelve dormitories had their sconces lit, and the boys began all sorts of amusement, some in their night-shirts, and others with their trousers slipped on.   Leap-frog was the prevalent game for a time, but at last Graham suggested theatricals, and they were agreed on.

" But we're making a regular knock-me-down shindy," said Llewellyn; " somebody must keep cavè."

" O, old Rose is safe enough at his Hebrew in the library; no fear of disturbing him if we were dancing hippopotami," answered Graham.

But it was generally considered safest to put some one at the top of the stairs, in case of an unexpected diversion in that direction, and little Wright consented to go first.   He had only to leave the lavatory door open, and stand at the top of the staircase, and he then com-manded for a great distance the only avenue in which danger was expected.   If any master's candle appeared in the hall, the boys had full three minutes' warning, and a single loudly-whispered " cavè " would cause some one in each dormitory instantly to " douse the glim," and shut the door ; so that by the time of the adversary's arrival, they would all be (of course) fast asleep in bed, some of them snoring in an alarming manner. Whatever noise the master might have heard, it would be impossible to fix it on any of the sleepers.

So at the top of the stairs stood little Wright, shoeless, and shivering in his night-gown, but keenly entering into the fun, and not unconscious of the dignity of his position. Meanwhile the rest were getting up a scenic representation of Bombastes Furioso, arranging a stage, piling a lot of beds together for a theatre, and dressing up the actors in the most fantastic apparel.

The impromptu Bombastes excited universal applause, and just at the end Wright ran in through the lavatory.

" I say," said the little fellow, " it's jolly cold standing at the top of the stairs. Won't some one relieve guard ? "

" O, I will," answered Eric, good-naturedly ; " it's a shame that one fellow should have all the bother and none of the fun ; " and he ran to take Wright's post.

After watching a minute or two, he felt sure that there was no danger, and therefore ran up to Upton's study for a change.

" Well, what's up ? " said the study-boy, approvingly, as he glanced at Eric's laughing eyes.

" O, we've been having leap-frog, and then Bombastes Furioso. But I'm keeping 'cavè' now; only it's so cold that I thought I'd run up to your study."

"Little traitor; we'll shoot you for a deserting sentinel."

"O no;" said Eric, "its all serene; Rowley's out, and dear old Rose 'd never dream of supposing us elsewhere than in the arms of Morpheus. Besides, the fellows are making less row now."

"Well! look here! let's go and look on, and I'll tell you a dodge; put one of the tin washing-basins against the iron door of the lavatory, and then if any one comes he'll make clang enough to wake the dead; and while he's amusing himself with this, there'll be lots of time to 'extinguish the superfluous abundance of the nocturnal illuminators.' Eh?"

"Capital!" said Eric, "come along."

They went down and arranged the signal very artistically, leaving the iron door ajar a little, and then neatly poising the large tin basin on its edge, so as to lean against it. Having extremely enjoyed this part of the proceeding, they went to look at the theatricals again, the boys being highly delighted at Upton's appearance among them.

They at once made Eric take a part in some very distant reminiscences of Macbeth, and corked his cheeks with whiskers and mustachios to make him resemble Banquo, his costume being completed by a girdle round his nightshirt, consisting of a very fine crimson silk handkerchief, richly broidered with gold, which had been

brought to him from India, and which at first, in the
innocence of his heart, he used to wear on Sundays,
until it acquired the soubriquet of " the Dragon."
Duncan made a superb Macbeth.

They were doing the dagger-scene, which was put
on the stage in a most novel manner. A sheet had
been pinned from the top of the room, on one side of
which stood a boy with a broken dinner knife, the
handle end of which he was pushing through a hole in
the middle of the sheet at the shadow of Duncan on
the other side.

Duncan himself, in an attitude of intensely affected
melodrama, was spouting—

> " Is this a dagger which I see before me ?
> The handle towards me now ? come, let me clutch thee ; "

And he snatched convulsively at the handle of the pro-
truded knife ; but as soon as he nearly touched it, this
end was immediately withdrawn, and the blade end
substituted, which made the comic Macbeth instantly
draw back again, and recommence his apostrophe.   This
scene had tickled the audience immensely, and Duncan,
amid shouts of laughter, was just drawing the somewhat
unwarrantable conclusion that it was

> " A dagger of the mind, a false creation,"

When a sudden grating, followed by a reverberated
clang, produced a dead silence.

" Cavè," shouted Eric, and took a flying leap into
his bed.   Instantly there was a bolt in different direc-

tions; the sheet was torn down, the candles dashed out, the beds shoved aside, and the dormitories at once plunged in profound silence, only broken by the heavy breathing of sleepers, when in strode—not Mr. Rose or any of the under masters—but—Dr. Rowlands himself!

He stood for a moment to survey the scene. All the dormitory doors were wide open; the sheet which had formed the stage curtain lay torn on the floor of No. 7; the beds in all the adjoining rooms were in the strangest positions; and half-extinguished wicks still smouldered in several of the sconces. Every boy was in bed, but the extraordinary way in which the bed-clothes were huddled about told an unmistakeable tale.

He glanced quickly round, but the moment he had passed into No. 8, he heard a run, and, turning, just caught sight of Upton's figure vanishing into the darkness of the lavatory, towards the study stairs.

He said not a word, but stalked hastily through all the dormitories, again stopping in No. 7 on his return. He heard nothing but the deep snores of Duncan, and instantly fixed on him as a chief culprit.

" Duncan !"

No reply; but calm stertorous music from Duncan's bed.

" Duncan !" he said, still louder and more sternly, " you sleep soundly, sir, too soundly; get up directly," and he laid his hand on the boy's arm.

" Get away you old donkey," said Duncan sleepily; " 't'aint time to get up yet. First bell hasn't rung."

"Come sir, this shamming will only increase your punishment;" but the imperturbable Duncan stretched himself lazily, gave a great yawn, and then awoke with such an admirably feigned start at seeing Dr. Rowlands, that Eric, who had been peeping at the scene from over his bed-clothes, burst into an irresistible explosion of laughter.

Dr. Rowlands swung round on his heel— "What! Williams! get out of bed, sir, this instant."

Eric, forgetful of his disguise, sheepishly obeyed ; but when he stood on the floor, he looked so odd in his crimson girdle and corked cheeks, with Dr. Rowlands surveying him in intense astonishment, that the scene became overpoweringly ludicrous to Duncan, who now in his turn was convulsed with a storm of laughter, faintly echoed in stifled titterings from other beds.

" *Very* good," said Dr. Rowlands, now thoroughly angry, " you will hear of this to-morrow;" and he walked away with a heavy step, stopping at the lavatory door to restore the tin basin to its proper place, and then mounting to the studies.

Standing in the passage into which the studies opened, he knocked at one of the doors, and told a boy to summon all their occupants at once to the library.

Meanwhile, the dormitory-boys were aghast, and as soon as they heard the Doctor's retreating footsteps, began flocking in the dark to No. 7, not daring to relight their candles.

" Good gracious !" said Attlay, " only to think of Rowly appearing ! How could he have twigged ? "

" He must have seen our lights in the window as he came home," said Eric.

" I say, what a row that tin-basin dodge of yours made! What a rage the Doctor will be in to-morrow!"

" Won't you just catch it!" said Barker to Duncan, but intending the remark for Eric.

" Just like your mean chaff," retorted Duncan. " But I say, Williams," he continued laughing, " you *did* look so funny in the whiskers."

At this juncture they heard all the study-boys running down stairs to the library, and, lost in conjecture, retired to their different rooms.

" What do you think he'll do to us?" asked Eric.

" I don't know," said Duncan uneasily; " flog us, for one thing, that's certain. I'm so sorry about that basin, Eric; but it's no good fretting. We've had our cake, and now we must pay for it, that's all."

Eric's cogitations began to be unpleasant, when the door opened, and somebody stole noiselessly in.

" Who's there?"

" Upton. I've come to have a chat. The Doctor's like a turkey-cock in sight of a red handkerchief. Never saw him in such a rage."

" Why, what's he been saying?" asked Eric, as Upton came and took a seat on his bed.

" Oh! he's been rowing us like six o'clock," said Upton, " about 'moral responsibility,' 'abetting the follies of children,' 'forgetting our position in the school,' and I don't know what all; and he ended by asking who'd been in the dormitories. Of course, I confessed the soft impeachment, whereon he snorted, 'Ha! I suspected so. Very well, Sir, you don't know how to use a study; you shall be deprived of it till the end of term.'"

"Did he really, Horace?" said Eric. "And it's all my doing that you've got into the scrape. Do forgive me."

"Bosh! My dear fellow," said Upton, "it's twice as much my fault as yours; and, after all, it was only a bit of fun. It's rather a bore losing the study, certainly; but never mind, we shall see all the more of each other. Good night; I must be off."

Next morning, prayers were no sooner over than Dr. Rowlands said to the boys, "Stop! I have a word to say to you."

"I find that there was the utmost disorder in the dormitories yesterday evening. All the candles were relighted at forbidden hours, and the noise made was so great that it was heard through the whole building. I am grieved that I cannot leave you, even for a few hours, without your taking such advantage of my absence; and that the upper boys, so far from using their influence to prevent these infractions of discipline, seem inclined rather to join in them themselves. On this occasion I have punished Upton, by depriving him of a privilege which he has abused; and as I myself detected Duncan and Williams, they will be flogged in the library at twelve. But I now come to the worst part of the proceeding.   Somebody had been reckless enough to try and prevent surprise by the dangerous expedient of putting a tin basin against the iron door. The consequence was, that I was severely hurt, and *might* have been seriously injured in entering the lavatory.   I must know the name of the delinquent."

Upton and Eric immediately stood up.   Dr. Rowlands looked surprised, and there was an expression of grieved interest in Mr. Rose's face.

" Very well," said the Doctor, " I shall speak to you both privately."

Twelve o'clock came, and Duncan and Eric received a severe caning.   Corporal punishment, however necessary and desirable for some dispositions, always produced on Eric the worst effects.   He burned, not with remorse or regret, but with shame and violent indignation, and listened, with a glare in his eye, to Dr. Rowlands' warnings.   When the flogging was over, he almost rushed out of the room, to choke in solitude his sense of humiliation, nor would he suffer any one for an instant to allude to his disgrace.   Dr. Rowlands had hinted that Upton was doing him no good; but he passionately resented the suggestion, and determined, with obstinate perversity, to cling more than ever to the boy whom he had helped to involve in the same trouble with himself.

Any attempt on the part of masters to interfere in the friendships of boys is usually unsuccessful.   The boy who has been warned against his new acquaintance

not seldom repeats to him the fact that Mr. So-and-so
doesn't like seeing them together, and after that they
fancy themselves bound in honour to shew that they
are not afraid of continuing their connection. It was
not strange, therefore, that Eric and Upton were thrown
more than ever into each other's society, and consequently, that Eric, while he improved daily in strength,
activity, and prowess, neglected more and more his
school duties and honourable ambitions.

Mr. Rose sadly remarked the failure of promise in
his character and abilities, and did all that could be
done, by gentle firmness and unwavering kindness, to
recal his pupil to a sense of duty. One night he sent
for him to supper, and invited no one else. During
the evening he drew out Eric's exercise, and compared
it with those of Russell and Owen, who were now
getting easily ahead of him in marks. Eric's was
careless, hurried, and untidy; the other two were neat,
spirited, and painstaking, and had, therefore, been
marked much higher.

"Your exercises *used* to be far better—I may say
incomparably better," said Mr. Rose; "what is the
cause of this falling off?"

Eric was silent.

Mr. Rose laid his hand gently on his head. " I
fear, my boy, you have not been improving lately. You
have got into many scrapes, and are letting boys beat
you in form who are far your inferiors in ability. That
is a very bad *sign*, Eric; in itself it is a discouraging

fact, but I fear it indicates worse evils. You are wasting the golden hours, my boy, that can never return. I only hope and trust that no other change for the worse is going on in your character."

And so he talked on till the boy's sorrow was undisguised. " Come," he said gently, " let us kneel down together before we part."

Boy and master knelt down humbly side by side, and, from a full heart, the young man poured out his fervent petitions for the child beside him. Eric's heart seemed to catch a glow from his words, and he loved him as a brother. He rose from his knees full of the strongest resolutions, and earnestly promised amendment for the future.

But poor Eric did not yet know his own infirmity. For a time, indeed, there was a marked improvement; but daily life flowed on with its usual allurements, and when the hours of temptation came, his good intentions melted away, so that, in a few more weeks, the prayer, and the vows that followed it, had been obliterated from his memory without leaving any traces in his life.

CHAPTER XI.

"And either greet him not
Or else disdainfully, which shall shake him more
Than if not looked on."—Troilus and Cressida, iii. 3.

PTON, expatriated from his study, was allowed to use one of the smaller class-rooms which were occupied during play-hours by those boys who were too high in the school for "the boarders' room," and who were waiting to succeed to the studies as they fell vacant. There were three or four others with him in this class-room, and although it was less pleasant than his old quarters, it was yet far more comfortable than the Pandemonium of the shell and fourth-form boys.

As a general rule, no boys were allowed to sit in any of the class-rooms except their legitimate occupants. The rule, however, was very generally overlooked, and hence Eric, always glad of an opportunity to escape from the company of Barker and his associates, became a constant frequenter of his friend's new abode. Here they used to make themselves very comfortable. Joining the rest, they would drink coffee or chocolate, and amuse themselves over the fire with Punch, or some warlike novel in a green or yellow cover. One of them very often read aloud to the rest; and Eric, being both a good reader and a merry, intelligent listener, soon became quite a favourite among the other boys.

Mr. Rose had often seen him sitting there, and left him unmolested; but if ever Mr. Gordon happened to come in and notice him, he invariably turned him out, and after the first offence or two, had several times set him an imposition. This treatment gave fresh intensity to his now deeply-seated disgust at his late master, and his expressions of indignation at " Gordon's spite " were loud and frequent.

One day Mr. Gordon had accidentally come in, and found no one there but Upton and Eric; they were standing very harmlessly by the window, with Upton's arm resting kindly on Eric's shoulder as they watched with admiration the network of rippled sunbeams that flashed over the sea. Upton had just been telling Eric the splendid phrase ἀνήριθμον γέλασμα πόντου, which he had stumbled upon in an Æschylus lesson that morning, and they were trying which would hit on the best rendering of it. Eric stuck up for the literal sublimity of " the innumerable laughter of the sea," while Upton was trying to win him over to " the many-twinkling smile of ocean." They were enjoying the discussion, and each stoutly maintaining his own rendering, when Mr. Gordon entered.

On this occasion he was particularly angry : he had an especial dislike of seeing the two boys together, because he fancied that the younger had grown more than usually conceited and neglectful, since he had been under the fifth-form patronage ; and he saw in Eric's presence there, a new case of wilful disobedience.

"Williams, here *again!*" he exclaimed sharply, "Why, sir, you seem to suppose that you may defy rules with impunity! How often have I told you that no one is allowed to sit here, except the regular occupants ?"

His voice startled the two boys from their pleasant discussion.

"No other master takes any notice of it, sir," said Upton.

"I have nothing to do with other masters. Williams, you will bring me the fourth Georgic, written out by Saturday morning, for your repeated disobedience. Upton, I have a great mind to punish you also, for tempting him to come here."

This was a mistake on Mr. Gordon's part, of which Upton took immediate advantage.

"I have no power to prevent it, sir, if he wishes it. Besides," he continued with annoying blandness of tone, "it would be inhospitable ; and I am too glad of his company."

Eric smiled ; and Mr. Gordon frowned, "Williams, leave the room instantly."

The boy obeyed slowly and doggedly. "Mr. Rose

never interferes with me, when he sees me here," he said as he retreated.

" Then I shall request Mr. Rose to do so in future ; your conceit and impertinence, are getting intolerable."

Eric only answered with a fiery glance ; the next minute Upton joined him on the stairs, and Mr. Gordon heard them laughing a little ostentatiously, as they ran out into the playground together. He went away full of strong contempt, and from that moment began to look on the friends as two of the worst boys in the school.

This incident had happened on Thursday, which was a half-holiday, and instead of being able to join in any of the games, Eric had to spend that weary afternoon in writing away at the fourth Georgic ; Upton staying in a part of the time to help him a little, by dictating the lines to him—an occupation not unfrequently interrupted by storms of furious denunciation against Mr. Gordon's injustice and tyranny ; Eric vowing " that he would pay him out somehow yet."

The imposition was not finished that evening, and it again consumed some of the next day's leisure, part of it being written between schools in the forbidden class-room. Still it was not quite finished on Friday afternoon at six, when school ended, and Eric stayed a few minutes behind the rest to scribble off the last ten lines ; which done, he banged down the lid of his desk, not locking it, and ran out.

The next morning an incident happened which

involved considerable consequences to some of the actors
in my story.

Mr. Rose and several other masters had not a room to
themselves, like Mr. Gordon, but heard their forms in
the great hall. At one end of this hall was a board
used for the various school notices, to which there were
always affixed two or three pieces of paper containing
announcements about examinations and other matters
of general interest.

On Saturday morning (when Eric was to give up
his Georgic), the boys, as they dropped into the hall
for morning school, observed a new notice on the board,
and, thronging round to see what it was, read these
words, written on a half-sheet of paper, attached by
wafers to the board—

" GORDON IS A SURLY DEVIL."

As may be supposed, so completely novel an announcement took them all very much by surprise, and they
wondered who had been so audacious as to play this
trick. But their wonder was cut short by the entrance
of the masters, and they all took their seats, without
any one tearing down the dangerous paper.

After a few minutes the eye of the second master,
Mr. Ready, fell on the paper, and, going up, he read it,
stood for a moment transfixed with astonishment, and
then called Mr. Rose.

Pointing to the inscription, he said, " I think we
had better leave that there, Rose, exactly as it is, till

Dr. Rowlands has seen it. Would you mind asking him to step in here?"

Just at this juncture Eric came in, having been delayed by Mr. Gordon while he rigidly inspected the imposition. As he took his seat, Montagu, who was next him, whispered—

"I say, have you seen the notice-board?"

"No. Why?"

"Why, some fellow has been writing up an opinion of Gordon not very favourable."

"And serve him right, too, brute!" said Eric, smarting with the memory of his imposition.

"Well, there'll be no end of a row; you'll see."

During this conversation, Dr. Rowlands came in with Mr. Rose. He read the paper, frowned, pondered a moment, and then said to Mr. Rose—"Would you kindly summon the lower school into the hall? As it would be painful to Mr. Gordon to be present, you had better explain to him how matters stand."

"Halloa! here's a rumpus!" whispered Montagu; "he never has the lower school down for nothing."

A noise was heard on the stairs, and in flocked the lower school. When they had ranged themselves on the vacant forms, there was a dead silence and hush of expectation."

"I have summoned you all together," said the Doctor, "on a most serious occasion. This morning, on coming into the school-room, the masters found that the notice-board had been abused for the purpose of

writing up an insult to one of our number, which is at
once coarse and wicked. As only a few of you have
seen it, it becomes my deeply painful duty to inform you
of its purport; the words are these—" Gordon is a surly
devil."—A *very* slight titter followed this statement,
which was instantly succeeded by a sort of thrilling
excitement; but Eric, when he heard the words, started
perceptibly, and coloured as he caught Montagu's eye
fixed on him.

Dr. Rowlands continued—" I suppose this dastardly
impertinence has been perpetrated by some boy out of
a spirit of revenge. I am perfectly amazed at the
unparalleled audacity and meanness of the attempt, and
it may be very difficult to discover the author of it.
But, depend upon it, discover him *we will*, at whatever
cost. Whoever the offender may be, and he must be
listening to me at this moment, let him be assured that
he shall *not* be unpunished. His guilty secret shall be
torn from him. His punishment can only be mitigated
by his instantly yielding himself up."

No one stirred, but during the latter part of this
address Eric was so uneasy, and his cheek burned with
such hot crimson, that several eyes were upon him,
and the suspicions of more than one boy were
awakened.

" Very well," said the head master, " the guilty
boy is not inclined to confess. Mark, then; if his
name has not been given up to me by to-day week,
every indulgence to the school will be forfeited, the

G

next whole holiday stopped, and the coming cricket-match prohibited."

"The handwriting may be some clue," suggested Mr. Ready. "Would you have any objection to my examining the note-books of the Shell?"

"None at all. The Shell-boys are to show their books to Mr. Ready immediately."

The head-boy of the Shell collected the books, and took them to the desk; the three masters glanced casually at about a dozen, and suddenly stopped at one. Eric's heart beat loud, as he saw Mr. Rose point towards him.

"We have discovered a handwriting which remarkably resembles that on the board. I give the offender one more chance of substituting confession for detection."

No one stirred; but Montagu felt that his friend was trembling violently.

"Eric Williams, stand out in the room."

Blushing scarlet, and deeply agitated, the boy obeyed.

"The writing on the notice is exactly like yours. Do you know anything of this shameful proceeding?"

"Nothing, sir," he murmured in a low tone.

"Nothing whatever?"

"Nothing whatever, sir."

Dr. Rowlands' look searched him through and through, and seemed to burn into his heart. He did not meet it, but hung his head. The Doctor felt certain from his manner that he was guilty. He chained him to the spot with his glance for a minute or two, and then said slowly, and with a deep sigh—

"Very well; I *hope* you have spoken the truth; but, whether you have or no, we shall soon discover. The school, and especially the upper boys, will remember what I have said. I shall now tear down the insulting notice, and put it into your hands, Avonley, as head of the school, that you may make further inquiries." He left the room, and the boys resumed their usual avocation till twelve o'clock. But poor Eric could hardly get through his ordinary pursuits; he felt sick and giddy, until everybody noticed his strange embarrassed manner, and random answers.

No sooner had twelve o'clock struck, than the whole school broke up into knots of buzzing and eager talkers.

"I wonder who did it," said a dozen voices at once.

"The writing was undoubtedly Williams'," suggested some.

"And did you notice how red and pale he got when the Doctor spoke to him, and how he hung his head?"

"Yes; and one knows how he hates Gordon."

"Ay; by the bye, Gordon set him a Georgic only on Thursday, and he has been swearing at him ever since."

"I noticed that he stayed in after all the rest last night," said Barker.

"Did he? By Jove, that looks bad."

"Has any one charged him with it?" asked Duncan.

" Yes," answered one of the group : " but he's as proud about it as Lucifer, and is furious if you mention it to him.   He says we ought to know him better than to think him capable of such a thing."

" And quite right, too," said Duncan.   " If he did it, he's done something totally unlike what one would have believed possible of him."

The various items of evidence were put together, and certainly they seemed to prove a strong case against Eric.   In addition to the probabilities already mentioned, it was found that the ink used was of a violet colour, and a peculiar kind, which Eric was known to patronise ; and not only so, but the wafers with which the paper had been attached to the board were yellow, and exactly of the same size with some which Eric was said to possess.   How the latter facts had been discovered, nobody exactly knew, but they began to be very generally whispered throughout the school.

In short, the almost universal conviction among the boys proclaimed that he was guilty, and many urged him to confess it at once, and save the school from the threatened punishment.   But he listened to such suggestions with the most passionate indignation.

" What !" he said, angrily, " tell a wilful lie to blacken my own innocent character ?   Never !"

The consequence was, they all began to shun him. Eric was put into Coventry.   Very few boys in the school still clung to him, and maintained his innocence in spite of appearances, but they were the boys whom he had most loved and valued, and they were most vigorous in his defence. They were Russell, Montagu, Duncan, Owen, and little Wright.

On the evening of the Saturday, Upton had sought out Eric, and said, in a very serious tone, " This is a bad business, Williams. I cannot forget how you have been abusing Gordon lately, and though I won't believe you guilty, yet you ought to explain."

" What? even *you*, then, suspect me?" said Eric, bursting into proud tears. " Very well. I shan't condescend to *deny* it. I won't speak to you again till you have repented of mistrusting me;" and he resolutely rejected all further overtures on Upton's part.

He was alone in his misery. Some one, he perceived, had plotted to destroy his character, and he saw too clearly how many causes of suspicion told against him. But it was very bitter to think that the whole school could so readily suppose that he would do a thing which from his soul he abhorred. " No," he thought; " bad I may be, but I *could* not have done such a base and cowardly trick."

Never in his life had he been so wretched. He wandered alone to the rocks, and watched the waves dashing against them with the rising tide. The tumult of the weather seemed to relieve and console the tumult of his heart. He drank in strength and defiance from the roar of the waters, and climbed to their very edge along the rocks, where every fresh rush of the waves enveloped him in white swirls of angry foam. The

look of the green, rough, hungry sea, harmonised with
his feelings, and he sat down and stared into it, to find
relief from the torment of his thoughts.

At last, with a deep sigh, he turned away to go
back, and meet the crowd of suspicious and unkindly companions, and brood alone over his sorrow in the midst
of them.   He had not gone many steps, when he caught
sight of Russell in the distance.   His first impulse was
to run away and escape; but Russell determined to stop
him, and when he came up, said, " Dear Eric, I have
sought you out on purpose to tell you that *I* don't suspect you, and have never done so for a moment.   I
know you too well, my boy, and be sure that *I* will
always stick to you, even if the whole school cut you."

" Oh, Edwin, I am *so* wretched.   I needn't tell
you that I am quite innocent of this.   What have I
done to be so suspected?   Why, even your cousin Upton
won't believe me."

" But he does, Eric," said Russell; " he told me so
just now, and several others said the same thing."

A transient gleam passed over Eric's face.

" O, I do so long for home again," he said.   " Except
you, I have no friend."

" Don't say so, Eric.   This cloud will soon blow
over.   Depend upon it, as the Doctor said, we shall discover the offender yet, and the fellows will soon make you
reparation for their false suspicions.   And you *have* one
friend, Eric," he continued, pointing reverently upwards.

Eric was overcome; he sat down on the grass and

hid his face till the tears flowed through his closed fingers. Russell sat silent and pitying beside him, and let Eric's head rest upon his shoulder.

When they got home, Eric found three notes in his drawer. One was from Mr. Gordon, and ran thus :—

" I have little doubt, Williams, that you have done this act. Believe me, I feel no anger, only pity for you. Come to me and confess, and I promise, by every means in my power, to befriend and save you."

This note he read, and then, stamping on the floor, tore it up furiously into twenty pieces, which he scattered about the room.

Another was from Mr. Rose ;

" Dear Eric—I *cannot, will* not, believe you guilty, although appearances look very black. You have many faults, but I feel sure that I cannot be mistaken in supposing you too noble-minded for a revenge so petty and so mean. Come to me, dear boy, if I can help you in any way. I *trust you*, Eric, and will use every endeavour to right you in the general estimation. You are innocent; pray to God for help under this cruel trial, and be sure that your character will yet be cleared. —Affectionately yours, WALTER ROSE."

" *P.S.*—I can easily understand that just now you will like quiet; come and sit with me in the library as much as you like."

He read this note two or three times with grateful emotion, and at that moment would have died for Mr. Rose. The third note was from Owen, as follows :—

"Dear Williams—We have been cool to each other lately; naturally, perhaps. But yet I think that it will be some consolation to you to be told, even by a rival, that I, for one, feel certain of your innocence. If you want company, I shall be delighted now to walk with you.—Yours truly,   D. OWEN."

This note, too, brought much comfort to the poor boy's lonely and passionate heart. He put it into his pocket, and determined at once to accept Mr. Rose's kind offer of allowing him to sit for the present in the library.

There were several boys in the room while he was reading his notes, but none of them spoke to him, and he was too proud to notice them, or interrupt the constrained silence. As he went out he met Duncan and Montagu, who at once addressed him in the hearing of the rest.

"Ha! Williams," said Duncan, "we have been looking everywhere for you, dear fellow. Cheer up, you shall be cleared yet. I, for one, and Monty for another, will maintain your innocence before the whole school."

Montagu *said* nothing, but Eric understood full well the trustful kindness of his soft pressure of the hand. His heart was too full to speak, and he went on towards the library.

"I wonder at your speaking to that fellow," said Bull, as the two new comers joined the group at the fire-place.

" You will be yourself ashamed of having ever suspected him before long," said Montagu warmly; " ay, the whole lot of you; and you are very unkind to condemn him before you are certain."

" I wish you joy of your *friend*, Duncan," sneered Barker.

" Friend?" said Duncan, firing up; "yes! he is my friend, and I'm not ashamed of him. It would be well for the school if *all* the fellows were as honourable as Williams."

Barker took the hint, and although he was too brazen to blush, thought it better to say no more.

CHAPTER XII.

> "A plot, a plot, a plot, to ruin all."
>
> TENNYSON, *The Princess*.

N the Monday evening, the head boy reported to Dr. Rowlands that the perpetrator of the offence had not been discovered, but that one boy was very generally suspected, and on grounds that seemed plausible. "I admit," he added, "that from the little I know of him he seems to me a very unlikely sort of boy to do it."

"I think," suggested the Doctor, "that the best way would be for you to have a regular trial on the subject, and hear the evidence. Do you think that you can be trusted to carry on the investigation publicly, with good order and fairness?"

"I think so, sir," said Avonley.

"Very well. Put up a notice, asking all the school to meet by themselves in the boarders' room to-morrow afternoon at three, and see what you can do among you."

Avonley did as the Doctor suggested. At first,
when the boys assembled, they seemed inclined to treat
the matter as a joke, and were rather disorderly; but
Avonley briefly begged them, if they determined to
have a trial, to see that it was conducted sensibly; and
by general consent he was himself voted into the desk
as president. He then got up and said—

"There must be no sham or nonsense about this
affair. Let all the boys take their seats quietly down
the room."

They did so, and Avonley asked, "Is Williams
here?"

Looking round, they discovered he was not. Russell
instantly went to the library to fetch him, and told him
what was going on. He took Eric's arm kindly as they
entered, to show the whole school that he was not
ashamed of him, and Eric deeply felt the delicacy of his
goodwill.

"Are you willing to be tried, Williams," asked
Avonley, "on the charge of having written the insulting
paper about Mr. Gordon? Of course we know very
little how these kind of things ought to be conducted,
but we will see that everything done is open and above
ground, and try to manage it properly."

"There is nothing I should like better," said Eric.

He had quite recovered his firm manly bearing. A
quiet conversation with his dearly loved friend and
master had reassured him in the confidence of innocence,
and though the colour on his cheek had through excite-

ment sunk into two bright red spots, he looked wonderfully noble and winning as he stood before the boys in the centre of the room. His appearance caused a little reaction in his favour, and a murmur of applause followed his answer.

"Good," said Avonley; "who will prosecute on the part of the school?"

There was a pause. Nobody seemed to covet the office.

"Very well; if no one is willing to prosecute, the charge drops."

"I will do it," said Gibson, a Rowlandite, one of the study boys at the top of the fifth form. He was a clever fellow, and Eric liked the little he had seen of him.

"Have you any objection, Williams, to the jury being composed of the sixth form? or are there any names among them which you wish to challenge?"

"No," said Eric, glancing round with confidence.

"Well, now, who will defend the accused?"

Another pause, and Upton got up.

"No," said Eric, at once. "You were inclined to distrust me, Upton, and I will only be defended by somebody who never doubted my innocence."

Another pause followed, and then, blushing crimson, Russell got up. "I am only a Shell-boy," he said, "but if Eric doesn't mind trusting his cause to me, I will defend him, since no other fifth-form fellow stirs."

"Thank you, Russell, I *wanted* you to offer, I could wish no better defender."

" Will Owen, Duncan, and Montagu help me, if they can?" asked Russell.

" Very willingly," they all three said, and went to take their seats by him. They conversed eagerly for a few minutes, and then declared themselves ready.

" All I have got to do," said Gibson, rising, " is to bring before the school the grounds for suspecting Williams, and all the evidence which makes it probable that he is the offender. Now, first of all, the thing must have been done between Friday evening and Saturday morning; and since the school-room door is generally locked soon after school, it was probably done in the short interval between six and a quarter past. I shall now examine some witnesses."

The first boy called upon was Pietrie, who deposed, that on Friday evening, when he left the room, having been detained a few minutes, the only boy remaining in it was Williams.

Carter, the school-servant, was then sent for, and deposed, that he had met Master Williams hastily running out of the room, when he went at a quarter past six to lock the door.

Examined by Gibson.—" Was any boy in the room when you did lock the door?"

" No one."

" Did you meet any one else in the passage?"

" No."

Cross-examined by Russell.—" Do boys ever get into the room after the door is locked?"

" Yes."

" By what means ? "

" Through the side windows."

" That will do."

Russell here whispered something to Duncan, who at once left the room, and on returning, after a few minutes' absence, gave Russell a significant nod.

Barker was next brought forward, and questioned by Gibson.

" Do you know that Williams is in the habit of using a particular kind of ink ?"

" Yes ; it is of a violet colour, and has a peculiar smell."

" Could you recognise anything written with it ?"

" Yes."

Gibson here handed to Barker the paper which had caused so much trouble.

" Is that the kind of ink ?"

" Yes."

" Do you know the handwriting on that paper ?"

" Yes ; it is Williams' hand."

" How can you tell ?"

" He makes his r's in a curious way."

" Turn the paper over.   Have you ever seen those kind of wafers before ?"

" Yes ; Williams has a box of them in his desk."

" Has any other boy, that you are aware of, wafers like them ?"

" No."

Cross-examined by Duncan.—"*How* do you know that Williams has wafers like those?"

"I have seen him use them."

"For what purpose?"

"To fasten letters."

"I can't help remarking that you seem very well acquainted with what he does. Several of those who know him best, and have seen him oftenest, never heard of these wafers. May I ask," he said, "if any one else in the school will witness to having seen Williams use these wafers?"

No one spoke, and Barker, whose malice seemed to have been changed into uneasiness, sat down.

Upton was the next witness. Gibson began—

"You have seen a good deal of Williams?"

"Yes," said Upton, smiling.

"Have you ever heard him express any opinions of Mr. Gordon?"

"Often."

"Of what kind?"

"Dislike and contempt," said Upton, amidst general laughter.

"Have you ever heard him say anything which implied a desire to injure him?"

"The other day Mr. Gordon gave him a Georgic as an imposition, and I heard Williams say that he would like to pay him out."

This last fact was new to the school, and excited a great sensation.

" When did he say this ? "

" On Friday afternoon."

Upton had given his evidence with great reluctance, although, being simply desirous that the truth should come out, he concealed nothing that he knew.   He brightened up a little when Russell rose to cross-examine him.

" Have you ever known Williams do any mean act ?"

" Never."

" Do you consider him a boy *likely* to have been guilty on this occasion."

" Distinctly the reverse.   I am convinced of his innocence."

The answer was given with vehement emphasis, and Eric felt greatly relieved by it.

One or two other boys were then called on as witnesses to the great agitation which Eric had shown during the investigation in the school-room, and then Gibson, who was a sensible self-contained fellow, said, " I have now done my part.   I have shown that the accused had a grudge against Mr. Gordon at the time of the occurrence, and had threatened to be revenged on him ; that he was the last boy in the room during the time when the offence must have been committed ; that the handwriting is known to resemble his, and that the ink and wafers employed were such as he, and he only, was known to possess.   In addition to all this, his behaviour, when the matter was first publicly noticed, was exactly such as coincides with the supposition of his guilt. I think you will all agree in considering these grounds of suspicion very strong; and leaving them to carry their full weight with you, I close the case for the prosecution."

The school listened to Gibson's quiet formality with a kind of grim and gloomy satisfaction, and when he had concluded, there were probably few but Eric's own immediate friends who were not fully convinced of his guilt, however sorry they might be to admit so unfavourable an opinion of a companion whom they all admired.

After a minute or two, Russell rose for the defence, and asked, "Has Williams any objection to his desk being brought, and any of its contents put in as evidence?"

"Not the least; there is the key, and you will find it in my place in school."

The desk was brought, but it was found to be already unlocked, and Russell looked at some of the note-paper which it contained. He then began—" In spite of the evidence adduced, I think I can show that Williams is not guilty. It is quite true that he dislikes Mr. Gordon, and would not object to any open way of showing it; it is quite true that he used the expressions attributed to him, and that the ink and wafers are such as may be found in his desk, and that the handwriting is not unlike his. But is it probable that a boy intending to post up an insult such as this, would do so in a manner, and at a time so likely to involve him in im-

mediate detection, and certain punishment? At any
rate, he would surely disguise his usual handwriting.
Now, I ask any one to look at this paper, and tell me
whether it is not clear, on the contrary, that these letters
were traced slowly and with care, as would be the case
with an elaborate attempt to imitate?"   Russell here
handed the paper to the jury, who again narrowly examined it.

"Now, the evidence of Pietrie and Carter is of no
use, because Carter himself admitted that boys often
enter the room by the window; a fact to which we
shall have to allude again.

"We admit the evidence about the ink and wafers.
But it is rather strange that Barker should know about
the wafers, since neither I, nor any other friend of Williams, often as we have sat by him when writing letters,
have ever observed that he possessed any like them."

Several boys began to look at Barker, who was
sitting very ill at ease on the corner of a form, in vain
trying to appear unconcerned.

"There is another fact which no one yet knows, but
which I must mention.   It will explain Williams' agitation when Dr. Rowlands read out the words on that
paper; and, confident of his innocence, I am indifferent
to its appearing to tell against him.   I myself once
heard Williams use the very words written on that
paper, and not only heard them, but expostulated with
him strongly for the use of them.   I need hardly say
how very unlikely it is, that remembering this, he should

thus publicly draw my suspicions on him, if he meant to insult Mr. Gordon undiscovered. But, besides myself, there was another boy who accidentally overheard that expression. That boy was Barker.

"I have to bring forward a new piece of evidence, which at least ought to go for something. Looking at this half-sheet of note-paper, I see that the printer's name on the stamp in the corner is 'Graves, York.' Now, I have just found that there is no paper at all like this in Williams' desk ; all the note-paper it contains is marked ' Blakes, Ayrton.'

"I might bring many witnesses to prove how very unlike Williams' general character a trick of this kind would be. But I am not going to do this. We think we know the real offender. We have had one trial, and now demand another. It is our painful duty to prove Williams' innocence by proving another's guilt. That other is a known enemy of mine, and of Montagu's, and of Owen's. We therefore leave the charge of stating the case against him to Duncan, with whom he has never quarrelled."

Russell sat down amid general applause ; he had performed his task with a wonderful modesty and self-possession, which filled every one with admiration, and Eric warmly pressed his hand.

The interest of the school was intensely excited, and Duncan, after a minute's pause, starting up, said—

"Williams has allowed his desk to be brought in and examined. Will Barker do the same?"

The real culprit now saw at once that his plot to ruin Eric was recoiling on himself. He got up, swore and blustered at Russell, Duncan, and Williams, and at first flatly refused to allow his desk to be brought. He was, however, forced to yield, and when opened, it was immediately seen that the note-paper it contained was identical with that on which the words had been written. At this he affected to be perfectly unconcerned, and merely protested against what he called the meanness of trying to fix the charge on him.

" And what have you been doing the whole of the last day or two," asked Gibson, quietly, " but endeavouring to fix the charge on another?"

" We have stronger evidence against you," said Duncan, confronting him with an undaunted look, before which his insolence quailed. " Russell, will you call Graham ?"

Graham was called, and put on his honour.

" You were in the sick-room on Friday evening ?"

" Yes."

" Did you see any one get in to the school-room through the side window ?"

" I may as well tell you all about it. I was sitting doing nothing in the sick-room, when I suddenly saw Barker clamber in to the school-room by the window, which he left open. I was looking on simply from curiosity, and saw him search Williams' desk, from which he took out something, I could not make out what. He then went to his own place, and wrote for about ten minutes, after which I observed him go up and stand by the notice-board. When he had done this, he got out by the window again, and ran off."

" Didn't this strike you as extraordinary ?"

" No ; I thought nothing more about it, till some one told me in the sick-room about this row. I then mentioned privately what I had seen, and it wasn't till I saw Duncan, half an hour ago, that I thought it worth while to make it generally known."

Duncan turned an inquiring eye to Barker (who sat black and silent), and then pulled some bits of torn paper from his pocket, put them together, and called Owen to stand up. Showing him the fragments of paper, he asked, " Have you ever seen these before ?"

" Yes. On Saturday, when the boys left the school-room, I stayed behind to think a little over what had occurred, feeling convinced that Williams was *not* guilty, spite of appearances. I was standing by the empty fire-place, when these bits of paper caught my eye. I picked them up, and, after a great deal of trouble, fitted them together. They are covered apparently with failures in an attempt at forgery, viz., first, ' Gordon is a sur——' and then a stop, as though the writer were dissatisfied, and several of the words written over again for practice, and then a number of r's made in the way that Williams makes them."

" There you may stop," said Barker, stamping fiercely ; " I did it all."

A perfect yell of scorn and execration followed this announcement.

" What! *you* did it, and caused all this misery, you ineffable blackguard!" shouted Upton, grasping him with one hand, while he struck him with the other.

" Stop!" said Avonley; " just see that he doesn't escape, while we decide on his punishment."

It was very soon decided by the sixth form that he should run the gauntlet of the school. The boys instantly took out their handkerchiefs, and knotted them tight. They then made a double line down each side of the corridor, and turned Barker loose. He stood stock-still at one end, while the fellows nearest him thrashed him unmercifully with the heavy knots. At last the pain was getting severe, and he moved on, finally beginning to run. Five times he was forced up and down the line, and five times did every boy in the line give him a blow, which, if it did not hurt much, at least spoke of no slight anger and contempt. He was dogged and unmoved to the last, and then Avonley hauled him into the presence of Dr. Rowlands. He was put in a secure room by himself, and the next morning was first flogged and then publicly expelled. Thenceforth he disappears from the history of Roslyn school.

I need hardly say that neither Eric nor his friends took any part in this retributive act. They sat together in the boarders' room till it was over, engaged in exciting discussion of the recent events. Most warmly did Eric thank them for their trustfulness. " Thank you," he said, " with all my heart, for proving my innocence; but thank you, even more a great deal, for first believing it."

Upton was the first to join them, and since he had but wavered for a moment, he was soon warmly reconciled with Eric. They had hardly shaken hands when the rest came flocking in. " We have all been unjust," said Avonley; " let's make up for it as well as we can. Three cheers for Eric Williams!"

They gave, not three, but a dozen, till they were tired; and meanwhile, every one was pressing round him, telling him how sorry they were for the false suspicion, and doing all they could to show their regret for his recent troubles. His genial, boyish heart readily forgave them, and his eyes were long wet with tears of joy. The delicious sensation of returning esteem made him almost think it worth while to have undergone his trial.

Most happily did he spend the remainder of that afternoon, and it was no small relief to all the Rowlandites in the evening to find themselves finally rid of Barker, whose fate no one pitied, and whose name no one mentioned without disgust. He had done more than any other boy to introduce meanness, quarrelling, and vice, and the very atmosphere of the rooms seemed healthier in his absence. One boy only forgave him, one boy only prayed for him, one boy only endeavoured to see him for one last kind word. That boy was Edwin Russell.

After prayers, Mr. Gordon, who had been at Dr.

Rowlands' to dinner, apologised to Eric amply and frankly for his note, and did and said all that could be done by an honourable man to repair the injury of an unjust doubt. Eric felt his generous humility, and from thenceforth, though they were never friends, he and Mr. Gordon ceased to be enemies.

That night Mr. Rose crowned his happiness by asking him and his defenders to supper in the library. A most bright and joyous evening they passed, for they were in the highest spirits; and when the master bade them "good night," he kindly detained Eric, and said to him, "Keep an innocent heart, my boy, and you need never fear trouble. Only think if you had been guilty, and were now in Barker's place!"

"O, I *couldn't* be guilty, sir," said Eric, gaily.

"Not of such a fault, perhaps. But," he added solemnly, "there are many kinds of temptation, Eric; many kinds. And they are easy to fall into. You will find it no light battle to resist them."

"Believe me, sir, I will try," he answered with humility.

"Jehovah-Nissi!" said Mr. Rose. "Let the Lord be your banner, Eric, and you will win the victory. God bless you."

And as the boy's graceful figure disappeared through the door, Mr. Rose drew his arm-chair to the fire, and sat and meditated long. He was imagining for Eric a sunny future—a future of splendid usefulness, of reciprocated love, of brilliant fame.

CHAPTER XIII.

THE ADVENTURE AT THE STACK.

"Ten cables from where green meadows,
  And quiet homes could be seen,
      No greater space
      From peril to peace,
  But the savage sea between!"—EDWIN ARNOLD.

HE Easter holidays at Roslyn lasted about ten days, and as most of the boys came from a distance, they usually spent them at school. Many of the usual rules were suspended during this time, and the boys were supplied every day with pocket-money; consequently the Easter holidays passed very pleasantly, and there was plenty of fun.

It was the great time for excursions all over the island, and the boys would often be out the whole day long among the hills, or about the coast. Eric enjoyed the time particularly, and was in great request among all the boys. He was now more gay and popular than ever, and felt as if nothing were wanting to his happiness. But this brilliant prosperity was not good for him, and

II

he felt continually that he cared far less for the reproaches of conscience than he had done in the hours of
his trial; sought far less for help from God than he
had done when he was lonely and neglected.

He always knew that his great safeguard was the
affection of Russell.   For Edwin's sake, and for shame
at the thought of Edwin's disapproval, he abstained
from many things into which he would otherwise have
insensibly glided in conformation to the general loose-
ness of the school morality.   But Russell's influence
worked on him powerfully, and tended to counteract a
multitude of temptations.

Among other dangerous lessons Upton had taught
Eric to smoke; and he was now one of those who often
spent a part of his holidays in lurking about with pipes
in their mouths at places where they were unlikely to
be disturbed, instead of joining in some hearty and
healthy game.   When he began to "learn" smoking,
he found it anything but pleasant; but a little practice
had made him an adept, and he found a certain amount
of enjoyable excitement in finding out cozy places by
the river, where he and Upton might go and lounge for
an hour to enjoy the forbidden luxury.

In reality he, like most boys, detested the habit;
but it seemed a fine thing to do, and to some, at any
rate, it was a refuge from vacuity.   Besides, they had a
confused notion that there was something "manly" in
it, and it derived an additional zest from the stringency
of the rules adopted to put it down.   So a number of the

boys smoked, and some few of them to such excess as to get them into great mischief, and form a habit which they could never afterwards abandon.

One morning of the Easter holidays, Eric, Montagu, and Russell started for an excursion down the coast to Rilby Head. As they passed through Ellan, Eric was deputed to go and buy Easter eggs and other provisions, as they did not mean to be back for dinner. In about ten minutes he caught up the other two, just as they were getting out of the town.

"What an age you've been buying a few Easter eggs," said Russell, laughing; "have you been waiting till the hens laid?"

"No; they're not the *only* things I've got."

"Well, but you might have got all the grub at the same shop."

"Ay; but I've procured a more refined article. Guess what it is?"

The two boys didn't guess, and Eric said, to enlighten them, "Will you have a whiff, Monty?"

"A whiff! Oh! I see you've been wasting your tin on cigars—*alias*, rolled cabbage-leaves. Oh fumose puer!"

"Well, will you have one?"

"If you like," said Montagu, wavering; "but I don't much care to smoke."

"Well, *I* shall, at any rate," said Eric, keeping off the wind with his cap, as he lighted a cigar, and began to puff.

They strolled on in silence; the smoking didn't promote conversation, and Russell thought that he had never seen his friend look so ridiculous, and entirely unlike himself, as he did while strutting along with the weed in his mouth. The fact was, Eric didn't guess how much he was hurting Edwin's feelings, and he was smoking more to "make things look like the holidays," by a little bravado, than anything else. But suddenly he caught the expression of Russell's face, and instantly said—

"O, I forgot, Edwin; I know you don't like smoking;" and he instantly flung the cigar over the hedge, being really rather glad to get rid of it. With the cigar, he seemed to have flung away the affected manner he displayed just before, and the spirits of all three rose at once.

"It isn't that I don't *like* smoking only, Eric, but I think it wrong—for *us* I mean."

"O, my dear fellow! surely there can't be any harm in it. Why, everybody smokes."

"It may be all very well for men, although I'm not so sure of that. But, at any rate, it's wrong and ridiculous in boys. You know yourself what harm it does in every way."

"O, it's a mere school rule against it. How can it be wrong? Why, I even know clergymen who smoke."

Montagu laughed. "Well, clergymen ain't immaculate," said he; "but I never met a man yet who didn't tell you that he was *sorry* he'd acquired the habit."

" I'm sure you won't thank that rascally cousin of mine for having taught you," said Russell; " but seriously, isn't it a very moping way of spending the afternoon, to go and lie down behind some hay-stack, or in some frowsy tumble-down barn, as you smokers do, instead of playing racquets or football?"

" O, it's pleasant enough sometimes," said Eric, speaking rather against his own convictions.

" As for me, I've pretty nearly left it off," said Montagu, " and I think Rose convinced me that it was a mistake. Not that he knows that I ever did smoke; I should be precious sorry if he did, for I know how he despises it in boys. Were you in school the other day when he caught Pietrie and Brooking?"

" No."

" Well, when Brooking went up to have his exercise corrected, Rose smelt that he had been smoking, and charged him with it. Brooking stoutly denied it, but after he had told the most robust lies, Rose made him empty his pockets, and there, sure enough, were a pipe and a cigar-case half full! You *should* have heard how Rose thundered and lightened at him for his lying, and then sent him to the Doctor. I never saw him so terrific before."

" You don't mean to say you were convinced it was wrong because Brooking was caught, and told lies—do you? *Non sequitur.*"

" Stop—not so fast. Very soon after Rose twigged Pietrie, who at once confessed, and was caned. I happened to be in the library when Rose sent for him, and Pietrie said mildly that " he didn't see the harm of it." Rose smiled in his kind way, and said, " Don't see the *harm* of it! Do you see any good in it?"

" No, sir."

" Well, isn't it forbidden?"

" Yes, sir."

" And doesn't it waste your money?"

" Yes, sir."

" And tempt you to break rules, and tell lies to screen yourself?"

" Yes, sir," said Pietrie, putting his tail between his legs.

" And don't your parents disapprove it? And doesn't it throw you among some of the worst boys, and get you into great troubles? Silly child," he said, pulling Pietrie's ear (as he sometimes does, you know), " don't talk nonsense; and remember next time you're caught, I shall have you punished." So off went Pietrie, ἀχρεῖον ἰδών, as our friend Homer says. And your humble servant was convinced."

" Well, well!" said Eric, laughing, " I suppose you're right. At any rate, I give in. Two to one ain't fair;—πρὸς δύο οὐδ' ὁ Ἡρακλῆς, since you're in a quoting humour."

Talking in this way they got to Rilby Head, where they found plenty to amuse them. It was a splendid headland, rising bluff four hundred feet out of the sea, and presenting magnificent reaches of rock scenery on all sides. The boys lay on the turf at the summit, and flung innocuous stones at the sea-gulls as they sailed far below them over the water, and every now and then pounced at some stray fish that came to the surface; or they watched the stately barques as they sailed by on the horizon, wondering at their cargo and destination; or chaffed the fishermen, whose boats heaved on the waves at the foot of the promontory. When they were rested, they visited a copper-mine by the side of the head, and filled their pockets with bits of bright quartz or red shining spar, which they found in plenty among the rocks.

In the afternoon they strolled towards home, determining to stop a little at the Stack on their way. The Stack formed one of the extremities of Ellan Bay, and was a huge mass of isolated schist, accessible at low water, but entirely surrounded at high tide. It was a very favourite resort of Eric's, as the coast all about it was bold and romantic; and he often went there with Russell on a Sunday evening to watch the long line of golden radiance slanting to them over the water from the setting sun—a sight which they often agreed to consider one of the most peaceful and mysteriously beautiful in nature.

They reached the Stack, and began to climb to its summit. The sun was just preparing to set, and the west was gorgeous with red and gold.

" We shan't see the line on the waters this evening," said Eric ; " there's too much of a breeze. But look, what a glorious sunset ! "

" Yes; it'll be stormy to-morrow," answered Russell; " but come along, let's get to the top; the wind's rising, and the waves will be rather grand."

" Ay, we'll sit and watch them; and let's finish our grub ; I've got several eggs left, and I want to get them out of my pocket."

They devoured the eggs, and then stood enjoying the sight of the waves, which sometimes climbed up the rock almost to their feet, and then fell back, hissing and discomfited. Suddenly they remembered that it was getting late, and that they ought to get home for tea at seven.

" Hallo ! " said Russell, looking at his watch, " it's half-past six. We must cut back as hard as we can. By the bye, I hope the tide hasn't been coming in all this time."

" Good God ! " said Montagu, with a violent start, " I'm afraid it has, though ! What asses we have been, with our waves and sunsets. Let's set off as hard as we can pelt."

Immediately they scrambled, by the aid of hands and knees, down the Stack, and made their way for the belt of rock which joined it to the mainland ; but, to their horror, they at once saw that the tide had come in, and that a narrow gulf of sea already divided them from the shore.

"There's only one way for it," said Eric; "if we're plucky we can jump that; but we mustn't wait till it gets worse. A good jump will take us *nearly* to the other side—far enough, at any rate, to let us flounder across somehow."

As fast as they could they hurried along down to the place where the momentarily increasing zone of water seemed as yet to be narrowest; and where the rocks on the other side were lower than those on which they stood. Their situation was by no means pleasant. The wind had been rising more and more, and the waves dashed into this little channel with such violence, that to swim it would have been a most hazardous experiment, particularly as they could not dive in from the ledge on which they stood, from their ignorance of the depth of water.

Eric's courage supported the other two. "There's no good *thinking* about it," said he, "jump we *must;* the sooner the better. We can but be a little hurt at the worst. Here, I'll set the example."

He drew back a step or two, and sprang out with all his force. He was a practised and agile jumper, and, to their great relief, he alighted near the water's edge, on the other side, where, after slipping once or twice on the wet and seaweed-covered rocks, he effected a safe landing, with no worse harm than a wetting up to the knees.

"Now then, you two," he shouted; "no time to lose."

" Will you jump first, Monty?" said Russell ; " both of you are better jumpers than I, and to tell the truth I'm rather afraid."

" Then I won't leave you," said Montagu ; " we'll both stay here."

" And perhaps be drowned or starved for our pains. No, Monty, *you* can clear it, I've no doubt."

" Couldn't we try to swim it together, Edwin?"

" Madness! look there." And as he spoke, a huge furious wave swept down the whole length of the gulf by which they stood, roaring and surging along till the whole water seethed, and tearing the seaweeds from their roots in the rock.

" Now's your time," shouted Eric again. " What *are* you waiting for? For God's sake, jump before another wave comes."

" Monty, you *must* jump now," said Russell, " if only to help me when I try."

Montagu went back as far as he could, which was only a few steps, and leapt wildly forward. He lighted into deep water, nearly up to his neck, and at first tried in vain to secure a footing on the sharp slippery schist ; but he stumbled forwards vigorously, and in half a minute, Eric leaning out as far as he could, caught his hand, and just pulled him to the other side in time to escape another rush of tumultuous and angry foam.

" Now, Edwin," they both shouted, " It'll be too late in another minute. Jump for your life."

Russell stood on the rock pale and irresolute.

Once or twice he prepared to spring, and stopped from fear at the critical instant. In truth, the leap was now most formidable ; to clear it was hopeless ; and the fury of the rock-tormented waves rendered the prospect of a swim on the other side terrible to contemplate. Once in the grasp of one of those billows, even a strong man must have been carried out of the narrow channel, and hurled against the towering sweep of rocks which lay beyond it.

" Oh Edwin, Edwin—dear Edwin—*do* jump," cried Eric with passionate excitement. " We will rush in for you."

Russell now seemed to have determined on running the risk ; he stepped back, ran to the edge, missed his footing, and with a sharp cry of pain, fell heavily forward into the water. For an instant, Eric and Montagu stood breathless,—but the next instant, they saw Russell's head emerge, and then another wave foaming madly by, made them run backwards for their lives, and hid him from their view. When it had passed, they saw him clinging with both hands, in the desperate instinct of self-preservation, to a projecting bit of rock, by the aid of which he gradually drew himself out of the water, and grasping at crevices or bits of seaweed, slowly and painfully reached the ledge on which they had stood before they took the leap. He presented a pitiable spectacle ; his face, pale as death, was dabbled with blood ; his head drooped on his breast ; his clothes were torn, and streamed with the salt water ; his cap was gone, and the wet hair, which he seemed too exhausted to push aside, hung over his forehead and eyes. He was evidently dizzy, and in pain; and they noticed that he only seemed to use one foot.

While he was regaining the ledge, neither of the boys spoke, lest their voices should startle him, and make him fall; but now, they both cried out, " Are you hurt, Edwin ?"

He did not answer, but supported his pale face on one hand, while he put the other to his head, from which the blood was flowing fast.

" O Edwin, for the love of God, try once more," said Montagu; " you will die if you spend the night on that rock."

They could not catch the reply, and called again. The wind and waves were both rising fast, and it was only by listening intently, that they caught the faint words, " I can't, my leg is hurt." Besides, they both saw that a jump was no longer possible; the channel was more than double the width which it had been when Eric leaped, and from the rapid ascent of the rocks on both sides, it was now far out of depth.

" O God, what can we do," said Montagu, bursting into tears. " We can never save him; and all but the very top of the Stack is covered at high tide."

Eric had not lost his presence of mind. " Cheer up, Edwin," he shouted; " I *will* get back to you somehow. If I fail, crawl up to the top again."

Again the wind carried away the reply, and Russell had sunk back on the rock.

"Monty," said Eric, "just watch for a minute or two. When I have got across, run to Ellan as hard as you can tear, and tell them that we are cut off by the tide on the Stack. They'll bring round the life-boat. It's our only chance."

"What are you going to do?" asked Montagu, terrified. "Why, Eric, it's death to attempt swimming that. Heavens!" And he drew Eric back hastily, as another vast swell of water came rolling along, shaking its white curled mane, like a sea-monster bent on destruction.

"Monty, it's no use," said Eric hastily, tearing off his jacket and waistcoat; "I'm not going to let Russell die on that ledge of rock. I shall try to reach him, whatever happens to me. Here; I want to keep these things dry. Be on the look out; if I get across, fling them over to me if you can, and then do as I told you."

He turned round; the wave had just spent its fury, and knowing that his only chance was to swim over before another came, he plunged in, and struck out like a man. He was a strong and expert swimmer, and as yet the channel was not more than a dozen yards across. He dashed over with the speed and strength of despair, and had just time to clutch the rocks on the other side before the next mighty swirl of the tide swept up in its white and tormented course.

In another minute he was on the ledge by Russell's side.

He took him tenderly in his arms, and called to Montagu for the dry clothes. Montagu tied them skilfully with his neck-handkerchief round a fragment of rock, adding his own jacket to the bundle, and then flung it over. Eric wrapped up his friend in the clothes, and once more shouted to Montagu to go on his errand. For a short time the boy lingered, reluctant to leave them, and then started off at a run. Looking back after a few minutes, he caught, through the gathering dusk, his last glimpse of the friends in their perilous situation. Eric was seated supporting Russell across his knees; when he saw Montagu turn, he waved his cap over his head as a signal of encouragement, and then began to carry Edwin higher up the rock for safety. It soon grew too dark to distinguish them, and Montagu at full speed flew to Ellan, which was a mile off. When he got to the harbour he told some sailors of the danger in which his friends were, and then ran on to the school. It was now eight o'clock, and quite dark. Tea was over, and lock-up time long past, when he stood excited, breathless, and without his jacket, at Dr. Rowlands' door.

" Good gracious! Master Montagu," said the servant; " what's the matter; have you been robbed?"

He pushed the girl aside, and ran straight to Dr. Rowlands' study. " O sir!" he exclaimed, bursting in, " Williams and Russell are on the Stack, cut off by the tide."

Dr. Rowlands started up hastily. "What! on this stormy night? Have you raised the alarm?"

"I told the life-boat people, sir, and then ran on."

"I will set off myself at once," said the Doctor, seizing his hat. "But, my poor boy, how pale and ill you look, and you are wet through too. You had better change your clothes at once, or go to bed."

"O no, sir," said Montagu, pleadingly; "do take me with you."

"Very well; but you must change first, or you may suffer in consequence. Make haste, and directly you are dressed, a cup of tea shall be ready for you down here, and we will start."

Montagu was off in an instant, and only stopped on his way to tell Duncan and the others of the danger which threatened their companions. The absence of the three boys from tea and lock-up had already excited general surmise, and Montagu's appearance, jacketless and wet, at the door of the boarders' room, at once attracted a group round him. He rapidly told them how things stood, and, hastening off, left them nearly as much agitated as himself. In a very short time he presented himself again before Dr. Rowlands, and when he had swallowed with difficulty the cup of tea, they sallied out.

It was pitch dark, and only one or two stars were seen at intervals struggling through the ragged masses of cloud. The wind howled in fitful gusts, and as their road led by the sea-side, Montagu shuddered to hear how

rough and turbulent the sea was, even on the sands.
He stumbled once or twice, and then the Doctor kindly
drew his trembling arm through his own, and made him
describe the whole occurrence, while the servant went
on in front with the lantern.   When Montagu told how
Williams had braved the danger of reaching his friend
at the risk of his life, Dr. Rowlands' admiration was
unbounded.   " Noble boy," he exclaimed, with enthusiasm ; " I shall find it hard to believe any evil of him
after this."

They reached Ellan, and went to the boat-house.

" Have you put out the life-boat? " said Dr. Rowlands anxiously.

" Ill luck, sir," said one of the sailors, touching his
cap ; " the life-boat went to a wreck at Port Vash two
days ago, and she hasn't been brought round again yet."

" Indeed ! but I do trust you have sent out another
boat to try and save those poor boys."

" We've been trying, sir, and a boat has just
managed to start ; but in a sea like that it's very dangerous, and it's so dark and gusty that I doubt it's no
use, so I expect they'll put back."

The Doctor sighed deeply.   " Don't alarm any
other people," he said; " it will merely raise a crowd
to no purpose.   Here, George," he continued to the
servant, " give me the lantern ; I will go with this
boy to the Stack ; you follow us with ropes, and order
a carriage from the King's Head.   Take care to bring
anything with you that seems likely to be useful."

Montagu and Dr. Rowlands again started, and with difficulty made their way through the storm to the shore opposite the Stack. Here they raised the lantern and shouted; but the wind was now screaming with such violence that they were not sure that they heard any answering shout. Their eyes, accustomed to the darkness, could just make out the huge black outline of the Stack rising from the yeast of boiling waves, and enveloped every moment in blinding sheets of spray. On the top of it Montagu half thought that he saw something, but he was not sure.

"Thank God, there is yet hope," said the Doctor, with difficulty making his young companion catch his words amid the uproar of the elements; "if they can but keep warm in their wet clothes, we may perhaps rescue them before morning."

Again he shouted to cheer them with his strong voice, and Montagu joined his clear ringing tones to the shout. This time they fancied that in one of the pauses of the wind they heard a faint cheer returned. Never was sound more welcome, and as they paced up and down they shouted at intervals, and held up the lantern, to show the boys that friends and help were near.

Eric heard them. When Montagu left, he had carried Russell to the highest point of the rock, and there, with gentle hands and soothing words, made him as comfortable as he could. He wrapped him in every piece of dry clothing he could find, and held him in his

H 2

arms, heedless of the blood which covered him. Very faintly Russell thanked him, and pressed his hand ; but he moaned in pain continually, and at last fainted away.

Meanwhile the wind rose higher, and the tide gained on the rocks, and the sacred darkness came down. At first Eric could think of nothing but storm and sea. Cold, and cruel,· and remorseless, the sea beat up, drenching them to the skin continually with its clammy spray ; and the storm shrieked round them pitilessly, and flung about the wet hair on Eric's bare head, and forced him to plant himself firmly, lest the rage of the gusts should hurl them from their narrow resting-place. The darkness made everything more fearful, for his eyes could distinguish nothing but the gulfs of black water glistening here and there with hissing foam, and he shuddered as his ears caught the unearthly noises that came to him in the mingled scream of weltering tempest and plangent wave. It was fearful to be isolated on the black rent rock, and see the waves gaining on them higher, higher, higher, every moment ; and he was in ceaseless terror lest they should be swept away by the violence of the breakers. " At least," thought he, as he looked down and saw that the ledge on which they had been standing had long been covered with deep and agitated waves, " at least I have saved Edwin's life." And he bravely made up his mind to keep up heart and hope, and weather the comfortless night with Russell in his arms.

And then his thoughts turned to Russell, who was still unconscious; and stooping down he kissed fondly the pale white forehead of his friend. He felt *then* how deeply he loved him, how much he owed him; and no mother could have nursed a child more tenderly than he did the fainting boy. Russell's head rested on his breast, and the soft hair, tangled with welling blood, stained his clothes. Eric feared that he would die, his fainting-fit continued so long, and from the helpless way in which one of his legs trailed on the ground he felt sure that he had received some dangerous hurt.

At last Russell stirred and groaned. "Where am I?" he said, and half opened his eyes; he started up frightened, and fell back heavily. He saw only the darkness; felt only the fierce wind and salt mist; heard only the relentless yell of the blast. Memory had no time to wake, and he screamed and fainted once more.

Poor Eric knew not what to do but to shelter him to the best of his power, and when he showed any signs of consciousness again, he bent over him, and said, "Don't you remember, Edwin? We're quite safe. I'm with you, and Monty's gone for help."

"Oh! I daren't jump," sobbed Russell; "oh mother, I shall be drowned. Save me! save me! I'm so glad they're safe, mother; but my leg hurts so." And he moaned again. He was delirious.

"How cold it is and wet too! where's Eric? are we bathing? run along, we shall be late. But stop, you're smoking. Dear Eric, don't smoke. Poor fel-

low, I'm afraid he's getting spoilt, and learning bad
ways. Oh save him." And as he wandered on, he
repeated a prayer for Eric, which evidently had been
often on his lips.

Eric was touched to the heart's core, and in one
rapid lightning-like glance, his memory revealed to him
the faultful past, in all its sorrowfulness. And *he* too
prayed wildly for help both for soul and body. Alone
on the crag, with the sea tumbling and plashing round
them, growing and gaining so much on their place of
refuge, that his terror began to summon up the image
of certain death ; alone, wet, hungry, and exhausted,
with the wounded and delirious boy, whose life depended
on his courage, he prayed as he had never prayed
before, and seemed to grow calmer by his prayer, and
to feel God nearer him than ever he had done in
the green cricket-field, or the safe dormitories of Roslyn
school.

A shout startled him. Lights on the water heaved
up and down, now disappearing, and now lifted high,
and at intervals there came the sound of voices.
Thank God! help was near; they were coming in a
boat to save them.

But the lights grew more distant; he saw them
disappearing towards the harbour. Yes! it was of no
use ; no boat could live in the surf at the foot of the
Stack cliffs, and the sailors had given it up in despair.
His heart sank again, all the more for its glimpse of
hope, and his strength began to give way. Russell's

delirium continued, and he grew too frightened even to pray.

A light from the land. The sound of shouts— yes, he could be sure of it; it was Dr. Rowlands' voice and Montagu's. He got convinced of this, and summoned all his strength to shout in return. The light kept moving up and down on the shore, not a hundred yards off. His fear vanished; they were no longer alone. The first moment that the tide suffered any one to reach them they would be rescued. His mind grew calm again, and he determined to hold up for Russell's sake until help should come; and every now and then, to make it feel less lonely, he answered the shouts which came from the friendly voices in the fitful pauses of the storm.

But Dr. Rowlands and Montagu paced up and down, and the master soothed the boy's fears, and talked to him so kindly, so gently, that Montagu began to wonder if this really could be the awful head-master, whose warm strong hand he was grasping, and who was comforting him as a father might. What a depth of genuine human kindness that stern exterior concealed! And every now and then, when the storm blew loudest, the Doctor would stand still for a moment, and offer up a short intense prayer, or ejaculation, that help and safety might come to his beloved charge in their exposure and peril.

Six or seven hours passed away; at last the wind began to sink, and the sea to be less violent. The

tide was on the turn. The carriage drove up with
more men and lights, and the thoughtful servant brought
with him the school surgeon, Dr. Underhay. Long
and anxiously did they watch the ebbing tide, and
when it had gone out sufficiently to allow of two stout
planks being laid across the channel, an active sailor
ventured over with a light, and in a few moments
stood by Eric's side. Eric saw him coming, but was
too weak and numb to move; and when the sailor
lifted up the unconscious Russell from his knees, Eric
was too much exhausted even to speak. The man
returned for him, and lifting him on his back crossed
the plank once more in safety, and carried them both
to the carriage, where Dr. Underhay had taken care
to have everything likely to revive and sustain them.
They were driven rapidly to the school, and the
Doctor raised to God tearful eyes of gratitude as the
boys were taken to the rooms prepared for them.
Mrs. Rowlands was anxiously awaiting their arrival,
and the noise of wheels was the signal for twenty
heads to be put through the dormitory windows, with
many an anxious inquiry, "Are they safe?"

"Yes, thank God!" called Dr. Rowlands; "so
now, boys, shut the windows, and get to sleep."

Russell was carefully undressed, and put to bed in
the Doctor's own house, and the wound in his head
was dressed. Eric and Montagu had beds provided
them in another room by themselves, away from the
dormitory; the room was bright and cheerful, with a

blazing fire, and looked like home; and when the two boys had drank some warm wine, and cried for weariness and joy, they sank to sleep after their dangers and fatigues, and slept the deep, calm, dreamless sleep of tired children.

So ended the perilous adventure of that eventful night of the Easter holidays.

CHAPTER XIV.

THE SILVER CORD BROKEN.

" Calm on the bosom of thy God,
    Fair spirit, rest thee now !
E'en while with us thy footsteps trod,
    His seal was on thy brow."—MRS. HEMANS.

HEY did not awake till noon. Montagu opened his eyes, and at first could not collect his thoughts, as he saw the carpeted little room, the bright fire, and the housekeeper seated in her arm-chair before it. But turning his head, he caught a glimpse of Eric, who was still asleep, and he then remembered all. He sprang out of bed, refreshed and perfectly well, and the sound of his voice woke Eric; but Eric was still languid and weak, and did not get up that day, nor was he able to go to work again for some days; but he was young and strong, and his vigorous constitution soon threw off the effects of his fast and exposure.

Their first inquiry was for Edwin. The nurse shook her head sadly. " He is very dangerously ill."

" Is he?" said they both anxiously. And then

they preserved a deep silence; and when Montagu, who immediately began to dress, knelt down to say his prayers, Eric, though unable to get up, knelt also over his pillow, and the two felt that their young earnest prayers were mingling for the one who seemed to have been taken while they were left.

The reports grew darker and darker about Edwin. At first it was thought that the blow on his head was dangerous, and that the exposure to wet, cold, fear, and hunger, had permanently weakened his constitution; and when his youth seemed to be triumphing over these dangers, another became more threatening. His leg never mended; he had both sprained the knee badly, and given the tibia an awkward twist, so that the least motion was agony to him.

In his fever he was constantly delirious. No one was allowed to see him, though many of the boys tried to do so, and many were the earnest inquiries for him day by day. It then became more fully apparent than ever, that, although Edwin was among them without being *of* them, no boy in the school was more deeply honoured and fondly loved than he. Even the elastic spirits of boyhood could not quite throw off the shadow of gloom which his illness cast over the school.

Very tenderly they nursed him. All that human kindness could do was done for him by the stranger hands. And yet not all; poor Edwin had no father, no mother, hardly any relatives. His only aunt, Mrs. Upton, would have come to nurse him, but she was an

I

invalid, and he was often left alone in his delirium and agony.

Alone, yet not alone. There was One with him— always in his thoughts, always leading, guiding, blessing him unseen—not deserting the hurt lamb of his flock; one who was once a boy himself, and who, when he was a boy, did his Father's business, and was subject unto his parents in the obscure home of the despised village. Alone! nay, to them whose eyes were opened, the room of sickness and pain was thronged and beautiful with angelic presences.

Often did Eric, and Upton, and Montagu, talk of their loved friend. Eric's life seemed absorbed in the thought of him, and in passionate, unspeakable longings for his recovery. Now he valued more than ever the sweet remembered hours spent with him; their games, and communings, and walks, and Russell's gentle influence, and brave, kindly rebukes. Yet he must not even see him, must not whisper one word of soothing to him in his anguish; he could only pray for him, and that he did with a depth of hope.

At last Upton, in virtue of his relationship, was allowed to visit him. His delirium had become more unfrequent, but he could not yet even recognise his cousin, and the visits to his sick-room were so sad and useless, that Upton forebore. "And yet you should hear him talk in his delirium," he said to Eric; "not one evil word, or bad thought, or wicked thing, ever escapes him. I'm afraid, Eric, it would hardly be so with you or me."

"No," said Eric, in a low and humble tone; and guilty conscience brought the deep colour, wave after wave, of crimson into his cheeks.

"And he talks with such affection of you, Eric. He speaks sometimes of all of us very gently; but you seem to be always in his thoughts, and every now and then he prays for you quite unconsciously."

Eric turned his head to brush away a tear. "When do you think I shall be allowed to see him?"

"Not just yet, I fear."

After a week or two of most anxious suspense, Russell's mind ceased to wander, but the state of his sprain gave more cause for alarm. Fresh advice was called in, and it was decided that the leg must be amputated.

When Eric was told of this, he burst into passionate complaints. "Only think, Monty, isn't it hard, isn't it cruel? When we see our brave, bright Edwin again, he will be a cripple." Eric hardly understood that he was railing at the providence of a merciful God.

The day for the operation came. When it was over, poor Russell seemed to amend, and the removal of the perpetual pain gave him relief. They were all deeply moved at his touching resignation; no murmur, no cry escaped him; no words but the sweetest thanks for every little office of kindness done to him. A few

days after, he asked Dr. Underhay " if he might see
Eric ?"

" Yes, my boy," said the doctor kindly, " you may
see him, and one or two other of your particular friends
if you like, provided you don't excite yourself too
much. I trust you will get better now."

So Eric and Montagu were told by Dr. Rowlands
that at six they might go and see their friend. " Be
sure, he added, " that you don't startle or excite
him."

They promised, and after school on that beautiful
evening of early summer they went to the sick-room
door. Stopping, they held their breath, and knocked
very gently. Yes! it was the well-known voice which
gave the answer, but it was faint and low. Full of
awe, they softly opened the door, which admitted them
into the presence of the dear companion whom they had
not seen for so long. Since then it seemed as though
gulfs far deeper than the sea had been flowing between
him and them.

Full of awe, and hand in hand, they entered the
room on tiptoe—the darkened room where Russell was.
What a hush and oppression there seemed to them at
first in the dim, silent chamber; what an awfulness in
all the appliances which showed how long and deeply
their schoolfellow had suffered. But all this vanished
directly they caught sight of his face. There he lay,
so calm, and weak, and still, with his bright, earnest
eyes turned towards them, as though to see whether

any of their affection for him had ceased or been forgotten !

In an instant they were kneeling in silence by the bed with bowed foreheads; and the sick boy tenderly put his hands on their heads, and pushed the frail white fingers through their hair, and looked at them tearfully without a word, till they hid their faces with their hands, and broke into deep suppressed sobs of compassion.

"Oh hush, hush!" he said, as he felt their tears dropping on his hands while they kissed them, "Dear Eric, dear Monty, why should you cry so for me? I am very happy."

But they caught the outline of his form as he lay on the bed, and had now for the first time realized that he was a cripple for life; and as the throng of memories came on them—memories of his skill and fame at cricket, and racquets, and football—of their sunny bathes together in sea and river, and all their happy holiday wanderings—they could not restrain their emotion, and wept uncontrollably. Neither of them could speak a word, or break the holy silence; and as he patted their heads and cheeks, his own tears flowed fast in sympathy and self-pity. But he felt the comforting affection which they could not utter; he felt it in his loneliness, and it did him good.

The nurse broke in upon the scene, which she feared would agitate Edwin too much; and with red eyes and heavy hearts the boys left, only whispering, "We will come again to-morrow, Edwin!"

They came the next day, and many days, and got
to talk quite cheerfully with him, and read to him.
They loved this occupation more than any game, and
devoted themselves to it. The sorrow of the sick-room
more than repaid them for the glad life without, when
they heard Russell's simple and heartfelt thanks. "Ah!
how good of you, dear fellows," he would say, "to give
up the merry playground for a wretched cripple," and
he would smile cheerfully to show that his trial had
not made him weary of life. Indeed, he often told them
that he believed they felt for him more than he did
himself.

One day Eric brought him a little bunch of .prim-
roses and violets. He seemed much better, and Eric's
spirits were high with the thoughts and hopes of the
coming holidays. "There, Edwin," he said, as the
boy gratefully and eagerly took the flowers, "don't they
make you glad? They are one of our *three* signs, you
know, of the approaching holidays. One sign was the
first sight of the summer steamer going across the bay;
another was May eve, when these island-fellows light
big gorse fires all over the mountains, and throw yellow
marsh-lilies at their doors to keep off the fairies. Do
you remember, Eddy, gathering some last May eve, and
sitting out in the playground till sunset, watching the
fires begin to twinkle on Cronck-Irey and Barrule for
miles away? What a jolly talk we had that evening
about the holidays; but my father and mother were
here then, you know, and we were all going to Fair-

holm. But the third sign—the first primrose and violet—was always the happiest. You can't think how I *grabbed* at the first primrose this year; I found it by a cave on the Ness. And though these are rather the last than the first, yet I knew you'd like them, Eddy, so I hunted for them everywhere. And how much better you're looking too; such shining eyes, and, yes! I positively declare, quite a ruddy cheek like your old one. You'll soon be out among us again, that's clear——"

He stopped abruptly: he had been rattling on just in the merry way that Russell now most loved to hear, but, as he was talking, he caught the touch of sadness on Russell's face, and saw his long, abstracted, eager look at the flowers.

"Dear fellow, you're not worse, are you?" he said quickly. "What a fool I am to chatter so; it makes you ill."

"No, no, Eric, talk on; you can't think how I love to hear you. Oh, how very beautiful these primroses are! Thank you, thank you, for bringing them." And he again fixed on them the eager dreamy look which had startled Eric—as though he were learning their colour and shape by heart.

"I wish I hadn't brought them, though," said Eric, "they are filling your mind with regrets. But, Eddy, you'll be well by the holidays—a month hence, you know—or else I shouldn't have talked so gladly about them."

"No Eric," said Russell sadly, "these dear flowers are the last spring blossoms that I shall see—*here* at least. Yes, I will keep them, for your sake Eric, till I die."

"Oh don't talk so," said Eric, shocked and flustered, "why everybody knows and says that you're getting better."

Russell smiled and shook his head. "No, Eric, I shall die. There stop, dear fellow, don't cry," said he, raising his hands quietly to Eric's face; "isn't it better for me so? I own it seemed sad at first to leave this bright world and the sea—yes, even that cruel sea," he continued smiling; "and to leave Roslyn, and Upton, and Monty, and, above all, to leave *you*, Eric, whom I love best in all the world. Yes, remember I've no home, Eric, and no prospects. There was nothing to be sorry for in this, so long as God gave me health and strength; but health went for ever into those waves at the Stack, where you saved my life, dear, gallant Eric; and what could I do now? It doesn't look so happy to *halt* through life. Oh Eric, Eric, I am young, but I am dying—dying, Eric," he said solemnly, "my brother; let me call you brother; I have no near relations, you know, to fill up the love in my yearning heart, but I *do* love *you*. Kiss me, Eric, as though I were a child, and you a child. There, that comforts me; I feel as if I *were* a child again, and had a dear brother;—and I *shall* be a child again soon, Eric, in the courts of a Father's house."

Eric could not speak. These words startled him; he never dreamt *recently* of Russell's death, but had begun to reckon on his recovery, and now life seemed darker to him than ever.

But Russell was pressing the flowers to his lips. " The grass withereth," he murmured, " the flower fadeth, and the glory of its beauty perisheth; but—*but* the word of the Lord endureth for ever." And here he too burst into natural tears, and Eric pressed his hand, with more than a brother's fondness, to his heart.

" Oh Eddy, Eddy, my heart is full," he said, " too full to speak to you. Let me read to you;" and with Russell's arm round his neck he sat down beside his pillow, and read to him about " the pure river of water of life, clear as crystal, proceeding out of the throne of God and of the Lamb." At first sobs choked his voice, but it gathered firmness as he went on.

" In the midst of the street of it, and on either side of the river, was there the tree of life, which bare twelve manner of fruits, and yielded her fruit every month; and the leaves of the tree were for the healing of the nations.

"And there shall be no more curse "—and here the reader's musical voice rose into deeper and steadier sweetness—" but the throne of God and of the Lamb shall be in it; and his servants shall serve him; and they shall see his face; and his name shall be in their foreheads."

" And they shall see his face," murmured Russell,

"*and they shall see his face.*"   Eric paused and looked
at him; a sort of rapture seemed to be lighted in his
eyes, as though they saw heavenly things, and his
countenance was like an angel's to look upon. Eric
closed the book reverently, and gazed.

"And now pray for me, Eric, will you?"   Eric
knelt down, but no prayer would come; his breast
swelled, and his heart beat fast, but emotion prevented
him from uttering a word. But Russell laid his hand
on his head and prayed.

"O gracious Lord God, look down, merciful Father,
on us, two erring, weak, sinful boys; look down and
bless us, Lord, for the love thou bearest unto thy
children. One thou art taking; Lord, take me to the
green pastures of thy home, where no curse is; and
one remains—O Lord! bless him with the dew of thy
blessing; lead and guide him, and keep him for ever in
thy fear and love, that he may continue thine for ever,
and hereafter we may meet together among the re-
deemed, in the immortal glory of the resurrection.
Hear us, O Father, for thy dear Son's sake.   Amen!
Amen!"

The childlike, holy, reverent voice ceased, and Eric
rose. One long brotherly kiss he printed on Russell's
forehead, and, full of sorrowful forebodings, bade him
good night.

He asked Dr. Underhay whether his fears were correct. "Yes," he said, "he may die at any time; he
must die soon. It is even best that he should; besides

the loss of a limb, that blow on the head would certainly affect the brain and the intellect if he lived."

Eric shuddered—a long cold shudder.

The holidays drew on; for Russell's sake, and at his earnest wish, Eric had worked harder than he ever did before. All his brilliant abilities, all his boyish ambition, were called into exercise; and, to the delight of every one, he gained ground rapidly, and seemed likely once more to dispute the palm with Owen. No one rejoiced more in this than Mr. Rose, and he often gladdened Russell's heart by telling him about it; for every day he had a long visit to the sick boy's room, which refreshed and comforted them both.

In other respects, too, Eric seemed to be turning over a new leaf. He and Upton, by common consent, had laid aside smoking, and every bad habit or disobedient custom which would have grieved the dying boy, whom they both loved so well. And although Eric's popularity, after the romantic Stack adventure and his chivalrous daring, was at its very zenith,—although he had received a medal and flattering letter from the Humane Society, who had been informed of the transaction by Dr. Rowlands,—although his success both physical and intellectual was higher than ever,—yet the dread of the great loss he was doomed to suffer, and the friendship which was to be snapped, overpowered every other feeling, and his heart was ennobled and purified by contact with his suffering friend.

It was a June evening, and he and Russell were

alone; he had drawn up the blind, and through the open window the summer breeze, pure from the sea and fragrant from the garden, was blowing refreshfully into the sick boy's room. Russell was very, very happy. No doubt, no fear, assailed him; all was peace and trustfulness. Long and earnestly that evening did he talk to Eric, and implore him to shun evil ways, striving to lead him gently to that love of God which was his only support and refuge now. Tearfully and humbly Eric listened, and every now and then the sufferer stopped to pray aloud.

"Good night, Eric," he said, "I am tired, *so* tired. I hope we shall meet again; I shall give you my desk and all my books, Eric, except a few for Horace, Owen, Duncan, and Monty. And my watch, that dear watch your mother, *my* mother, gave me, I shall leave to Rose as a remembrance of us both. Good night, brother."

A little before ten that night Eric was again summoned with Upton and Montagu to Russell's bedside. He was sinking fast; and as he had but a short time to live, he expressed a desire to see them, though he could see no others.

They came, and were amazed to see how bright the dying boy looked. They received his last farewells—he would die that night. Sweetly he blessed them, and made them promise to avoid all evil, and read the Bible, and pray to God. But he had only strength to speak at intervals. Mr. Rose, too, was there; it seemed as though he held the boy by the hand, as fearlessly now, yea, joyously, he entered the waters of the dark river.

" Oh, I should *so* like to stay with you, Monty, Horace, dear, dear Eric, but God calls me. I am going —a long way—to my father and mother—and to the light. I shall not be a cripple there—nor be in pain." His words grew slow and difficult. " God bless you, dear fellows; God bless you, dear Eric ; I am going— to God."

He sighed very gently; there was a slight sound in his throat, and he was dead. The gentle, holy, pure spirit of Edwin Russell had passed into the presence of its Saviour and its God. O happy and blameless boy, no fairer soul has ever stood in the light of the rain- bow-circled throne.

A terrible scene of boyish anguish followed, as they kissed again and again the lifeless brow. But quietly, calmly, Mr. Rose checked them, and they knelt down with streaming eyes while he prayed.

They rose a little calmer, and as for the last time they kissed the corpse with everlasting farewells, Mr. Rose said in a solemn tone,—

" For ever with the Lord,
    Amen ! so let it be !
  Life from the dead is in that word,
    And Immortality."

CHAPTER XV.

HOME AGAIN.

"O far beyond the waters
  The fickle feet may roam,
But they find no light so pure and bright
  As the one fair star of home;
The star of tender hearts, lady,
  That glows in an English home."

F. W. F.

THAT night when Eric returned to No. 7, full of grief, and weighed down with the sense of desolation and mystery, the other boys were silent from sympathy in his sorrow. Duncan and Llewellyn both knew and loved Russell themselves, and they were awestruck to hear of his death; they asked some of the particulars, but Eric was not calm enough to tell them that evening. The one sense of infinite loss agitated him, and he indulged his paroxysms of emotion unrestrained, yet silently. Reader, if ever the life has been cut short which you most dearly loved, if ever you have been made to feel absolutely lonely in the world, then, and then only, will you appreciate the depth of his affliction.

But, like all affliction, it purified and sanctified. To Eric, as he rested his aching head on a pillow wet with tears, and vainly sought for the sleep whose blessing he had never learned to prize before, how odious seemed all the vice which he had seen and partaken in since he became an inmate of that little room. How his soul revolted with infinite disgust from the language which he had heard, and the open glorying in sin of which he had so often been a witness. The stain and the shame of sin fell heavier than ever on his heart; it rode on his breast like a nightmare; it haunted his fancy with visions of guilty memory, and shapes of horrible regret. The ghosts of buried misdoings, which he had thought long lost in the mists of recollection, started up menacingly from their forgotten graves, and made him shrink with a sense of their awful reality. Behind him, like a wilderness, lay years which the locust had eaten; the intrusted hours which had passed away, and been reckoned to him as they past.

And the thought of Russell mingled with all — Russell, as he fondly imaged him now, glorified with the glory of heaven, crowned, and in white robes, and with a palm in his hand. Yes, he had walked and talked with one of the Holy Ones. Had Edwin's death quenched his human affections, and altered his human heart? If not, might not he be there even now, leaning over his friend with the beauty of his invisible presence? The thought startled him, and seemed to give an awful lustre to the moonbeam which fell into the room. No! he could not endure such a presence now, with his weak conscience and corrupted heart; and Eric hid his head under the clothes, and shut his eyes.

Once more the pang of separation entered like iron into his soul. Should he ever meet Russell again? What if *he* had died instead of Edwin, where would he have been? "Oh, no! no!" he murmured aloud, as the terrible thought came over him of his own utter unfitness for death, and the possibility that he might never never again hear the beloved accents, or gaze on the cherished countenance of his school friend.

In this tumult of accusing thoughts he fell asleep; but that night the dew of blessing did not fall for him on the fields of sleep. He was frightened by unbidden dreams, in all of which his conscience obtruded on him his sinfulness, and his affection called up the haunting lineaments of the dear dead face. He was wandering down a path, at the end of which Russell stood with open arms inviting him earnestly to join him there; he saw his bright ingenuous smile, and heard, as of old, his joyous words, and he hastened to meet him; when suddenly the boy-figure disappeared, and in its place he saw the stern brow, and gleaming garments, and drawn flaming sword of the Avenger. And then he was in a great wood alone, and wandering, when the well-known voice called his name, and intreated him to turn from that evil place; and he longed to turn,—but, whenever he tried, ghostly hands seemed to wave him back again, and irresistible cords to drag him into the dark forest, amid the sound of mocking laughs. Then he was sinking, sinking, sinking into a gulf, deep and darker even than the inner darkness of a sin-desolated heart;

sinking, helplessly, hopelessly, everlastingly; while far away, like a star, stood the loved figure in light infinitely above him, and with pleading hands implored his deliverance, but could not prevail; and Eric was still sinking, sinking, infinitely, when the agony awoke him with a violent start and stifled scream.

He could sleep no longer. Whenever he closed his eyes he saw the pale, dead, holy features of Edwin, and at last he fancied that he was praying beside his corpse, praying to be more like *him*, who lay there so white and calm; sorrowing beside it, sorrowing that he had so often rejected his kind warnings, and pained his affectionate heart. So Eric began again to make good resolutions about all his future life. Ah! how often he had done so before, and how often they had failed. He had not yet learned the lesson which David learned by sad experience; " Then I said, it is mine own infirmity, *but I will remember the years of the right hand of the Most High.*"

That, too, was an eventful night for Montagu. He had grown of late far more thoughtful than before; under Edwin's influence he had been laying aside, one by one, the careless sins of school life, and his tone was nobler and manlier than it had ever been. Montagu had never known or heard much about godliness; his father, a gentleman, a scholar, and a man of the world, had trained him in the principles of refinement and good taste, and given him a high standard of conventional honour; but he passed through life lightly, and had

taught his son to do the same. Possessed of an ample
fortune, which Montagu was to inherit, he troubled
himself with none of the deep mysteries of life, and

> " Pampered the coward heart
> With feelings all too delicate for use ;
> Nursing in some delicious solitude
> His dainty loves and slothful sympathies."

But Montagu in Edwin's sick-room and by his death-
bed ; in the terrible storm at the Stack, and by contact
with Dr. Rowlands' earnestness, and Mr. Rose's deep,
unaffected, sorrow-mingled piety ; by witnessing Eric's
failures and recoveries ; and by beginning to take in his
course the same heartfelt interest which Edwin taught
him—Montagu, in consequence of these things, had
begun to see another side of life, which awoke all his
dormant affections and profoundest reasonings.   It
seemed as though, for the first time, he began to catch
some of

> " The still sad music of humanity,"

and to listen with deep eagerness to the strain. Hitherto,
to be well dressed, handsome, agreeable, rich, and
popular, had been to him a realised ideal of life ; but
now he awoke to higher and worthier aims ; and once,
when Russell, whose intelligent interest in his work
exceeded that of any other boy, had pointed out to him
that solemn question of Euripides—

> " Οἴει σὺ τοὺς θανόντας ὦ Νικήρατε
> Τρυφῆς ἀπάσης μεταλαβόντας ἐν βίῳ
> Πεφευγέναι τὸ θεῖον;"

he had entered into its meaning with wonderful vividness. So that, without losing any of that winning gracefulness of address which made him so great a favourite with the school, it became evident to all that he combined with it a touching earnestness. Sometimes when he read the Bible to Edwin he began to wonder at his past ignorance and selfishness, and humbly hope for better things. All that night of death he had truer comfort than Eric—for he cast his cares on God; more calm than Eric—for he fixed his hopes on the Son of God; greater strength granted him than Eric—because he had learned not to rely upon his own; less fear and torment than Eric—because he laid the burden of his sins before the cross, and, as a child, believed in their forgiveness for His sake who died thereon.

The holidays were approaching. Eric, to escape as much as possible from his sorrow, plunged into the excitement of working for the examination, and rapidly made up for lost ground. He now spent most of his time with the best of his friends, particularly Montagu. Owen, and Upton; for Upton, like himself, had been much sobered by sorrow at their loss. This time he came out *second* in his form, and gained more than one prize. This was his first glimpse of real delight since Russell's death; and when the prize-day came, and he stood with his companions in the flower-decorated room. and went up amid universal applause to take his prize-books, and receive a few words of compliment from the governor who took the chair, he felt almost happy, and keenly entered into the pleasure which his success caused, as well as into the honours won by his friends. One outward sign only remained of his late bereavement— his mourning dress. All the prize-boys wore rosebuds or lilies of the valley in their button-holes on the occasion, but on this day Eric would not wear them. Little Wright, who was a great friend of theirs, had brought some as a present both to Eric and Montagu, as they stood together on the prize-day morning; they took them with thanks, and, as their eyes met, they understood each other's thought.

"No," said Eric to Wright, "we won't wear these to-day, although we have both got prizes. Come along; I know what we will do with them."

They all three walked together to the little green, quiet churchyard, where, by his own request, Edwin had been buried. Many a silent visit had the friends paid to that grave, on which the turf was now green again, and the daisies had begun to blossom. A stone had just been placed to mark the spot, and they read—

SACRED TO THE MEMORY

OF

AN ORPHAN,

WHO DIED AT ROSLYN SCHOOL, MAY 1847,

AGED FIFTEEN YEARS.

"*Is it well with the child?   It is well.*"

1 KINGS iv. 26.

The three boys stood by the grave in silence and sorrow for a time.

"He would have been the gladdest at our success, Monty," said Eric; "let us leave the signs of it upon his grave."

And, with reverent hand, scattering over that small mound the choice rosebuds and fragrant lilies with their green leaves, they turned away without another word.

The next morning the great piles of corded boxes which crowded the passage were put on the coach, and the boys, gladly leaving the deserted building, drove in every sort of vehicle to the steamer. What joyous triumphant mornings those were! How the heart exulted and bounded with the sense of life and pleasure, and how universal was the gladness and good humour of every one. Never were voyages so merry as those of the steamer that day, and even the "good-byes" that had to be said at Southpool were lightly borne. From thence the boys quickly scattered to the different railways, and the numbers of those who were travelling together got thinner and thinner as the distance increased. Wright and one or two others went nearly all the way with Eric, and when he got down at the little roadside station, from whence started the branch rail to Ayrton, he bade them a merry and affectionate farewell. The branch train soon started, and in another hour he would be at Fairholm.

It was not till then that his home feelings woke in all their intensity. He had not been there for a year.

At Roslyn the summer holidays were nine weeks, and the holidays at Christmas and Easter were short, so that it had not been worth while to travel so far as Fairholm, and Eric had spent his Christmas with friends in another part of the island. But now he was once more to see dear Fairholm, and his aunt, his cousin Fanny, and above all, his little brother. His heart was beating fast with joy, and his eyes sparkling with pleasure and excitement. As he thrust his head out of the window, each well-remembered landmark gave him the delicious sensation of meeting again an old friend. "Ah! there's the white bridge, and there's the canal, and the stile; and *there* runs the river, and there's Velvet Lawn. Hurrah! here we are." And springing out of the train before it had well stopped, he had shaken hands heartily with the old coachman, who was expecting him, and jumped up into the carriage in a moment.

Through the lanes he knew so well, by whose hedgerows he had so often plucked sorrel and wild roses; past the old church with its sleeping churchyard; through the quiet village, where every ten yards he met old acquaintances who looked pleased to see him, and whom he greeted with glad smiles and nods of recognition; past the Latin school, from which came murmurs and voices as of yore (what a man he felt himself now by comparison!);—by the old Roman camp, where he had imagined such heroic things when he was a little child; through all the scenes so rich with the memories and associations of his happy childhood, they flew along;

and now they had entered the avenue, and Eric was painfully on the look-out.

Yes! there they were all three—Mrs. Trevor, and Fanny, and Vernon, on the mound at the end of the avenue; and the younger ones ran to meet him. It was a joyous meeting; he gave Fanny a hearty kiss, and put his arm round Vernon's neck, and then held him in front to have a look at him.

"How tall you've grown, Verny, and how well you look," he said, gazing proudly at him; and indeed the boy was a brother to be justly proud of. And Vernon quite returned the admiration as he saw the healthy glow of Eric's features, and the strong graceful development of his limbs.

And so they quickly joined Mrs. Trevor, who embraced her nephew with a mother's love; and, amid all that nameless questioning of delightful trifles, that "blossoming vein" of household talk, which gives such an incommunicable charm to the revisiting of home, they all three turned into the house, where Eric, hungry with his travels, did ample justice to the "jolly spread" prepared for him, luxurious beyond anything he had seen for his last year at school. When he and Vernon went up to their room at night—the same little room in which they slept on the night when they first had met— they marked their heights on the door again, which showed Eric that in the last year he had grown two inches, a fact which he pointed out to Vernon with no little exultation. And then they went to bed, and to a sleep over which brooded the indefinite sensation of a great unknown joy ;—that rare heavenly sleep which only comes once or twice or thrice in life, on occasions such as this.

He was up early next morning, and, opening his window, leaned out with his hands among the green vine-leaves which encircled it. The garden looked beautiful as ever, and he promised himself an early enjoyment of those currants which hung in ruby clusters over the walls. Everything was bathed in the dewy balm of summer morning, and he felt very happy as, with his little spaniel frisking round him, he visited the great Newfoundland in his kennel, and his old pet the pony in the stable. He had barely finished his rounds when breakfast was ready, and he once more met the home-circle from which he had been separated for a year. And yet over all his happiness hung a sense of change and half melancholy ; they were not changed, but *he* was changed. Mrs. Trevor, and Fanny, and Vernon were the same as ever, but over *him* had come an alteration of feeling and circumstance ; an unknown or half-known *something* which cast a shadow between them and him, and sometimes made him half shrink and start as he met their loving looks. Can no schoolboy, who reads his history, understand and explain the feeling which I mean ?

By that mail he wrote to his father and mother an account of Russell's death, and he felt that they would guess why the letter was so blurred. " But," he wrote,

"I have some friends still; especially Mr. Rose among the masters, and Monty and Upton among the boys. Monty you know; he is more like Edwin than any other boy, and I like him very much. You didn't know Upton, but I am a great deal with him, though he is much older than I am. He is a fine handsome fellow, and one of the most popular in the school. I hope you will know him some day."

The very next morning Eric received a letter which he at once recognised to be in Upton's handwriting. He eagerly tore off the envelope, and read—

"My dearest Eric—I have got bad news to tell you, at least, I feel it to be bad news for me, and I flatter myself that you will feel it to be bad news for you. In short, I am going to leave Roslyn, and probably we shall never meet there again. The reason is, I have had a cadetship given me, and I am to sail for India in September. I have already written to the school to tell them to pack up and send me all my books and clothes.

"I feel leaving very much; it has made me quite miserable. I wanted to stay at school another year at least; and I will honestly tell you, Eric, one reason: I'm very much afraid that I've done you, and Graham, and other fellows, no good; and I wanted, if I possibly could, to undo the harm I had done. Poor Edwin's death opened my eyes to a good many things, and now I'd give all I have never to have taught or encouraged you in wrong things. Unluckily it's too late;—only, I hope

K

that you already see, as I do, that the things I mean lead to evil far greater than we ever used to dream of.

" Good-bye now, old fellow ! Do write to me soon, and forgive me, and believe me ever—Your most affectionate,   HORACE UPTON."

" P.S.—Is that jolly little Vernon going back to school with you this time? I remember seeing him running about the shore with my poor cousin when you were a home-boarder, and thinking what a nice little chap he looked. I hope you'll look after him as a brother should, and keep him out of mischief."

Eric folded the letter sadly, and put it into his pocket; he didn't often show them his school letters, because, like this one, they often contained allusions to things which he did not like his aunt to know. The thought of Upton's leaving made him quite unhappy, and he wrote him a long letter by that post, indignantly denying the supposition that his friendship had ever done him anything but good.

The postscript about Vernon suggested a thought that had been often in his mind. He could not but shudder in himself, when he thought of that bright little brother of his being initiated in the mysteries of evil which he himself had learnt, and sinking like himself into slow degeneracy of heart and life. It often puzzled and perplexed him, and at last he determined to open his heart, partially at least, in a letter to Mr. Rose. The master fully understood his doubts, and wrote him the following reply :—

"My dear Eric—I have just received your letter about your brother Vernon, and I think that it does you honour. I will briefly give you my own opinion.

"You mean, no doubt, that, from your own experience, you fear that Vernon will hear at school many things which will shock his modesty, and much language which is evil and blasphemous; you fear that he will meet with many bad examples, and learn to look on God and godliness in a way far different from that to which he has been accustomed at home. You fear, in short, that he must pass through the same painful temptations to which you have yourself been subjected; to which, perhaps, you have even succumbed.

"Well, Eric, this is all true. Yet, knowing this, I say, by all means let Vernon come to Roslyn. The innocence of mere ignorance is a poor thing; it *cannot*, under any circumstances, be permanent, nor is it at all valuable as a foundation of character. The true preparation for life, the true basis of a manly character, is not to have been ignorant of evil, but to have known it and avoided it; not to have been sheltered from temptation, but to have passed through it and overcome it by God's help. Many have drawn exaggerated pictures of the lowness of public school morality; the best answer is to point to the good and splendid men that have been trained in public schools, and who lose no opportunity of recurring to them with affection. It is quite possible to be *in* the little world of school-life, and yet not *of* it. The ruin of human souls can never be achieved by enemies from without, unless they be aided by traitors from within. Remember our lost friend; the peculiar lustre of his piety was caused by the circumstances under which he was placed. He often told me before his last hour, that he rejoiced to have been at Roslyn; that he had experienced there much real happiness, and derived in every way lasting good.

"I hope you have been enjoying your holidays, and that you will come back with the 'spell of home affection' alive in your heart. I shall rejoice to make Vernon's acquaintance, and will do for him all I can. Bring him with you to me in the library as soon as you arrive.—Ever, dear Eric,

Affectionately yours,

"WALTER ROSE."

END OF PART I.

PART II.

"Sed revocare gradum."—VIRGIL.

---◆---

CHAPTER I.

ABDIEL.

Φθείρουσιν ἤθη χρήσθ᾽ ὁμιλίαι κακαί.—MENANDER.

YEAR had passed since the events narrated in the last chapter, and had brought with it many changes.

To Eric the changes were not for good. The memories of Russell were getting dim; the resolutions made during his illness had vanished; the bad habits laid aside after his death had been resumed. All this took place very gradually; there were many inward struggles, much occasional remorse, but the struggles by degrees grew weaker, and remorse lost its sting, and Eric Williams soon learned again to follow the multitude to do evil.

He was now sixteen years old, and high in the fifth form, and, besides this, he was captain of the school eleven. In work he had fallen off, and no one now expected the fulfilment of that promise of genius which he had given when he first came. But in all school

sports he had improved, and was the acknowledged
leader and champion in matters requiring boldness and
courage.   His popularity made him giddy ; favour of
man led to forgetfulness of God ; and even a glance at
his countenance showed a self-sufficiency and arrogance
which ill became the refinement of his features, and ill
replaced the ingenuous modesty of former days.

And Vernon Williams was no longer a new boy.
The worst had happened to him, which Eric in his better
moments could have feared.   He had fallen into
thoroughly bad hands, and Eric, who should have been
his natural guardian and guide, began to treat him with
indifference, and scarcely ever had any affectionate intercourse with him.   It is by no means unfrequent that
brothers at school see but little of each other, and follow
their several pursuits, and choose their various companions, with small regard to the relationship between
them.

Yet Eric could not overlook or be blind to the fact,
that Vernon's chief friend or leader was the most
undesirable whom he could have chosen.   It was a
new boy named Brigson.   This boy had been expelled
from one of the most ill-managed schools in Ireland,
although, of course, the fact had been most treacherously
concealed from the authorities at Roslyn ; and now he
was let loose, without warning or caution, among the
Roslyn boys.   Better for them if their gates had been
open to the pestilence ! the pestilence could but have
killed the body, but this boy—this fore-front fighter in

the devil's battle—did much to ruin many an immortal
soul. He systematically, from the very first, called evil
good and good evil, put bitter for sweet and sweet for
bitter. He openly threw aside the admission of any
one moral obligation. Never did some of the Roslyn
boys, to their dying day, forget the deep, intolerable,
unfathomable flood of moral turpitude and iniquity which
he bore with him ; a flood, which seemed so irresistible,
that the influence of such boys as Montagu and Owen
to stay its onrush seemed as futile as the weight of a
feather to bar the fury of a mountain stream. Eric
might have done much, Duncan might have done much,
to aid the better cause, had they tried ; but they resisted
at first but faintly, and then not at all, until they too
were swept away in the broadening tide of degeneracy
and sin.

Big, burly, and strong, though much younger than
he looked (if he stated his age correctly, which I doubt),
Brigson, being low in the school, naturally became the
bully and the Coryphæus of all the lower forms—the
bully if they opposed him, the Coryphæus if they
accepted his guidance. A little army of small boys
attended him, and were ever ready for the schemes of
mischief to which he deliberately trained them, until
they grew almost as turbulent, as disobedient, and as
wicked, as himself. He taught, both by precept and
example, that towards masters neither honour was to be
recognized, nor respect to be considered due. To cheat
them, to lie to them, to annoy them in every possible

way—to misrepresent their motives, mimic their defects,
and calumniate their actions—was the conduct which he
inaugurated towards them; and for the time that he
continued at Roslyn the whole lower school was a
Pandemonium of evil passions and despicable habits.

Every one of the little boys became more or less
amenable to his influence, and among them Vernon
Williams.   Had Eric done his duty, this would never
have been; but he was half-ashamed to be often with
his brother, and disliked to find him so often creeping
to his side.   He flattered himself that in this feeling he
was only anxious that Vernon should grow spirited and
independent; but, had he examined himself, he would
have found selfishness at the bottom of it.   Once or
twice his manner showed harshness to Vernon, and the
little boy both observed and resented it.   Montagu and
others noticed him for Eric's sake; but, being in the
same form with Brigson, Vernon was thrown much
with him, and feeling, as he did, deserted and lonely, he
was easily caught by the ascendancy of his physical
strength and reckless daring.   Before three months
were over, he became, to Eric's intolerable disgust, a
ringleader in the band of troublesome scapegraces, whose
increasing numbers were the despair of all who had the
interests of the school at heart.

Unfortunately, Owen was now head of the school,
and from his constitutional want of geniality, he was
so little of a boy that he had no sympathy from the
others, and little authority over them.   He simply kept

aloof, holding his own way, and retiring into his own tastes and pursuits, and the society of one or two congenial spirits in the school, so as in no way to come in contact with the spreading corruption.

Montagu, now Owen's chief friend, was also in the sixth, and fearlessly expressed at once his contempt for Brigson, and his dread of the evil he was effecting. Had the monitorial system existed, that contagion could have been checked at once; but, as it was, brute force had the unlimited authority. Ill indeed are those informed who raise a cry, and join in the ignorant abuse of that noble safeguard of English schools. Any who have had personal and intimate experience of how schools work *with* it and *without* it, know what a Palladium it is of happiness and morality; how it prevents bullying, upholds manliness, is the bulwark of discipline, and makes boys more earnest and thoughtful, often at the most critical periods of their lives, by enlisting all their sympathies and interests on the side of the honourable and the just.

Brigson knew at a glance whom he had most to fear; Bull, Attlay, Llewellyn, Graham, all tolerated or even approved of him. Owen did not come in his way, so he left him unmolested. To Eric and Duncan he was scrupulously civil, and by flattery and deference managed to keep apparently on excellent terms with them. Eric pretended to be ignorant of the harm he was bringing about, and in answer to the indignant and measureless invectives of Montagu and others, professed to see in Brigson a very good fellow; rather wild, perhaps, but still a very good fellow.

Brigson hated Montagu, because he read on his features the unvarying glance of withering contempt. He dared not come across him openly, since Montagu was so high in the school; and besides, though much the bigger of the two, Brigson was decidedly afraid of him. But he chose sly methods of perpetual annoyance. He nick-named him "Rosebud;" he talked *at* him whenever he had an opportunity; he poisoned the minds of the gang of youngsters against him; he spread malicious reports about him; he diminished his popularity, and embittered his feelings, by every secret and underhand means which lay in his power.

One method of torment was most successful. As a study-boy, Montagu did not come to bed till an hour later than the lower part of the school, and Brigson taught some of the little fellows to play all kinds of tricks to his bed and room, so that, when he came down, it was with the certainty of finding everything in confusion. Sometimes his bed would be turned right on end, and he would have to put it to the ground and remake it before he could lie down. Sometimes all the furniture in the room would be thrown about in different corners, with no trace of the offender. Sometimes he would find all sorts of things put inside the bed itself. The intolerable part of the vexation was, to be certain that this was done by Brigson's instigation, or by his own hand, without having the means of convicting or preventing him. Poor Monty grew very sad at heart, and this perpetual dastardly annoyance weighed the more heavily on his spirits, from its being of a kind which peculiarly grated on his refined taste, and his natural sense of what was gentlemanly and fair.

One night, coming down, as usual, in melancholy dread, he saw a light under the door of his room. It struck him that he was earlier than usual, and he walked up quickly and noiselessly. There they were at it! The instant he entered, there was a rush through the opposite door, and he felt convinced that one of the retreating figures was Brigson's. In a second he had sprung across, so as to prevent the rest from running, and with heaving breast and flaming eyes, glared at the intruders as they stood there, sheepish and afraid.

" What!" he said angrily, " so *you* are the fellows who have had the cowardice to annoy me thus, night after night, for weeks; you miserable, degraded young animals!" And he looked at the four or five who had not made their escape. " What! and *you* among them," he said with a start, as he caught the eye of Vernon Williams.—" Oh, this is too bad." His tone showed the deepest sorrow and vexation, and for a moment he said no more. Instantly Vernon was by him.

" *Do* forgive me, *do* forgive me, Montagu," he said ; " I really didn't know it teased you so much."

But Montagu shook him off, and at once recovered himself. " Wretched boys! let me see what you have been doing to-night. Oh, as usual," he said, glancing at the complete disorder which they had been effecting. "Ha! but what is this? So Brigson has introduced another vile secret among you. Well, he shall rue it!" and he pointed to some small, almost invisible flakes of a whitish substance scattered here and there over his pillow. It was a kind of powder which, if once it touched the skin, caused the most violent and painful irritation.

"By heavens, this is *too* bad!" he exclaimed, stamping his foot with anger. "What have I ever done to you young blackguards, that you should treat me thus? Have I ever been a bully? Have I ever harmed one of you? And *you*, too, Vernon Williams!"

The little boy trembled and looked ashamed under his noble glance of sorrow and scorn.

"Well, I *know* who has put you up to this; but you shall not escape so. I shall thrash you every one."

Very quietly he suited the action to the word, sparing none. They took it patiently enough, conscious of richly deserving it; and when it was over, Vernon said, "Forgive me, Montagu. I am very sorry, and will never do so again." Montagu, without deigning a reply, motioned them to go, and then sat down, full of grief, on his bed. But the outrage was not over for that night, and no sooner had he put out the light than he became painfully aware that several boys were stealing into the room, and the next moment he felt a bolster fall on his head. He was out of bed in an instant, and with a few fierce and indignant blows, had scattered the crowd of his cowardly assailants, and driven them away. A number of fellows had set on him in the dark—on *him*, of all others. Oh, what a change must have happened in the school that this should be possible! He felt that the contagion of Brigson's base-ness had spread far indeed.

He fought like a lion, and several of the conspirators had reason to repent their miscalculation in assaulting so spirited an antagonist. But this did not content him; his blood was up, and he determined to attack the evil at its source. He strode through his discom-fited enemies straight into Brigson's room, struck a match, and said, " Brigson, get out of bed this instant."

" Hullo!" grunted Brigson, pretending to be only just awake.

" None of that, you blackguard! Will you take a thrashing?"

" No!" roared Brigson, " I should think not."

" Well, then, take *that!*" he shouted, striking him in the face.

The fight that followed was very short. In a single round Montagu had utterly thrashed, and stricken to the earth, and forced to beg for mercy, his cumbrous and brutal opponent. He seemed to tower above him with a magnificent superiority, and there was a self-controlled passion about him which gave tremendous energy to every blow. Brigson was utterly dashed, confounded, and cowed, and took without a word the parting kick of ineffable contempt which Montagu bestowed on him.

" There," he said to the fellows, who had thronged

in from all the dormitories at the first hint of a fight,
" I, a sixth-form fellow, have condescended to thrash
that base coward there, whom all you miserable lower
boys have been making an idol and hero of, and from
whom you have been so readily learning every sort of
blackguardly and debasing trick. But let me tell you
and your hero, that if any of you dare to annoy or lift
a finger at me again, you shall do it at your peril. I
despise you all; there is hardly one gentlemanly or
honourable fellow left among you since that fellow
Brigson has come here; yes, I despise you, and you
know that you deserve it." And every one of them
did shrink before his just and fiery rebuke.

The scene was not over when the door suddenly
opened, and Mr. Rose appeared. He stood amazed to
see Montagu there in his night-shirt, the boys all round,
and Brigson washing his nose, which was bleeding pro-
fusely, at his basin.

Montagu instantly stepped up to him. " You can
trust me, sir; may I ask you kindly to say nothing of
this ? I have been thrashing some one that deserved it,
and teaching these fellows a lesson."

Mr. Rose saw and allowed for his excited manner.
" I can trust you," he said, " Montagu, and shall take
no further notice of this irregularity. And now get
instantly to your beds."

But Montagu, slipping on his clothes, went straight
up to the studies, and called the upper boys together.
He briefly told them what had occurred, and they

rejoiced greatly, binding themselves for the future to check, if they could, by all fair means, Brigson's pernicious influence and abominable example.

But it was too late now; the mischief was done.

" O Eric," said Montagu, " why did you not make a stand against all this before ? Your own brother was one of them."

" Little wretch. I'll kick him well for it," said Eric.

" No, no!" said Montagu, " that'll do no good. Try rather to look after him a little more."

" I hope *you* will forgive him, and try and rescue him."

" I will do what I can," said Montagu, coldly.

Eric sighed, and they parted.

Montagu had hoped that after this Eric would at least break off all open connection with Brigson ; and, indeed, Eric had meant to do so. But that personage kept carefully out of his way until the first burst of indignation against him had subsided, and after a time began to address Eric as if nothing had happened. Meanwhile he had completely regained his ascendancy over the lower part of the school, which was not difficult, because they were wincing under Montagu's contempt, and mingled no little dislike with it ; a dislike which all are too apt to feel towards those whose very presence and moral superiority are a tacit rebuke of their own failings. But while Montagu was hated, Eric was at the zenith of popular favour, a favour which Brigson ostentatiously encouraged. He was openly flattered and caressed, and if ever he got a large score at cricket, it was chalked triumphantly over the walls. All this he was weak enough to enjoy immensely, and it was one of the reasons why he did not wish to risk his popularity by breaking with Brigson. So, after a little constraint and coldness, he began to stand in much the same relation to him as before.

The best-disposed of the upper boys disliked all this very much, and the sixth and fifth forms began to be split up into two main parties—the one, headed by Eric, and, to a much less degree, by Duncan, who devoted themselves to the games and diversions of the school, and troubled themselves comparatively little about anything else ; the other, headed by Montagu, who took the lead in intellectual pursuits, and endeavoured, by every means in their power, to counteract the pernicious effects of the spreading immorality.

And so at Roslyn, owing mainly to the wickedness of one depraved boy, and the weak fear of man which actuated others, all was disunion, misery, and deterioration. The community which had once been peaceful, happy, and united, was filled with violent jealousy and heart-burnings ; every boy's hand seemed to be against his neighbour ; lying, bad language, dishonesty, grew fearfully rife, and the few who, like Owen and Montagu, remained uncontaminated by the general mischief, walked alone and despondent amid their uncongenial and degraded schoolfellows.

CHAPTER II.

WILDNEY.

"That punishment's the best to bear
  That follows soonest on the sin,
And guilt's a game where losers fare
  Better than those who seem to win."

Cov. PATMORE.

AT the beginning of this quarter Eric and Duncan had succeeded to one of the studies, and Owen shared with Montagu the one which adjoined it.

Latterly the small boys, in the universal spirit of disobedience, had frequented the studies a good deal, but it was generally understood that no study-boy might ask any one to be a regular visitor to his room without the leave of its other occupant.

So one evening Duncan said to Eric, " Do you know little Wildney ?"

" You mean that jolly fearless-looking little fellow, with the great black eyes, who came at the beginning of the quarter ? No, I don't know him."

" Well, he's a very nice little fellow ; a regular devil."

" Humph !" said Eric, laughing ; " I shall bring out a new Duncan-dictionary, in which $\varkappa\varepsilon\varrho\varkappa o\varkappa\varepsilon\varrho\acute{\omega}\nu\nu\chi o\varsigma =$ very nice little fellow."

" Pooh !" said Duncan ; " you know well enough what I mean ; I mean he 's not one of your white-faced, lily-hearted new boys, but has lots of fun in him."

" Well, what of him ? "

" Have you any objection to my asking him to sit in the study when he likes ? "

" Not the least in the world."

" Very well, I 'll go and fetch him now. But wouldn't you like to ask your brother Vernon to come in too whenever he 's inclined ?"

" No," said Eric, " I don't care. He does come every now and then."

Duncan went to fetch Wildney, and while he was gone, Eric was thinking *why* he didn't give Vernon the free run of his study. He would not admit to himself the true reason, which was, that he had too much ground to fear that his example would do his brother no good.

Eric soon learned to like Wildney, who was a very bright, engaging, spirited boy, with a dash of pleasant impudence about him which took Eric's fancy. He had been one of the most mischievous of the lower fellows, but, although clever, did little or nothing in school, and was in the worst repute with the masters. Until he was " taken up" by Eric, he had been a regular little hero among his compeers, because he was game for any kind of mischief, and, in the new tone of popular morality, his fearless disregard of rules made him the object of general admiration. From this time, however, he was much in the studies, and unhappily carried with him to those upper regions the temptation to a deeper and more injurious class of transgressions than had yet penetrated there.

It was an ill day for General Wildney when he sent his idolised little son to Roslyn ; it was an ill day for Eric when Duncan first asked the child to frequent their study.

It was past nine at night, and the lower school had gone to bed, but there was Wildney quietly sitting on Eric's knee by the study fire, while Duncan was doing some Arnold's verses for him to be shown up next day.

" Bother these verses," said Duncan, " I shall have a whiff. Do you mind, Eric ?"

" No; not at all."

" Give me a weed, too," said Wildney.

" What ! young un—you don't mean to say you smoke ?" asked Eric in surprise.

" Don't I, though ? let me show you. Why, a whole lot of us went and smoked two or three pipes by Riverbend only yesterday."

" Phew !" said Eric, " then I suppose I must smoke too to keep you in countenance ;" and he took a cigar. It was the first time he had touched one since the day at the Stack. The remembrance made him gloomy and silent. "Tempora mutantur," thought he, "nos et mutamur in illis."

"Why, how glum you are," said Wildney, patting him on the head.

"O no!" said Eric, shaking off unpleasant memories. "Look," he continued, pointing out of the window to change the subject, "what a glorious night it is! Nothing but stars, stars, stars."

"Yes," said Duncan, yawning; "this smoking makes one very thirsty. I wish I'd some beer."

"Well, why shouldn't we get some?" said Wildney; "it would be very jolly."

"Get some! What! at this time of night?"

"Yes; I'll go now, if you like, to Ellan, and be back before ten."

"Nonsense," said Eric; "it aint worth while."

"I believe you think I'm afraid," said Wildney, laughing, and looking at Eric with his dark eyes; "and what's more, I believe *you're* afraid."

"Little whippersnapper!" said Eric, colouring, "as if I was afraid to do anything *you* dare do. I'll go with you at once, if you like."

"What are you thinking of?" asked Duncan, "I don't care twopence about the beer, and I hope you won't go."

"But I will, though," said Eric, a little nettled that Wildney, of all people, should think him wanting in pluck.

"But how will you get out?"

"Oh, *I'll* show you a dodge there," said Wildney. "Come along. Have you a dark lantern?"

" No, but I'll get Llewellyn's."

" Come along, then."

So the little boy of twelve took the initiative, and, carrying the dark lantern, instructed the two study-boys of sixteen in a secret which had long been known to the lower part of the school.

" Ibant obscuri dubiâ sub luce." He led them quietly down stairs, stole with them noiselessly past the library door, and took them to a window in the passage, where a pane was broken.

" Could you get through that?" he whispered to Eric, " if we broke away the rest of the glass?"

" I don't know. But, then, there's the bar outside."

" Oh, I'll manage that. But will you go and peep through the key-hole of the library, and see who's there, Duncan?"

" No," said Duncan, bluntly, " no key-holes for me."

" Hush! then *I* will," and he glided away, while Eric, as quietly as he could, broke away the glass until it was all removed.

" There's only old Stupid," whispered he, irreverently designating an under-master named Harley, " and he's asleep before the fire. Now, then, just lift me up, Eric, will you?"

Eric lifted him, and he removed the nails which fastened the end of the bar. They looked secure enough, and were nails an inch long driven into the mortar; but they had been successfully loosened, and only wanted a little pull to bring them out. In one

minute Wildney had unfastened and pushed down one
end of the bar.   He then got through the broken pane,
and dropped down outside.   Eric followed with some
little difficulty, for the aperture would only just admit
his passage; and Duncan, going back to the study,
anxiously awaited their return.

It was a bright moonlight night, and the autumn
air was pleasant and cool.   But Eric's first thought, as
he dropped on to the ground, was one of shame that
he should suffer his new friend, a mere child, so easily
to tempt him into disobedience and sin.   He had hardly
thought till then of what their errand was to be, but
now he couldn't help so strongly disapproving of it,
that he was half-inclined to turn back.   He did not,
however, dare to suggest this, lest Wildney should
charge him with cowardice, and betray it to the rest.
Besides, the adventure had its own excitement, the stars
looked splendid, and the stolen waters were sweet.

" I hope we shan't be seen crossing the playground," said Wildney.   " My eye, should'nt we catch
it !"

He was obviously beginning to be afraid; so Eric
assumed an air of nonchalance, and played the part of
protector.

" Here, take my arm," he said; and as Wildney
grasped it tight, instead of feeling angry and ashamed
at having been misled by one so much his junior, Eric
felt strongly drawn towards him by community of
danger and interest.   Reaching Ellan, it suddenly

struck him that he did'nt know where they were going to buy the beer. He asked Wildney.

"Oh, I see you're not half up to snuff," said Wildney, whose courage had risen; "I'll show you."

He led to a little low public-house, whence tipsy songs were booming, and tapped at a side-door three times. As they looked in they saw some sailors boozing in a dirty tap-room, and enveloped in tobacco-smoke.

The side-door was opened, and a cunning wicked-looking man held up a light to see who they were.

"Hallo, Billy," said Wildney, confidentially, "all serene; give us two bottles of beer—on tick, you know."

"Yessir—d'reckly," said the man, with a hateful twinkle of the eyes. "So you're out for a spree," he continued, winking in a knowing way. "Won't you walk in to the back-parlour while I get them?" And he showed them into a dingy horrid room behind the house, stale with smoke, and begrimed with dust.

Eric was silent and disgusted, but Wildney seemed quite at home. The man soon returned with the beer. "Wouldn't you like a glass of summat now, young gen'lmen?" he asked, in an insinuating way.

"No, Billy! don't jabber—we must be off. Here, open the door."

"Stop, I'll pay," said Eric. "What's the damage?"

"Three shilling, sir," said the man. "Glad to see a new customer, sir." He pocketed the money, and showed them out, standing to look after them with a malicious leer as they disappeared, and jerking his left thumb over his shoulder.

"Faugh!" said Eric, taking a long breath as they got out again into the moonlight, "what a poisonous place! Good gracious, Charlie, who introduced you there?"

"Oh, I don't think much of going *there*," said Wildney, carelessly; "we go every week almost."

"We! who?"

"Oh, Brigson and a lot of us. We have a club there which we call 'the Anti-muffs,' and that's our smoking-room."

"And is that horrid beast the landlord?"

"Yes; he was an old school-servant, and there's no harm in him that I know of."

But Eric only "phewed" again two or three times, and thought of Montagu.

Suddenly Wildney clutched him by the arm, and pulled him into the deep shadow of a porch, whispering, in a low tone, "Look!"

Under a lamp-post, directly opposite them, stood Mr. Rose! He had heard voices and footsteps a moment before, and, puzzled at their sudden cessation in the noiseless street, he was looking round.

"We must run for it," whispered Wildney hastily, as Mr. Rose approached the porch; and the two boys took to their heels, and scampered away as hard as they could, Eric helping on Wildney by taking his hand, and neither of them looking behind. They heard Mr. Rose following them at first, but soon distanced him, and reached a place where two roads met, either of which would lead to the school.

"We won't go by the road; I know a short cut by the fields. What fun!" said Wildney, laughing.

"What an audacious little monkey you are; you know all sorts of dodges," said Eric.

They had no time to talk, but with a speed winged by fear got to the school, sprang on the buttress beneath the window, effected their entrance, and vanished after replacing the bar—Eric to his study, and Wildney to his dormitory.

"Here's a go!" said the latter, as they ran up stairs; "I've smashed one of the beer-bottles in getting through the window, and my trousers are deluged with the stuff."

They had hardly separated when Mr. Rose's step was heard on the stairs. He was just returning from a dinner-party, when the sight of two boys and the sound of their voices startled him in the street, and their sudden disappearance made him sure that they were Roslyn boys, particularly when they began to run. He strongly suspected that he recognised Wildney as one of them, and therefore made straight for his dormitory, which he entered, just as that worthy had thrust the beer-stained trousers under his bed. Mr. Rose walked up quietly to his bedside, and observed that he was not asleep, and that he still had half his clothes

on.   He was going away when he saw a little bit of the
trousers protruding under the mattress, and giving a
pull, out they came, wringing wet with the streams of
beer.   He could not tell at first what this imported,
but a fragment of the bottle fell out of the pocket
with a crash on the floor, and he then discovered.
Taking no notice of Wildney's pretended sleep, he
said, quietly, " Come to me before breakfast to-morrow,
Wildney," and went down stairs.

Eric came in soon after, and found the little fellow
vainly attempting to appear indifferent, as he related to
his admiring auditors the night's adventure; being
evidently rather proud of the " Eric and I," which he
introduced every now and then into his story.

" Has he twigged you ?"

" Yes."

" And me ?"

" I don't know; we shall see to-morrow."

" I hope not," said Eric; " I'm sorry for you,
Charlie."

" Can't be cured, must be endured," said Wildney.

" Well, good night! and don't lose heart."

Eric went back to Duncan in the study, and they
finished the other bottle of beer between them, though
without much enjoyment, because they were full of
surmises as to the extent of the discovery, and the
nature of the punishment.

Eric went in to tell Montagu of their escapade.

He listened very coldly, and said, "Well, Eric, it

would serve you right to be caught. What business have you to be going out at night, at the invitation of contemptible small fry, like this little Wildney?"

"I beg you won't speak of any friend of mine in those terms," said Eric, drawing up haughtily.

"I hope you don't call a bad little boy like Wildney, who'd be no credit to any one, *your* friend, Eric?"

"Yes I do, though. He's one of the pluckiest, finest, most promising fellows in the lower school."

"How I begin to hate that word plucky," said Montagu; "it's made the excuse here for everything that's wrong, base, and unmanly. It seems to me it's infinitely more 'plucky' just now to do your duty and not be ashamed of it."

"You've certainly required *that* kind of pluck to bear you up lately, Monty," said Owen, looking up from his books.

"Pluck!" said Montagu, scornfully; "you seem to me to think it consists in lowering yourself down to the level of that odious Brigson, and joining hand and glove with the dregs of the school."

"Dregs of the school! Upon my word, you're cool, to speak of any of my associates in that way," said Eric, now thoroughly angry.

"Associates!" retorted Montagu, hotly; "pretty associates! How do you expect anything good to go on, when fellows high in the school like you have such dealings with the refined honourable Brigson, and the exemplary intellectual Wildney?"

"You're a couple of confounded muffs," shouted Eric, banging the door, and flinging into his own study again without further reply.

"Havn't you been a little hard on him, considering the row he's in?" asked Owen.

Montagu's head was resting on his hand as he bent over the table. "Perhaps I have, indeed. But who could help it, Owen, in the present state of things? Yes, you're right," he said, after a pause; "*this* wasn't the time to speak. I'll go and talk to him again. But how utterly changed he is!"

He found Eric on the stairs going down to bed with an affectation of noise and gaiety. He ran after him, and said—

"Forgive me my passion and sarcasm, Williams. You know I am apt to express myself strongly." He could not trust himself to say more, but held out his hand.

Eric got red, and hesitated for a moment.

"Come, Eric, it isn't *wholly* my fault, is it, that we are not so warm to each other as we were when . . ."

"Oh, Monty, Monty!" said Eric, softened by the allusion; and he warmly grasped his friend's proffered hand.

"Oh, Eric!"

The two shook hands in silence, and as they left each other they felt that while things continued thus their friendship could not last. It was a sad thought for both.

Next morning Wildney received a severe flogging, but gained great reputation by not betraying his companion, and refusing to drop the least hint as to their means of getting out, or their purpose in visiting Ellan. So the secret of the bar remained undiscovered, and when any boy wanted to get out at night—(unhappily the trick now became common enough)—he had only to break a pane of glass in that particular window, which, as it was in the passage, often remained unmended and undiscovered for weeks.

After the flogging, Mr. Rose said shortly to Eric, " I want to speak to you."

The boy's heart misgave him as they entered the familiar library.

" I think I suspect who was Wildney's companion."

Eric was silent.

" I have no proof, and shall not therefore act on vague suspicion ; but the boy whom I *do* suspect is one whose course lately has given me the deepest pain ; one who has violated all the early promise he gave ; one who seems to be going farther and farther astray, and sacrificing all moral principle to the ghost of a fleeting and most despicable popularity—to the approval of those whom he cannot himself approve."

Eric still silent.

" Whatever you do *yourself*, Williams"—(it was the first time for two years that Mr. Rose had called him " Williams," and he winced a little)—" whatever you do

yourself, Williams, rests with *you ;* but remember it is a
ten-thousandfold heavier and more accursed crime to set
stumbling-blocks in the way of others, and abuse your
influence to cause any of Christ's little ones to perish."

" I wasn't the tempter, however," thought Eric,
still silent.

" Well, you seem hardened, and give no sign.
Believe, me, Williams, I grieve for you, and that bitterly.
My interest in you is no less warm, though my affection
for you cannot be the same.   You may go."

" Another friend alienated, and oh, how true a one !
He has not asked me to see him once this term,"
thought Eric, sadly ; but a shout of pleasure greeted
him directly he joined the football in the play-ground,
and, half consoled, he hoped Mr. Rose had heard it, and
understood that it was meant for the boy whom he had
just been rebuking.   " Well, after all," he thought, " I
have *some* friends still."

Yes, friends, such as they were !   Except Duncan,
hardly one boy whom he really respected ever walked
with him now.   Even little Wright, one of the very
few lower boys who had risen superior to Brigson's
temptations, seemed to keep clear of him as much as he
could ; and, in absolute vacuity, he was obliged to asso-
ciate with fellows like Attlay, and Graham, and Llewellyn,
and Bull.

Even with Bull !   All Eric's repugnance for this boy
seemed to have evaporated ; they were often together,
and, to all appearance, were sworn friends.   Eric did

not shrink now from such conversation as was pursued unchecked in his presence by nearly every one ; nay, worse, it had lost its horror, and he was neither afraid nor ashamed to join in it himself. This plague-spot had fretted more deeply than any other into the heart of the school morality, and the least boys seemed the greatest proficients in unbaring, without a blush, its hideous ugliness.

CHAPTER III.

"THE JOLLY HERRING."

"Velut unda supervenit undam."—VIRGIL.

THE Anti-muffs request the honour of Williams' company to a spread they are going to have to-morrow evening at half-past four, in their smoking-room."

A note to this effect was put into Eric's hands by Wildney after prayers. He read it when he got into his study, and hardly knew whether to be pleased or disgusted at it.

He tossed it to Duncan, and said, "What shall I do?"

Duncan turned up his nose, and chucked the note into the fire.

"I'd give them that answer, and no other."

"Why?"

"Because, Eric," said Duncan, with more seriousness than was usual with him, "I can't help thinking things have gone too far lately."

"How do you mean?"

"Well, I'm no saint myself, Heaven knows; but I

do think that the fellows are worse now than I have
ever known them—far worse. Your friend Brigson
reigns supreme out of the studies; he has laid down a
law that *no work* is to be done down stairs ever under
any pretence, and it's only by getting into one of the
studies that good little chaps like Wright can get on at
all. Even in the class-rooms there's so much row and
confusion that the mere thought of work is ridiculous."

"Well, there's no great harm in a little noise, if
that's all."

"But it isn't all. The talk of nearly the whole
school is getting most blackguardly; shamelessly so.
Only yesterday Wildney was chatting with Vernon up
here (you were out, or Vernon would not have been
here) while I was reading; they didn't seem to mind
me, and I'm sure you'd have been vexed to the heart
if you'd heard how they talked to each other. At last
I couldn't stand it any longer, and bouncing up, I boxed
both their ears smartly, and kicked them down stairs."

As Eric said nothing, Duncan continued, "And I
wish it ended in talk, but——"

"But I believe you're turning Owenite. Why,
bless me, we're only schoolboys; it'll be lots of time
to turn saint some other day."

Eric was talking at random, and in the spirit of
opposition. "You don't want to make the whole
school such a muffish set as the Rosebuds, do you?"

There was something of assumed bravado in Eric's
whole manner which jarred on Duncan exceedingly.

"Do as you like," he said, curtly, and went into another study.

Immediately after came a rap at the door, and in walked Wildney, as he often did after the rest were gone to bed, merely slipping his trousers over his night-shirt, and running up to the studies.

"Well, you'll come to the Anti-muffs, won't you?" he said.

"To that pestilential place again?—not I."

Wildney looked offended. "Not after we've all asked you? The fellows won't half like your refusing."

He had touched Eric's weak point.

"Do come," he said, looking up in Eric's face.

"Confound it all," answered Eric, hastily. "Yes, I've no friends, I'll come, Charlie. Anything to please you, boy."

"That's a brick. Then I shall cut down and tell the fellows. They'll be no end glad. No friends! why all the school like you." And he scampered off, leaving Eric ill at ease.

Duncan didn't re-enter the study that evening.

The next day, about half-past four, Eric found himself on the way to Ellan. As he was starting, Bull caught him up, and said—

"Are you going to the Anti-muffs?"

"Yes; why? are you going too?"

"Yes; do you mind our going together?"

"Not at all."

In fact, Eric was very glad of some one—no matter who—to keep him in countenance, for he felt considerably more than half ashamed of himself.

They went to "The Jolly Herring," as the pothouse was called, and passed through the dingy beery tap-room into the back parlour, to which Eric had already been introduced by Wildney. About a dozen boys were assembled, and there was a great clapping on the table as the two new-comers entered. A long table was laid down the room, which was regularly spread for dinner.

"Now then, Billy; make haste with the goose," called Brigson. "I vote, boys, that Eric Williams takes the chair."

"Hear! hear!" said half a dozen; and Eric, rather against his will, found himself ensconced at the end of the table, with Brigson and Bull on either hand. The villainous-low-foreheaded man, whom they called Billy, soon brought in a tough goose at one end of the table, and some fowls at the other; and they fell to, doing ample justice to the δαὶς ἐίση, while Billy waited on them. There was immense uproar during the dinner, every one eating as fast, and talking as loud, as he could.

The birds soon vanished, and were succeeded by long rolly-polly puddings, which the boys called Goliahs; and they, too, rapidly disappeared. Meanwhile beer was circling only too plentifully.

"Now for the dessert, Billy," called several voices;

and that worthy proceeded to put on the table some
figs, cakes, oranges, and four black bottles of wine.
There was a general grab for these dainties, and one
boy shouted, " I say, I've had no wine."

" Well, it's all gone. We must get some brandy—
it's cheaper," said Brigson ; and accordingly some
brandy was brought in, which the boys diluted with
hot water, and soon despatched.

" Here ! before you're all done swilling," said
Brigson, " I've got a health ; ' Confound muffs and
masters, and success to the anti's.'"

" And their chairman," suggested Wildney.

" And their chairman, the best fellow in the school,"
added Brigson.

The health was drunk with due clamour, and Eric
got up to thank them.

" I'm not going to spout," he said ; " but boys
must be boys, and there's no harm in a bit of fun. I
for one have enjoyed it, and am much obliged to you
for asking me ; and now I call for a song."

'' Wildney ! Wildney's song," called several.

Wildney had a good voice, and struck up, without
the least bashfulness—

> " Come, landlord, fill the flowing bowl,
>   Until it does run over !
> Come, landlord, fill," &c.

" Now," he said, " join in the chorus !" The
boys, all more or less excited, joined in heartily and
uproariously—

" For to-night we 'll merry merry be !
For to-night we 'll merry merry be !
For to-night we 'll merry merry be !
  To-morrow we 'll be sober ! "

While Wildney sang, Eric had time to think. As he glanced round the room, at the flushed faces of the boys, some of whom he could not recognise in the dusky atmosphere, a qualm of disgust and shame passed over him. Several of them were smoking, and, with Bull and Brigson heading the line on each side of the table, he could not help observing what a bad set they looked. The remembrance of Russell came back to him. Oh, if Edwin could have known that he was in such company at such a place ! And by the door stood Billy, watching them all like an evil spirit, with a leer of saturnine malice on his evil face.

But the bright little Wildney, unconscious of Eric's bitter thoughts, sang on with overflowing mirth. As Eric looked at him, shining out like a sunbeam among the rest, he felt something like blood-guiltiness on his soul, when he felt that he was sanctioning the young boy's presence in that degraded assemblage.

Wildney meanwhile was just beginning the next verse, when he was interrupted by a general cry of " cavé, cavé." In an instant the room was in confusion ; some one dashed the candles upon the floor, the table was overturned with a mighty crash, and plates, glasses, and bottles rushed on to the ground in shivers. Nearly every one bolted for the door, which led through the passage into the street; and in their headlong flight and selfishness, they stumbled over each other, and prevented all egress, several being knocked down and bruised in the crush. Others made for the tap-room; but, as they opened the door leading into it, there stood Mr. Ready and Mr. Gordon! and as it was impossible to pass without being seen, they made no further attempt at escape. All this was the work of a minute. Entering the back parlour, the two masters quickly took down the names of full half the boys who, in the suddenness of the surprise, had been unable to make their exit.

And Eric?

The instant that the candles were knocked over, he felt Wildney seize his hand, and whisper, " This way; all serene;" following, he groped his way in the dark to the end of the room, where Wildney, shoving aside a green baize curtain, noiselessly opened a door, which at once let them into a little garden. There they both crouched down under a lilac tree beside the house, and listened intently.

There was no need for this precaution; their door remained unsuspected, and in five minutes the coast was clear. Creeping into the house again, they whistled, and Billy coming in, told them that the masters had gone, and all was safe.

" Glad ye're not twigged, gen'lmen," he said; " but there'll be a pretty sight of damage for all this glass and plates."

" Shut up with your glass and plates," said Wildney. " Here, Eric, we must cut for it again."

It was the dusk of a winter evening when they got out from the close room into the open air, and they had to consider which way they would choose to avoid discovery. They happened to choose the wrong, but escaped by dint of hard running, and Wildney's old short cut. As they ran they passed several boys (who having been caught, were walking home leisurely), and managed to get back undiscovered, when they both answered their names quite innocently at the roll-call, immediately after lock up.

" What lucky dogs you are to get off," said many boys to them.

" Yes, it's precious lucky for me," said Wildney. " If I'd been caught at this kind of thing a second time, I should have got something worse than a swishing."

" Well, it's all through you I escaped," said Eric, " you knowing little scamp."

" I'm glad of it, Eric," said Wildney in his fascinating way, " since it was all through me you went. It's rather too hazardous though ; we must manage better another time."

During tea-time Eric was silent, as he felt pretty sure that none of the sixth form or other study boys would particularly sympathise with his late associates. Since the previous evening he had been cool with Duncan, and the rest had long rather despised him as a boy who'd do anything to be popular; so he sat there silent, looking as disdainful as he could, and not touching the tea, for which he felt disinclined after the recent potations. But the contemptuous exterior hid a self-reproving heart, and he felt how far more noble Owen and Montagu were than he. How gladly would he have changed places with them! how much he would have given to recover some of their forfeited esteem!

The master on duty was Mr. Rose, and after tea he left the room for a few minutes while the tables were cleared for "preparation," and the boys were getting out their books and exercises. All the study and class-room boys were expected to go away during this interval; but Eric, not noticing Mr. Rose's entrance, sat gossipping with Wildney about the dinner and its possible consequences to the school.

He was sitting on the desk carelessly, with one leg over the other, and bending down towards Wildney. He had just told him that he looked like a regular little sunbeam in the smoking-room of the Jolly Herring, and Wildney was pretending to be immensely offended by the simile.

"Hush! no more talking," said Mr. Rose, who did everything very gently and quietly. Eric heard him, but he was inclined to linger, and had always received such mild treatment from Mr. Rose, that he didn't think he would take much notice of the delay. For the moment he did not, so Wildney began to chatter again.

"All study boys to leave the room," said Mr. Rose.

Eric just glanced round and moved slightly; he might have gone away, but that he caught a satirical look in Wildney's eye, and besides wanted to show off a little indifference to his old master, with whom he had had no intercourse since their last-mentioned conversation.

"Williams, go away instantly; what do you mean by staying after I have dismissed you?" said Mr. Rose sternly.

Every one knew what a favourite Eric had once been, so this speech created a slight titter. The boy heard it just as he was going out of the room, and it annoyed him, and called to arms all his proud and dogged obstinacy. Pretending to have forgotten something, he walked conceitedly back to Wildney, and whispered to him, " I shan't go if he chooses to speak like that."

A red flush passed over Mr. Rose's cheek; he took two strides to Eric, and laid the cane sharply once across his back.

Eric was not quite himself, or he would not have acted as he had done. His potations, though not deep, had, with the exciting events of the evening, made his head giddy, and the stroke of the cane, which he had not felt now for two years, roused him to madness. He bounded up, sprang towards Mr. Rose, and almost before he knew what he was about, had wrenched the cane out of his hands, twisted it violently in the middle until it broke, and flung one of the pieces furiously into the fire.

For one instant, boy and master—Eric Williams and Mr. Rose—stood facing each other amid breathless silence, the boy panting and passionate, with his brain swimming, and his heart on fire ; the master pale, grieved, amazed beyond measure, but perfectly self-collected.

"After that exhibition," said Mr. Rose, with cold and quiet dignity, "you had better leave the room."

"Yes I had," answered Eric bitterly ; "there's your cane." And, flinging the other fragment at Mr. Rose's head, he strode blindly out of the room, sweeping books from the table, and overturning several boys in his way. He then banged the door with all his force, and rushed up into his study.

Duncan was there, and remarking his wild look and demeanour, asked, after a moment's awkward silence "Is anything the matter, Williams ?"

"Williams !" echoed Eric with a scornful laugh ; "yes, that's always the way with a fellow when he's in trouble. I always know what's coming when you begin to leave off calling me by my Christian name."

"Very well, then," said Duncan, good-humouredly, "what's the matter, Eric ?"

"Matter ?" answered Eric, pacing up and down the little room with an angry to-and-fro like a caged wild beast, and kicking everything which came in his way, "Matter ? hang you all, you are all turning against me, because you are a set of muffs, and——"

"Take care !" said Duncan ; but suddenly he caught Eric's look, and stopped.

"——And I've been breaking Rose's cane over his head, because he had the impudence to touch me with it, and——"

"Eric, you're not yourself to-night," said Duncan, interrupting, but speaking in the kindest tone ; and taking Eric's hand, he looked him steadily in the face.

Their eyes met; the boy's false self once more slipped off. By a strong effort he repressed the rising passion which the fumes of drink had caused, and flinging himself on his chair, refused to speak again, or even to go down stairs when the prayer-bell rang.

Seeing that in his present mood there was nothing to be done with him, Duncan, instead of returning to the study, went after prayers into Montagu's, and talked with him over the recent events, of which the boys' minds were all full.

But Eric sat lonely, sulky, and miserable, in his study, doing nothing, and when Montagu came in to visit him, felt inclined to resent his presence.

"So !" he said, looking up at the ceiling, "another saint come to cast a stone at me ! Well ! I suppose I must be resigned," he continued, dropping his cheek on his hand again; "only don't let the sermon be long."

But Montagu took no notice of his sardonic harshness, and seated himself by his side, though Eric pettishly pushed him away.

"Come, Eric," said Montagu, taking the hand which was repelling him ; "I won't be repulsed in this way. Look at me. What? won't you even look? Oh Eric, one wouldn't have fancied this in past days, when we were so much together with one who is dead. It's a long long time since we've even alluded to him, but *I* shall never forget those happy days."

Eric heaved a deep sigh.

" I'm not come to reproach you. You don't give me a friend's right to reprove. But still, Eric, for your own sake, dear fellow, I can't help being sorry for all this. I did hope you'd have broken with Brigson after the thrashing I gave him, for the foul way in which he treated me. I don't think you *can* know the mischief he is doing."

The large tears began to soften the fire of Eric's eye. " Ah !" he said, " it's all of no use ; you're all giving me the cold shoulder, and I'm going to the bad, that's the long and short of it."

" Oh, Eric ! for your own sake, for your parents' sake, for the school's sake, for all your real friends' sake, don't talk in that bitter hopeless way. You are too noble a fellow to be made the tool or the patron of the boys who lead, while they seem to follow you. I *do* hope you'll join us even yet in resisting them."

Eric had laid his head on the table, which shook with his emotion. " I can't talk, Monty," he said, in an altered tone ; " but leave me now ; and if you like, we will have a walk to-morrow."

" Most willingly, Eric." And again, warmly pressing his hand, Montagu returned to his own study.

Soon after, there came a timid knock at Eric's door.

He expected Wildney as usual; a little before, he had been looking out for him, and hoping he would come, but he did n't want to see him now, so he answered rather peevishly, "Come in; but I don't want to be bothered to-night."

Not Wildney, but Vernon appeared at the door. "May I come in? not if it bothers you, Eric," he said gently.

"Oh, Verny, I did n't know it was you; I thought it would be Wildney. You *never* come now."

The little boy came in, and his pleading look seemed to say, "Whose fault is that?"

"Come here, Verny;" and Eric drew him towards him, and put him on his knee, while the tears trembled large and luminous in the child's eyes.

It was the first time for many a long day that the brothers had been alone together, the first time for many a long day that any acts of kindness had passed between them. Both seemed to remember this, and, at the same time, to remember home, and their absent parents, and their mother's prayers, and all the quiet half-forgotten vista of innocent pleasures, and sacred relationships, and holy affections. And why did they see each other so little at school? Their consciences told them both, that either wished to conceal from the other his wickedness and forgetfulness of God.

They wept together; and once more, as they had not done since they were children, each brother put his arm round the other's neck. And remorseful Eric

could not help being amazed, how, in his cruel heartless
selfishness, he had let that fair child go so far far astray ;
left him as a prey to such boys as were his companions
in the lower school.

"Eric, did you know I was caught to-night at the
dinner ?"

"You !" said Eric, with a start and a deep blush.
"Good heavens ! I didn't notice you, and should not have
dreamt of coming, if I'd known you were there.   Oh,
Vernon, forgive me for setting you such a bad example."

"Yes, I was there, and I was caught."

"Poor boy ! but never mind ; there are such a lot
that you can't get much done to you."

"It isn't *that* I care for ; I've been flogged before,
you know.   But——may I say something ?"

"Yes, Vernon, anything you like."

"Well, then,—oh, Eric ! I'm *so so* sorry that you
did that to Mr. Rose to-night.   All the fellows are
praising you up, of course ; but I could have cried to
see it, and I did.   I wouldn't have minded if it had
been anybody but Rose."

"But why ?"

"Because, Eric, he's been so good, so kind to both
of us.   You've often told me about him, you know, at
Fairholm, and he's done such lots of kind things to
me.   And only to-night, when he heard I was caught,
he sent for me to the library, and spoke so firmly, yet
so gently, about the wickedness of going to such low
places, and about so young a boy as I am learning to

drink, and the ruin of it —— and—and "——His voice
was choked by sobs for a time,—"and then he knelt
down and prayed for me, so as I have never heard any
one pray but mother;—and do you know, Eric, it was
strange, but I thought I *did* hear our mother's voice
praying for me too, while he prayed, and "——He tried
in vain to go on; but Eric's conscience continued for
him; "and just as he had ceased doing this for one
brother, the other brother, for whom he has often done
the same, treated him with coarseness, violence, and
insolence."

"Oh, I am utterly wretched, Verny. I hate myself.
And to think that while I'm like this, they are yet
loving and praising me at home. And, oh, Verny, I
was so sorry to hear from Duncan, how you were talking
the other day."

Vernon hid his face on Eric's shoulder; and as his
brother stooped over him, and folded him to his heart,
they cried in silence, for there seemed no more to say,
until wearied with sorrow, the younger fell asleep; and
then Eric carried him tenderly down stairs, and laid him,
still half-sleeping, upon his bed.

He laid him down, and looked at him as he slumbered.
The other boys had not been disturbed by their noiseless
entrance, and he sat down on his brother's bed to think,
shading off the light of the candle with his hand. It
was rarely now that Eric's thoughts were so rich with
the memories of childhood, and sombre with the consciousness of sin, as they were that night, while he

gazed on his brother Vernon's face. He did not know what made him look so long and earnestly; an indistinct sorrow, an unconjectured foreboding, passed over his mind, like the shadow of a summer cloud. Vernon was now slumbering deeply; his soft childish curls fell off his forehead, and his head nestled in the pillow; but there was an expression of uneasiness on his sleeping features, and the long eyelashes were still wet with tears.

"Poor child," thought Eric; "dear little Vernon; and he is to be flogged, perhaps birched, to-morrow."

He went off sadly to bed, and hardly once remembered, that *he* too would come in for certain punishment the next day.

CHAPTER IV.

"Raro antecedentem scelestum
Deseruit pede Pœna claudo."—Hor.

FTER prayers the next morning Dr. Rowlands
spoke to his boarders on the previous day's
discovery, and in a few forcible vivid words
set before them the enormity of the offence.
He ended by announcing that the boys who were
caught would be birched,—"except the elder ones,
Bull and Brigson, who will bring me one hundred
lines every hour of the half-holidays till further
notice. There are some," he said, "I am well aware,
who, though present yesterday, were not detected. I
am sorry for it, for *their* sakes; they will be more
likely to sin again. In cases like this, punishment is
a blessing, and impunity a burden." On leaving the
room he bade Eric follow him into his study. Eric
obeyed, and stood before the head-master with downcast
eyes.

"Williams," he said, "I have had a great regard
for you, and felt a deep interest in you from the day I

M

first saw you, and knew your excellent parents. At one time I had conceived great hopes of your future course, and your abilities seemed likely to blossom into noble fruit. But you fell off greatly, and grew idle and careless. At last an event happened, in which for a time you acted worthily of yourself, and which seemed to arouse you from your negligence and indifference. All my hopes in you revived; but as I continued to watch your course (more closely, perhaps, than you supposed), I observed with pain that those hopes must be again disappointed. It needs but a glance at your countenance to be sure that you are not so upright or right-minded a boy as you were two years ago. I can judge only from your outward course; but I deeply fear, Williams, I deeply fear, that in *other* respects also you are going the down-hill road. And what am I to think now, when, on the *same* morning, you and your little brother *both* come before me for such serious and heavy faults? I cannot free you from blame even for *his* misdoings, for you are his natural guardian here; I am only glad that you were not involved with him in that charge."

"Let *me* bear the punishment, sir, instead of him," said Eric, by a sudden impulse; "for I misled him, and was there myself."

Dr. Rowlands paced the room in deep sorrow. "You, Williams! on the verge of the sixth form. Alas! I fear, from this, that the state of things among you is even worse than I had supposed."

Eric again hung his head.

" No ; you have confessed the sin voluntarily, and therefore at present I shall notice it; only, let me entreat you to beware. But I must turn to the other matter. What excuse have you for your intolerable conduct to Mr. Rose, who, as I know, has shown you from the first the most unusual and disinterested kindness ? "

" I cannot defend myself, sir. I was excited, and could not control my passion."

" Then you must sit down here, and write an apology, which I shall make you read aloud before the whole school at twelve to-day."

Eric, with trembling hand, wrote his apology, and Dr. Rowlands glanced at it. " Come to me again at twelve," he said.

At twelve all the school were assembled, and Eric, pale and miserable, followed the Doctor into the great school-room. The masters stood at one end of the room, and among them Mr. Rose, who, however, appeared an indifferent and uninterested spectator of the transaction. Every glance was fixed on Eric, and every one pitied him.

" We are assembled," said Dr. Rowlands, " for an act of justice. One of your number has insulted a master publicly, and is ashamed of his conduct, and has himself written the apology which he will read. I had intended to add a still severer punishment, but Mr. Rose has earnestly begged me not to do so, and I have succumbed to his wishes. Williams, read your apology."

There was a dead hush, and Eric tried once or

twice in vain to utter a word. At last, by a spasmodic effort, he regained his voice, and read, but in so low and nervous a tone, that not even those nearest him heard what he was saying.

Dr. Rowlands took the paper from him. " Owing," he said, " to a very natural and pardonable emotion, the apology has been read in such a way that you could not have understood it. I will therefore read it myself. It is to this effect—

"'I, Eric Williams, beg humbly and sincerely to apologise for my passionate and ungrateful insult to Mr. Rose.'

" You will understand that he was left quite free to choose his own expressions; and as he has acknowledged his shame and compunction for the act, I trust that none of you will be tempted to elevate him into a hero, for a folly which he himself so much regrets. This affair,—as I should wish all bad deeds to be after they have once been punished,—will now be forgiven, and I hope forgotten."

They left the room and dispersed, and Eric fancied that all shunned and looked coldly on his degradation. But not so: Montagu came, and taking his arm in the old friendly way, went a walk with him. It was a constrained and silent walk, and they were both glad when it was over, although Montagu did all he could to show that he loved Eric no less than before. Still it was weeks since they had been much together, and they had far fewer things in common now than they used to have before.

" I'm so wretched, Monty," said Eric at last ; " do you think Rose despises me ? "

" I am *sure* of the contrary. Won't you go to him, Eric, and say all you feel ? "

" Heigh ho ! I shall never get right again. Oh, to recover the last two years ! "

" You can redeem them, Eric, by a nobler present. Let the same words comfort you that have often brought hopé to me—' I will restore the years which the locust hath eaten.' "

They reached the school-door, and Eric went straight to the library. Mr. Rose was there alone. He received him kindly, as usual, and Eric went up to the fire-place where he was standing. They had often stood by that library fire on far different terms.

" Forgive me, sir," was all Eric could say, as the tears rushed to his eyes.

" Freely, my boy," said Mr. Rose, sadly. " I wish you could feel how fully I forgive you ; but," he added, laying his hand for the last time on Eric's head, " you have far more, Eric, to forgive yourself. I will not talk to you, Eric ; it would be little good I fear ; but you little know how much I pity and tremble for you."

While these scenes were being enacted with Eric, a large group was collected round the fire-place in the boarders' room, and many tongues were loudly discussing the recent events.

Alas for gratitude ! there was not a boy in that group to whom Mr. Rose had not done many an act of kindness; and to most of them far more than they ever knew. Many a weary hour had he toiled for them in private, when his weak frame was harassed by suffering; many a sleepless night had he wrestled for them in prayer, when, for their sakes, his own many troubles were laid aside. Work on, Walter Rose, and He who seeth in secret will reward you openly! but expect no gratitude from those for whose salvation you, like the great tender-hearted apostle, would almost be ready to wish yourself accursed.

Nearly every one in that noisy group was abusing Mr. Rose. It had long been Brigson's cue to do so; he derided him on every opportunity, and delighted to represent him as hypocritical and insincere. Even his weak health was the subject of Brigson s coarse ridicule, and the bad boy paid, in deep hatred, the natural tribute which vice must ever accord to excellence.

"You see how he turns on his pets if they offend him," said Brigson; "why, even that old beast Gordon isn't as bad."

"Yes; while poor Eric was reading, Rose reminded me of Milton's serpent," drawled Bull;

"Hope elevates and joy brightens his crest."

"He-e-ar! He-e-ar!" said Pietrie; "*vide* the last fifth form Rep."

"I expect Eric won't see everything so much *couleur de Rose* now, as the French frog hath it," remarked Graham.

" It was too bad to stand by and triumph, certainly," observed Wildney.

"I say, you fellows," remonstrated Wright, who, with Vernon, was sitting reading a book at one of the desks, " all that isn't fair. I'm sure you all saw how really sorry Rose looked about it ; and he said, you know, that it was merely for the sake of school discipline that he put the matter in Rowlands' hands."

" Discipline be hanged," shouted Brigson ; " we 'll have our revenge on him yet, discipline or no."

" I hope you won't, though," said Vernon ; " I know Eric will be sorry if you do."

" The more muff he. We shall do as we like."

" Well, I shall tell him ; and I 'm sure he 'll ask you not. You know how often he tries to stick up for Rose."

" If you say a word more," said Brigson, unaccustomed to being opposed among his knot of courtiers, " I 'll kick you out of the room ; you and that wretched little fool there with you."

"You may do as you like," answered Wright, quietly ; " but you won't go on like this long, I can tell you."

Brigson tried to seize him, but failing, contented himself with flinging a big coal at him as he ran out of the room, which narrowly missed his head.

" I have it !" said Brigson ; " that little donkey's given me an idea. We 'll *crust* Rose to-night.

" To crust," gentle reader, means to pelt an obnoxious person with crusts.

" Capital !" said some of the worst boys present ; " we will."

" Well, who'll take part ?"

No one offered. " What ! are we all turning sneaks and cowards ? Here, Wildney, won't you ? you were abusing Rose just now."

" Yes, I will," said Wildney, but with no great alacrity. " You'll not have done till you've got us all expelled, I believe."

" Fiddle-stick end ! and what if we are ? besides, he can't expel half the school."

First two or three more offered, and then a whole lot, gaining courage by numbers. So the plot was regularly laid. Pietrie and Graham were to put out the lights at each end of one table immediately after tea, and Wildney and Brooking at the other, when the study fellows had gone out. There would then be only Mr. Rose's candle burning, and the two middle candles, which, in so large a room, would just give enough light for their purpose. Then all the conspirators were to throng around the door, and from it aim their crusts at Mr. Rose's head. Not nearly so many would have volunteered to join, but that they fancied Mr. Rose was too gentle to take up the matter with vigour, and they were encouraged by his quiet leniency towards Eric the night before. It was agreed that no study-boy should be told of the intention, lest any of them should interfere.

Many hearts beat fast at tea that night as they

observed that numbers of boys, instead of eating all their
bread, were cutting off the crusts, and breaking them
into good-sized bits.

Tea finished, Mr. Rose said grace, and then sat
down quietly reading in his desk. The signal agreed
on was the (accidental) dropping of a plate by Brigson.
The study-boys left the room.

Crash !—down fell a plate on the floor, breaking to
pieces in the fall.

Instantly the four candles went out, and there was
a hurried movement towards the door, and a murmur
of voices.

" Now then," said Brigson, in a loud whisper,
" what a funky set you are ! Here goes ! "

The master, surprised at the sudden gloom and
confusion, had just looked up, unable to conjecture what
was the matter. Brigson's crust caught him a sharp
rap on the forehead as he moved.

In an instant he started up, and ten or twelve more
crusts flew by or hit him on the head, as he strode out
of the desk towards the door. Directly he stirred,
there was a rush of boys into the passage, and if he
had once lost his judgment or temper, worse harm might
have followed. But he did not. Going to the door, he
said, " Preparation will be in five minutes; every boy
not then in his place will be punished."

During that five minutes the servants had cleared
away the tea, full of wonder ; but Mr. Rose paced up and
down the room, taking no notice of any one. Imme-

diately after, all the boys were in their places, with
their books open before them, and in the thrilling
silence you might have heard a pin drop. Every one
felt that Mr. Rose was master of the occasion, and
awaited his next step in terrified suspense.

They all perceived how thoroughly they had mistaken their subject. The ringleaders would have given
all they had to be well out of the scrape. Mr, Rose
ruled by kindness, but he never suffered his will to be
disputed for an instant. He governed with such con-
summate tact, that they hardly felt it to be govern-
ment at all, and hence arose their stupid miscalculation.
But he felt that the time was now come to assert his
paramount authority, and determined to do so at once
and for ever.

"Some of you have mistaken me," he said, in a
voice so strong and stern that it almost startled them.
"The silly display of passion in one boy yesterday has
led you to presume that you may trifle with me. You
are wrong. For Williams' sake, as a boy who has, or
at least once *had*, something noble in him, I left that
matter in the Doctor's hands. I shall *not* do so to-
night. Which of you put out the candles?"

Dead silence. A pause.

"Which of you had the audacity to throw pieces
of bread at me?"

Still silence.

"I warn you that I *will* know, and it will be far

worse for all the guilty if I do not know at once."
There was unmistakeable decision in the tone.

"Very well. I know many boys who were *not*
guilty, because I saw them in parts of the room where
to throw was impossible. I shall now *ask* all the rest,
one by one, if they took any part in this. And beware
of telling me a lie.

There was an uneasy sensation in the room, and
several boys began to whisper aloud, " Brigson ! Brigson !" The whisper grew louder, and Mr. Rose heard
it. He turned on Brigson like a lion, and said—

" They call your name ; stand out !"

The awkward, big, ungainly boy, with his repulsive
countenance, shambled out of his place into the middle
of the room. Mr. Rose swept him with one flashing
glance. " *That* is the boy," thought he to himself,
" who has been like an ulcer to this school. These
boys shall have a good look at their hero." It was
but recently that Mr. Rose knew all the harm which
Brigson had been doing, though he had discovered,
almost from the first, what *sort* of character he had.

So Brigson stood out in the room, and as they
looked at him, many a boy cursed him in their hearts
for evil taught them, such as a lifetime's struggle could
not unteach. And it was *that* fellow, that stupid,
clumsy, base compound of meanness and malice, that
had ruled like a king among them. Faugh !

" They call your name ! Do you know anything
of this ?"

"No!" said Brigson; "I'll swear I'd nothing to do with it."

"Oh-h-h-h!"—the long, intense, deep-drawn expression of disgust and contempt ran round the room.

"You have told me a lie!" said Mr. Rose, slowly, and with ineffable contempt. "No words can express my loathing for your false and dishonourable conduct. Nor shall your lie save you, as you shall find immediately. Still, you shall escape if you can or dare to deny it again. I repeat my question—Were you engaged in this?"

He fixed his full, piercing eye on the culprit, whom it seemed to scorch and wither. Brigson winced back, and said nothing. "As I thought," said Mr. Rose.

"Not *one* boy only, but many, were engaged. I shall call you up one by one to answer me. Wildney, come here."

The boy walked in front of the desk.

"Were you one of those who threw?"

Wildney, full as he was of dangerous and deadly faults, was no coward, and not a liar. He knew, or at least feared, that this new scrape might be fatal to him, but, raising his dark and glistening eyes to Mr. Rose, he said penitently—

"I didn't throw, sir, but I *did* put out one of the candles that it might be done."

The contrast with Brigson was very great; the dark cloud hung a little less darkly on Mr. Rose's forehead, and there was a very faint murmur of applause.

"Good! stand back. Pietrie, come up."

Pietrie, too, confessed, and indeed all the rest of the plotters except Brooking. Mr. Rose's lip curled with scorn as he heard the exclamation which his denial caused; but he suffered him to sit down.

When Wright's turn came to be asked, Mr. Rose said—"No! I shall not even ask you, Wright. I know well that your character is too good to be involved in such an attempt."

The boy bowed humbly, and sat down. Among the last questioned was Vernon Williams, and Mr. Rose seemed anxious for his answer.

"No," he said at once,—and seemed to wish to add something.

"Go on," said Mr. Rose, encouragingly.

"Oh, sir! I only wanted to say that I hope you won't think Eric knew of this. He would have hated it, sir, more even than I do."

"Good," said Mr. Rose; "I am sure of it. And now," turning to the offenders, "I shall teach you never to dare again to be guilty of such presumption and wickedness as to-night. I shall punish you according to my notion of your degrees of guilt. Brigson, bring me a cane from that desk."

He brought it.

"Hold out your hand."

The cane fell, and instantly split up from top to bottom. Mr. Rose looked at it, for it was new that morning.

" Ha ! I see ; more mischief; there is a hair in it."

The boys were too much frightened to smile at the complete success of the trick.

" Who did this ?   I must be told at once."

" *I* did, sir," said Wildney, stepping forward.

" Ha ! very well," said Mr. Rose, while, in spite of his anger, a smile hovered at the corner of his lips. " Go and borrow me a cane from Mr. Harley."

While he went there was unbroken silence.

" Now, sir," said he to Brigson, " I shall flog you."

Corporal punishment was avoided with the bigger boys, and Brigson had never undergone it before.   At the first stroke he writhed and yelled ; at the second he retreated, twisting like a serpent, and blubbering like a baby ; at the third he flung himself on his knees, and, as the strokes fell fast, clasped Mr. Rose's arm, and implored and besought for mercy.

" *Miserable* coward," said Mr. Rose, throwing into the word such ringing scorn that no one who heard it ever forgot it.   He indignantly shook the boy off, and caned him till he rolled on the floor, losing every particle of self-control, and calling out, " The devil—the devil—the devil !" (" invoking his patron saint," as Wildney maliciously observed).

" There ! cease to blaspheme, and get up," said the master, blowing out a cloud of fiery indignation. " There, sir.   Retribution comes at last, leaden-footed but iron-handed.   A long catalogue of sins is visited on you to-day, and not only on your shrinking body, but on your conscience too, if you have one left. Let those red marks betoken that your reign is ended. Liar and tempter, you have led boys into the sins which you then meanly deny! And now, you boys, *there* in that coward, who cannot even endure his richly-merited punishment, see the boy whom you have suffered to be your *leader* for well-nigh six months!"

"Now, sir"—again he turned upon Brigson—"that flogging shall be repeated with interest on your next offence. At present you will take each boy on your back while I cane him. It is fit that they should see where *you* lead them to."

Trembling violently, and cowed beyond description, he did as he was bid. No other boy cried, or even winced; a few sharp cuts was all which Mr. Rose gave them, and even they grew fewer each time, for he was tired, and displeased to be an executioner.

"And now," he said, "since that disgusting but necessary scene is over, *never* let me have to repeat it again."

But his authority was established like a rock from that night forward. No one ever ventured to dispute it again, or forgot that evening. Mr. Rose's noble moral influence gained tenfold strength from the respect and wholesome fear that he then inspired.

But, as he had said, Brigson's reign was over. Looks of the most unmitigated disgust and contempt were darted at him, as he sat alone and shunned at the end of the table; and the boys seemed now to loathe and nauseate the golden calf they had been worshipping. He had not done blubbering even yet, when the prayer-bell rang. No sooner had Mr. Rose left the room than Wildney, his dark eyes sparkling with rage, leaped on the table, and shouted—

"Three groans, hoots, and hisses, for a liar and a coward," a sign of execration which he was the first to lead off, and which the boys echoed like a storm.

Astonished at the tumult, Mr. Rose reappeared at the door. "Oh, we're not hissing you, sir," said Wildney excitedly; "we're all hissing at lying and cowardice."

Mr. Rose thought the revulsion of feeling might do good, and he was striding out again without a word, when—

"Three times three for Mr. Rose," sang out Wildney.

Never did a more hearty or spontaneous cheer burst from the lips and lungs of fifty boys than that. The news had spread like wildfire to the studies, and the other boys came flocking in during the uproar, to join in it heartily. Cheer after cheer rang out like a sound of silver clarions from the clear boy-voices; and in the midst of the excited throng stood Eric and Montagu, side by side, hurrahing more lustily than all the rest.

But Mr. Rose, in the library, was on his knees, with moving lips and lifted hands. He coveted the popular applause as little as he had dreaded the popular opposition; and the evening's painful experiences had

taught him anew the bitter lesson to expect no gratitude, and hope for no reward, but simply, and con-
tentedly, and unmurmuringly, to work on in God's
vineyard so long as life and health should last.

Brigson's brazen forehead bore him through the
disgrace which would have crushed another. But still
he felt that his position at Roslyn could never be what
it had been before, and he therefore determined to leave
at once. By grossly calumniating the school, he got
his father to remove him, and announced, to every one's
great delight, that he was going in a fortnight. On his
last day, by way of bravado, he smashed and damaged
as much of the school property as he could, a proceeding
which failed to gain him any admiration, and merely
put his father to ruinous expense.

The day after his exposure Eric had cut him dead,
without the least pretence of concealment; an example
pretty generally followed throughout the school.

In the evening Brigson went up to Eric and hissed
in his ear, "You cut me, curse you; but, *never fear,
I'll be revenged on you yet.*"

"Do your worst," answered Eric, contemptuously;
"and never speak to me again."

CHAPTER V.

RIPPLES.

"Our echoes roll from soul to soul,
And live for ever and for ever."—TENNYSON.

WEN and Montagu were walking by Silver-burn, and talking over the affairs of the school. During their walk they saw Wright and Vernon Williams in front of them.

"I am so glad to see those two together," said Montagu; "I really think Wright is one of the best little fellows in the school, and he'll be the saving of Vernon. He's already persuaded him to leave off smoking and other bad things, and has got him to work a little harder, and turn over a new leaf altogether."

"Yes," answered Owen; "I've seen a marvellous improvement in little Williams lately. I think that Duncan gave him a rough lesson the other night which did him good, and dear old Rose too has been leading him by the hand; but the best thing is that, through Wright, he sees less of Eric's *friend*, that young scape-grace Wildney."

" Yes ; that little wretch has a good deal to answer for. What a pity that Eric spoils him so, or rather suffers himself to be spoilt by him. I'm glad Vernon's escaped his influence now : he's too fine a boy to be made as bad as the general run of them. What a brilliant little fellow he is ; just like his brother."

" Just like what his brother *was*," said Owen ; " his face, like his mind, has suffered lately."

" Too true," answered Montagu, with a sigh ; " and yet, cool as we now are in our outward intercourse, he little knows how I love him, and yearn for the Eric I once knew. Would to God poor Russell had lived, and then I believe that Williams wouldn't have gone so far wrong."

" Well, I think there's another chance for him now that—that—what name is bad enough for that Brigson ? —is gone."

" I hope so. But"—he added after a pause— " his works do follow him. Look there ! " He took a large stone and threw it into the Silverburn stream ; there was a great splash, and then ever-widening circles of blue ripple broke the surface of the water, dying away one by one in the sedges on the bank. " There," he said, " see how long those ripples last, and how numerous they are."

Owen understood him. " Poor Williams ! What a gleam of new hope there was in him after Russell's death ! "

" Yes, for a time," said Montagu ; " heigh ho ! I

fear we shall never be warm friends again. We can't
be while he goes on as he is doing. And yet I love
him."

A sudden turn of the stream brought them to the
place called Riverbend.

" If you want a practical comment on what we've
been talking about, you'll see it there," said Montagu.

He pointed to a party of boys, four or five, all
lying on a pleasant grass bank, smoking pipes. Prominent among them was Eric, stretched at ease, and
looking up at the clouds, towards which curled the
puffed fumes of his meerschaum—a gift of Wildney's.
That worthy was beside him similarly employed.

The two sixth-form boys hoped to pass by unobserved, as they did not wish for a rencontre with our
hero under such circumstances. But they saw Wildney
pointing to them, and, from the fits of laughter which
followed his remarks, they had little doubt that they
were the subject of the young gentleman's wit. This
is never a pleasant sensation ; but they observed that
Eric made a point of not looking their way, and went
on in silence.

" How very sad !" said Montagu.

" How very contemptible !" said Owen.

" Did you observe what they were doing ?"

" Smoking ?"

" Worse than that a good deal. They were doing
something which, if Eric doesn't take care, will one day
be his ruin."

" What ? "

" I saw them drinking. I have little doubt it was brandy."

" Good heavens ! "

" It is getting a common practice with some fellows. One of the ripples, you see, of Brigson's influence."

Before they got home they caught up Wright and Vernon, and walked in together.

" We've been talking," said Wright, " about a bad matter. Vernon here says that there's no good working for a prize in his form, because the cribbing's so atrocious. Indeed, it's very nearly as bad in my form. It always is under Gordon ; he *can't* understand fellows doing dishonourable things."

" It's a great bore in the weekly examinations," said Vernon ; " every now and then Gordon will even leave the room for a few minutes, and then out come dozens of books."

" Well, Wright," said Montagu, " if that happens again next examination, I'd speak out about it."

" How ? "

" Why, I'd get every fellow who disapproves of it to give me his name, and get up and read the list, and say that you at least have pledged yourselves not to do it."

" Humph ! I don't know how that would answer. They'd half kill me for one thing."

" Never mind ; do your duty. I wish I'd such an opportunity, if only to show how sorry I am for my own past unfairness."

And so talking, the four went in, and the two elder went to their study.

It was too true that drinking had become a common vice at Roslyn school. Accordingly, when Eric came in with Wildney about half an hour after, Owen and Montagu heard them talk about ordering some brandy, and then arrange to have a " jollification," as they called it, that evening.

They got the brandy through " Billy." One of Brigson's most cursed legacies to the school was the introduction of this man to a nefarious intercourse with the boys. His character was so well known that it had long been forbidden, under the strictest penalty, for any boy ever to speak to him; yet, strange to say, they seemed to take a pleasure in doing so, and just now particularly it was thought a fine thing, a sign of " pluck" and " anti-muffishness," to be on familiar and intimate terms with that degraded and villainous scoundrel.

Duncan had made friends again with Eric ; but he did not join him in his escapades and excesses, and sat much in other studies. He had not been altogether a good boy, but yet there was a sort of rough honesty and good sense in him, which preserved him from the worst and most dangerous failings, and his character had been gradually improving as he mounted higher in the school. He was getting steadier, more diligent, more thoughtful, more manly ; he was passing through that change so frequent in boys as they grow older, to which

Eric was so sad an exception. Accordingly Duncan, though sincerely fond of Eric, had latterly disapproved vehemently of his proceedings, and had therefore taken to snubbing his old friend Wildney, in whose favour Eric seemed to have an infatuation, and who was the means of involving him in every kind of impropriety and mischief. So that night Duncan, hearing of what was intended, sat in the next study, and Eric, with Bull, Wildney, Graham, and Pietrie, had the room to themselves. Several of them were lower boys still, but they came up to the studies after bed-time, according to Wildney's almost nightly custom.

A little pebble struck the study window.

" Hurrah !" said Wildney, clapping his hands, " here's the grub."

They opened the window and looked out. Billy was there, and they let down to him a long piece of cord, to which he attached a basket, and, after bidding them " Good night, and a merry drink," retired. No sooner had they shut the window, than he grimaced as usual towards them, and shook his fist in a sort of demoniacal exultation, muttering, " Oh, I'll have you all under my thumb yet, you fine young fools ! "

Meanwhile the unconscious boys had opened the basket, and spread its contents on the table. They were, bread, a large dish of sausages, a tart, beer, and, alas ! a bottle of brandy.

They soon got very noisy, and at last uproarious. The snatches of songs, peals of laughter, and rattle of plates, at last grew so loud that the other study-boys were afraid lest one of the masters should come up and catch the revellers. All of them heard every word that was spoken by Eric and his party, as the walls between the rooms were very thin; and very objectionable much of the conversation was.

"This *won't* do," said Duncan emphatically, after a louder burst of merriment than usual; "those fellows are getting drunk; I can tell it to a certainty from the confused and random way in which some of them are talking."

"We'd better go in and speak to them," said Montagu; "at any rate, they've no right to disturb us all night. Will you come?"

"I'll join you," said Owen; "though I'm afraid my presence won't do you much good."

The three boys went to the door of Eric's study, and their knock could not at first be heard for the noise. When they went in they found a scene of reckless disorder; books were scattered about, plates and glasses lay broken on the floor, beer was spilt on sides, and there was an intolerable smell of brandy.

"If you fellows don't care," said Duncan, sharply, "Rose or somebody'll be coming up and catching you. It's ten now."

"What's that to you?" answered Graham, with an insolent look.

"It's something to me that you nice young men have been making such a row that none of the rest of us can hear our own voices, and that, between you, you've made this study in such a mess that I can't endure it."

" Pooh !" said Pietrie ; " we're all getting such saints, that one can't have the least bit of spree now-a-days."

" Spree !" burst in Montagu indignantly; " fine spree, to make sots of yourselves with spirits ; fine spree, to ————"

" Amen !" said Wildney, who was perched on the back of a chair ; and he turned up his eyes and clasped his hands with a mock-heroic air.

" There, Williams," continued Montagu, pointing to the mischievous-looking little boy ; " see that spectacle, and be ashamed of yourself, if you can. That's what you lead boys to ! Are you anxious to become the teacher of drunkenness ? "

In truth, there was good ground for his sorrowful apostrophe, for the scene was very painful to a high-minded witness.

They hardly understood the look on Eric's countenance ; he had been taking far more than was good for him ; his eyes sparkled fiercely, and though as yet he said nothing, he seemed to be resenting the intrusion in furious silence.

" How much longer is this interesting lecture to last ?" asked Bull, with his usual insufferable drawl ; " for I want to finish my brandy."

Montagu rather looked as if he intended to give

the speaker a box on the ear; but he was just deciding that Bull wasn't worth the trouble, when Wildney, who had been grimacing all the time, burst into a fit of satirical laughter.

"Let's turn out these impudent lower-school fellows," said Montagu, speaking to Duncan. "Here! you go first," he said, seizing Wildney by the arm, and giving him a swing, which, as he was by no means steady on his legs, brought him sprawling to the ground.

"By Jove, I won't stand this any longer," shouted Eric, springing up ferociously. "What on earth do you mean by daring to come in like this? Do you hear?"

Montagu took no sort of notice of his threatening gesture, for he was looking to see if Wildney was hurt, and finding he was not, proceeded to drag him out, struggling and kicking frantically.

"Drop me, you fellow, drop me, I say. I won't go for you," cried Wildney, shaking with passion. "Eric, why do you let him bully me?"

"You let him go this minute," repeated Eric, hoarsely.

"I shall do no such thing. You don't know what you're about."

"Don't I? Well, then, take *that*, to show whether I do or no!" and suddenly leaning forward, he struck Montagu a violent back-handed blow on the mouth.

Everybody saw it, everybody heard it; and it

instantly astounded them into silence. That Montagu
should have been so struck in public, and that by Eric
—by a boy who had loved him, and whom he had loved
—by a boy who had been his schoolfellow for three years
now, and whose whole life seemed bound to him by so
many associations; it was strange, and sad indeed.

Montagu sprang straight upright; for an instant
he took one stride towards his striker with lifted hand
and lightning eyes, while the blood started to his lips
in consequence of the blow. But he stopped suddenly,
and his hand fell to his side; by a strong effort of self-
control he contrived to master himself, and sitting
down quite quietly on a chair, he put his white handkerchief to his wounded mouth, and took it away stained
with blood.

No one spoke; and rising with quiet dignity, he
went back into his study without a word.

"Very well," said Duncan; "you may all do as
you like; only I heartily hope now you will be caught.
Come, Owen."

"Oh, Williams," said Owen, "you are changed
indeed, to treat your best friend so."

But Eric was excited with drink, and the slave of
every evil passion at that moment. "Serve him right,"
he said; "what business has he to interfere with what
I choose to do?"

There was no more noise that night. Wildney
and the rest slunk off ashamed and frightened, and
Eric, leaving his candle flaring on the table, went down

to his bed-room, where he was very sick. He had neither strength nor spirit to undress, and flung himself
into bed just as he was. When they heard that he
was gone, Owen and Duncan (for Montagu was silent
and melancholy) went into his study, put out the candle, and had only just cleared away, to the best of their
power, the traces of the carouse, when Dr. Rowlands
came up stairs on his usual nightly rounds. They had
been lighting brown paper to take away the fumes of
the brandy, and the Doctor asked them casually the
cause of the smell of burning. Neither of them
answered, and seeing Owen there, in whom he placed
implicit trust, the Doctor thought no more about it.

Eric awoke with a bad headache, and a sense of
shame and sickness. When he got up he felt most
wretched, and while washing he thought to himself,
" Ah! that I could thus wash away the memory of last
night!" Of course, after what had occurred, Eric
and Montagu were no longer on speaking terms, and
miserable as poor Eric felt when he saw how his blow
had bruised and disfigured his friend's face, he made no
advances. He longed, indeed, from his inmost heart,
to be reconciled to him; but feeling that he had done
grievous wrong, he dreaded a repulse, and his pride
would not suffer him to run the risk. So he pretended
to feel no regret, and, supported by his late boon-com-
panions, represented the matter as occurring in the
defence of Wildney, whom Montagu was bullying.

Montagu, too, was very miserable; but he felt that,

although ready to forgive Eric, he could not, in common
self-respect, take the first step to a reconciliation;
indeed, he rightly thought that it was not for Eric's
good that he should do so.

" You and Williams appear never to speak to each
other now," said Mr. Rose. " I am sorry for it, Monty; I think you are the only boy who has any influence over him."

" I fear you are mistaken, sir, in that. Little
Wildney has much more."

" Wildney?" asked Mr. Rose, in sorrowful surprise. " Wildney more influence than *you?* "

" Yes, sir."

" Ah, that our poor Edwin had lived ! "

So, with a sigh, Walter Rose and Harry Montagu
buried their friendship for Eric until happier days.

CHAPTER VI.

ERIC AND MONTAGU.

"And constancy lives in realms above;
    And life is thorny; and youth is vain;
    And to be wroth with one we love,
    Doth work like madness in the brain.
    *   *   *   *
    Each spoke words of high disdain
    And insult to his heart's best brother.
                        COLERIDGE'S *Christabel.*

RIGHT had not forgotten Montagu's advice, and had endeavoured to get the names of boys who weren't afraid to scout publicly the disgrace of cheating in form. But he could only get one name promised him—the name of Vernon Williams; and feeling how little could be gained by using it, he determined to spare Vernon the trial, and speak, if he spoke at all, on his own responsibility.

As usual, the cribbing at the next weekly examination was well-nigh universal, and when Mr. Gordon went out to fetch something he had forgotten, merely saying, " I trust to your honour not to abuse my absence," books and papers were immediately pulled out with the coolest and most unblushing indifference.

This was the time for Wright to deliver his conscience; he had counted the cost, and, rightly or wrongly, considering it to be his duty, he had decided that speak he would. He well knew that his interference would be attributed to jealousy, meanness, sneaking, and every kind of wrong motive, since he was himself one of the greatest sufferers from the prevalent dishonesty; but still he had come to the conclusion that he *ought* not draw back, and therefore he bravely determined that he would make his protest, whatever happened.

So, very nervously, he rose and said, "I want to tell you all that I think this cheating very wrong and blackguardly. I don't mind losing by it myself; but if Vernon Williams loses the prize in the lower fourth, and any one gets it by copying, I've made up my mind to tell Gordon."

His voice trembled a little at first, but he spoke fast, and acquired firmness as he went on. Absolute astonishment and curiosity had held the boys silent with amazement, but by the end of this sentence they had recovered themselves, and a perfect burst of derision and indignation followed.

"Let's see if *that*'ll cut short his oration," said Wildney, throwing a book at his head, which was instantly followed by others from all quarters.

"My word! we've had nothing but lectures lately," said Brooking. "Horrid little Owenite saint."

"Saint!—sneak, you mean. I'll teach him," growled Pietrie, and jumping up, he belaboured Wright's head with the Latin grammar out of which he had just been cribbing.

The whole room was in confusion and hubbub, during which Wright sat stock still, quietly enduring without bowing to the storm.

Only one boy sympathised with him, but he did so deeply—poor little penitent Vernon. He felt his position hard because Wright had alluded so prominently to him, and he knew how much he must be misconstrued; but he had his brother's spirit, and would not shrink. Amid the tumult he got up in his seat, and they heard his pleasant, childish voice saying boldly, "I hope Wright won't tell; but he's the best fellow in the room, and cribbing *is* a shame, as he says."

What notice would have been taken of this speech is doubtful, for at the critical moment Mr. Gordon reappeared, and the whispered cavè caused instantaneous quiet.

Poor Wright awaited with some dread the end of school; and many an angry kick and blow he got, though he disarmed malice by the spirit and heroism with which he endured them. The news of his impudence spread like wildfire, and not five boys in the school approved of what he had done, while most of them were furious at his ill-judged threat of informing Mr. Gordon. There was a general agreement to thrash him after roll-call that afternoon.

Eric had lately taken a violent dislike to Wright, though he had been fond of him in better days. He used to denounce him as a disagreeable and pragmatical little muff, and was as loud as any of them in condemning his announced determination to " sneak." Had he known that Wright had acted under Montagu's well-meant, though rather mistaken advice, he might have abstained from having anything more to do with the matter, but now he promised to kick Wright himself after the four o'clock bell.

Four o'clock came; the names were called; the master left the room. Wright, who perfectly knew what was threatened, stood there pale but fearless. His indifferent look was an additional annoyance to Eric, who walked up to him carelessly, and boxing his ears, though without hurting him, said contemptuously, " Conceited little sneak.".

Montagu had been told of the intended kicking, and had determined even single-handed to prevent it. He did *not*, however, expect that Eric would have taken part in it, and was therefore unprepared. The colour rushed into his cheeks; he went up, took Wright quietly by the hand, and said with firm determination, " No one in the school shall touch Wright again."

" What? no one! just hark to that," said Graham ; " I suppose he thinks himself cock of the school."

Eric quite misunderstood Montagu's proceeding; he took it for a public challenge. All the Rowlandites were round, and to yield would have looked like cowardice. Above all, his evil genius Wildney was by, and said, " How very nice ! another dictation lesson ! "

A threatening circle had formed round Montagu, but his closed lips, and flushing brow, and dilated nostrils, betrayed a spirit which made them waver, and he quietly repeated, " No one shall touch you, Wright."

" They *will*, though," said Eric instantly ; " *I* will, for one, and I should like to see you prevent me." And so saying he gave Wright another slight blow.

Montagu dropped Wright's hand, and said slowly, " Eric Williams, I have taken one unexpected blow from you without a word, and bear the marks of it yet. It is time to show that it was *not* through cowardice that I did not return it. Will you fight ?"

The answer was not prompt by any means, though every one in the school knew that Eric was not afraid. So sure was he of this, that, for the sake of " auld lang syne," he would probably have declined to fight with Montagu had he been left to his own impulses.

" I have been in the wrong, Montagu, more than once," he answered, falteringly, " and we have been friends—"

But it was the object of many of the worst boys that the two should fight—not only that they might see the fun, but that Montagu's authority, which stood in their way, might be flung aside. So Brooking whispered in an audible voice—

" Faith ! he's showing the white feather."

" You're a liar ! " flung in Eric ; and turning to Montagu, he said—" There ! I'll fight you this moment."

Instantly they had stripped off their coats and

prepared for action. A ring of excited boys crowded round them. Fellows of sixteen, like Montagu and Eric, rarely fight, because their battles have usually been decided in their earlier school-days; and it was also but seldom that two boys so strong, active, and prominent (above all, so high in the school), took this method of settling their differences.

The fight began, and at first the popular favour was entirely on the side of Eric, while Montagu found few or none to back him. But he fought with a fire and courage which soon won applause; and as Eric, on the other hand, was random and spiritless, the cry was soon pretty fairly divided between them.

After a sharp round they paused for breath, and Owen, who had been a silent and disgusted spectator of such a combat between boys of such high standing, said with much feeling—

" This is not a very creditable affair, Montagu."

" It is necessary," was Montagu's laconic reply.

Among other boys who had left the room before the fracas had taken place, was Vernon Williams, who shrank away to avoid the pain of seeing his new friend Wright bullied and tormented. But curiosity soon took him back, and he came in just as the second round began. At first he only saw a crowd of boys in the middle of the room, but jumping on a desk he had a full view of what was going on.

There was a tremendous hubbub of voices, and Eric, now thoroughly roused by the remarks he overheard, and especially by Wildney's whisper that "he was letting himself be licked," was exerting himself with more vigour and effect. It was anything but a noble sight; the faces of the combatants were streaked with blood and sweat, and as the miserable gang of lower school-boys backed them on with eager shouts of— " Now Eric, now Eric," " Now Montagu, go it, sixth form," etc., both of them fought under a sense of deep disgrace, increased by the recollections which they shared in common.

All this Vernon marked in a moment, and, filled with pain and vexation, he said in a voice which, though low, could be heard amid all the uproar, " Oh Eric, Eric, fighting with Montagu ! " There was reproach and sorrow in the tone, which touched more than one boy there, for Vernon, spite of the recent change in him, could not but continue a popular favourite.

" Shut up there, you little donkey," shouted one or two, looking back at him for a moment.

But Eric heard the words, and knew that it was his brother's voice. The thought rushed on him how degraded his whole position was, and how different it might have been. He felt that he was utterly in the wrong, and Montagu altogether in the right; and from that moment his blows once more grew feeble and ill-directed. When they again stopped to take rest, the general shout for Montagu showed that he was considered to have the best of it.

" I'm getting so tired of this," muttered Eric, during the pause.

" Why, you're fighting like a regular muff," said Graham ; " you'll have to acknowledge yourself thrashed in a minute."

" That I'll *never* do," he said, once more firing up.

Just as the third round began, Duncan came striding in, for Owen, who had left the room, told him what was going on. He had always been a leading fellow, and quite recently his influence had several times been exerted in the right direction, and he was very much looked up to by all the boys alike, good or bad. He determined, for the credit of the sixth, that the fight should not go on, and bursting into the ring, with his strong shoulders he hurled on each side the boys who stood in his way, and struck down the lifted arms of the fighters.

" You *shan't* fight," he said, doggedly, thrusting himself between them ; " so there's an end of it. If you do, you'll both have to fight me first."

" Shame !" said several of the boys, and the cry was caught up by Bull and others.

" Shame, is it ?" said Duncan, and his lip curled with scorn. " There's only one way to argue with you fellows. Bull, if you, or any other boy, repeat that word, I'll thrash him. Here, Monty, come away from this disgraceful scene."

" I'm sick enough of it," said Montagu, " and am ready to stop if Williams is,—provided no one touches Wright."

" I'm sick of it too," said Eric sullenly.

" Then you two shall shake hands," said Duncan.

For one instant—an instant which he regretted till the end of his life—Montagu drew himself up and hesitated. He had been deeply wronged, deeply provoked, and no one could blame him for the momentary feeling; but Eric had observed the gesture, and his passionate pride took the alarm. "It's come to this, then," he thought; "Montagu doesn't think me good enough to be shaken hands with."

" Pish!" he said aloud, in a tone of sarcasm; "it may be an awful honour to shake hands with such an immaculate person as Montagu, but I'm not proud on the subject;" and he turned away.

Montagu's hesitation was but momentary, and without a particle of anger or indignation he sorrowfully held out his hand. It was too late; that moment had done the mischief, and it was now Eric's turn coldly to withdraw.

" You don't think me worthy of your friendship, and what's the good of grasping hands if we don't do it with cordial hearts?"

Montagu's lip trembled, but he said nothing, and quietly putting on his coat, waved back the throng of boys with a proud sweep of his arm, and left the room with Duncan.

" Come along, Wright," he said.

" Nay, leave him," said Eric with a touch of remorse. " Much as you think me beneath you, I have honour enough to see that no one hurts him."

The group of boys gradually dispersed, but one or two remained with Eric, although he was excessively wearied by their observations.

" You didn't fight half like yourself," said Wildney.

" Can't you tell why? I had the wrong side to fight for." And getting up abruptly, he left the room, to be alone in his study, and bathe his swollen and aching face.

In a few minutes Vernon joined him, and at the mere sight of him Eric burst into tears of shame. That evening with Vernon in the study, after the dinner at the Jolly Herring, had revived all his really warm affection for his little brother; and as he could no longer conceal the line he took in the school, they had been often together since then; and Eric's moral obliquity was not so great as to prevent him from feeling deep joy at the change for the better in Vernon's character.

" Verny, Verny," he said, as the boy came up and affectionately took his hand, " it was you who lost me that fight."

" Oh, but, Eric, you were fighting with Montagu."

" Don't you remember the days, Eric," he continued, " when we were home-boarders, and how kind Monty used to be to me even then, and how mother liked him, and thought him quite your truest friend, except poor Russell?"

" I do, indeed. I didn't think then that it would come to this."

" I 've always been *so* sorry," said Vernon, " that I joined the fellows in playing him tricks. I can't think how I came to do it, except that I 've done such lots of bad things here. But he 's forgiven and forgotten that long ago, and is very kind to me now."

It was true; but Eric didn't know that half the kindness which Montagu showed to his brother was shown solely for *his* sake.

" Do you know, I 've thought of a plan for making you two friends again? I 've written to Aunt Trevor to ask him to Fairholm with us next holidays."

" Oh, have you? Good Verny! Yes; *there* we might be friends. Perhaps there," he added, half to himself, " I might be more like what I was in better days."

" But it 's a long time to look forward to. Easter hasn't come yet," said Vernon.

So the two young boys proposed; but God had disposed it otherwise.

CHAPTER VII.

THE PIGEONS.

" Et motæ ad Lunam trepidabis arundinis umbram."—

Juv. x. 21.

OW awfully dull it is, Charlie," said Eric, a few weeks before Easter, as he sat with Wildney in his study one holiday afternoon.

" Yes ; too late for football, too early for cricket." And Wildney stretched himself and yawned.

" I suppose this is what they call ennui," said Eric again, after a pause. " What's to be done, Sunbeam ? "

" You *shan't* call me that, so there 's an end of it," said Wildney, hitting him on the arm.

" By the bye, Eric, you remind me to-morrow's my birth-day, and I've got a parcel coming this afternoon full of grub from home. Let 's go and see if it 's come ? "

" Capital ! We will."

So Eric and Wildney started off to the coach-office, where they found the hamper, and ordered it to be brought at once to the school, and carried up to Eric's study.

N 2

On opening it they found it rich in dainties, among which were a pair of fowls and a large plum-cake.

"Hurrah!" said Wildney, "you were talking of nothing to do; I vote we have a carouse to-morrow."

"Very well; only let's have it *before* prayers, because we so nearly got caught last time."

"Ay, and let it be in one of the class-rooms, Eric; not up here, lest we have another incursion of the "Rosebuds." I shall have to cut preparation, but that don't matter. It's Harley's night, and old Stupid will never twig."

"Well, whom shall we ask?" said Eric.

"Old Llewellyn for one," said Wildney. "We haven't seen him for an age, and he's getting too lazy even for a bit of fun."

"Good; and Graham," suggested Eric. He and Wildney regarded their possessions so much as common property, that he hadn't the least delicacy in mentioning the boys whom he wanted to invite.

"Yes; Graham's a jolly bird; and Bull?"

"I've no objection; and Pietrie?"

"Well; and your brother Vernon?"

"No!" said Eric, emphatically. "At any rate I won't lead *him* into mischief any more."

"Attlay, then; and what do you say to Brooking?"

"No, again," said Eric; "he's a blackguard."

"I wonder you haven't mentioned Duncan," said Wildney.

"Duncan! why, my dear child, you might as well

ask Owen, or even old Rose, at once. Bless you, Charlie, he's a great deal too correct to come now."

"Well; we've got six already, that's quite enough."

"Yes; but two fowls isn't enough for six hungry boys."

"No, it isn't," said Wildney. He thought a little, and then, clapping his hands, danced about, and said, "Are you game for a *regular* lark, Eric?"

"Yes; anything to make it less dull. I declare I've very nearly been taking to work again to fill up the time."

Eric often talked now of work in this slighting way, partly as an excuse for the low places in form to which he was gradually sinking. Everybody knew that had he properly exerted his abilities he was capable of beating almost any boy; so, to quiet his conscience, he professed to ridicule diligence as an unboyish piece of muffishness, and was never slow to sneer at the "grinders," as he contemptuously called all those who laid themselves out to win school distinctions.

"Ha, ha!" said Wildney, "that's rather good! No, Eric, it's too late for you to turn 'grinder' now. I might as well think of doing it myself, and I've never been higher than five from lag in my form yet."

"Haven't you? But what's the regular lark you hinted at?"

"Why, we'll go and seize the Gordonites' *pigeons*, and make another dish of them."

"Seize the Gordonites' pigeons! Why, when do you mean?"

"To-night."

Eric gave a long whistle. "But wouldn't it be st—t—— ?"

"Stealing?" said Wildney, with a loud laugh. "Pooh! ' *convey* the wise it call.' "

But Eric still looked serious. "Why, my dear old boy," continued Wildney, " the Gordonites'll be the first to laugh at the trick when we tell them of it next morning, as of course we will do. There, now, don't look grumpy. I shall cut away and arrange it with Graham, and tell you the whole dodge ready prepared to-night at bed-time."

After lights were put out, Wildney came up to the study according to promise, and threw out hints about the proposed plan. He didn't tell it plainly, because Duncan was there, but Duncan caught quite enough to guess what was intended, and said, when Wildney had gone—

"Take my advice, and have nothing to do with this, Eric."

Eric had grown very touchy lately about advice, particularly from any fellow of his own standing; and after the checks he had recently received, a coolness had sprung up between him and nearly all the study-boys, which made him more than ever inclined to assert his independence, and defy and thwart them in every way.

"Keep your advice to yourself, Duncan, till it's

asked for," he answered, roughly. "You've done nothing but *advise* lately, and I'm rather sick of it."

"Comme vous voulez," replied Duncan, with a shrug. "Gang your own gait; I'll have nothing more to do with trying to stop you since you *will* ruin yourself."

Nothing more was said in the study that evening, and when Eric went down he didn't even bid Duncan good-night.

"Charlie," he said, as he stole on tiptoe into Wildney's dormitory.

"Hush!" whispered Wildney, "the other fellows are asleep. Come and sit by my bedside, and I'll tell you what we're going to do."

Eric went and sat by him, and he sat up in his bed. "First of all, *you're* to keep awake till twelve to-night," he whispered; "old Rowly'll have gone round by that time, and it'll be all safe. Then come and awake me again, and I'll watch till one, Pietrie till two, and Graham till three. Then Graham'll awake us all, and we'll dress."

"Very well. But how will you get the key of the lavatory?"

"Oh, I'll manage that," said Wildney, chuckling. "But come again and awake me at twelve, will you?"

Eric went to his room and lay down, but he didn't take off his clothes, for fear he should go to sleep. Dr. Rowlands came round as usual at eleven, and then Eric closed his eyes for a few minutes, till the head-master

had disappeared.   After that he lay awake thinking for
an hour, but his thoughts weren't very pleasant.

At twelve he went and awoke Wildney.

" I don't feel very sleepy.   Shall I sit with you for
your hour, Charlie ? "

" Oh, do ! I should like it of all things.   But douse
the glim there ; we shan't want it, and it might give
the alarm."

" All right."

So Eric went and sat by his dangerous little friend,
and they talked in low voices until they heard the great
school clock strike one.   They then woke Pietrie, and
Eric went off to bed again.

At three Graham awoke him, and dressing hastily,
he joined the others in the lavatory.

" Now, I 'm going to get the key," said Wildney,
" and mean to have a bad stomach-ache for the purpose."

Laughing quietly he went up to the door of Mr.
Harley's bed-room, which opened out of the lavatory,
and knocked.

No answer.

He knocked a little louder.

Still no answer.

Louder still.

" Bother the fellow," said Wildney ; " he sleeps like
a grampus.   Won't one of you try to wake him ?"

" No," said Graham ; " 'taint dignified for fifth-form
boys to have stomach-aches."

"Well, I must try again." But it seemed no use knocking, and Wildney at last, in a fit of impatience, thumped a regular tattoo on the bed-room door.

"Who's there?" said the startled voice of Mr. Harley.

"Only me, sir!" answered Wildney, in a mild and innocent way.

"What do you want?"

"Please, sir, I want the key of the lavatory. I'm indisposed," said Wildney again, in a tone of such disciplined suavity, that the others shook with laughing.

Mr. Harley opened the door about an inch, and peered out suspiciously.

"Oh, well, you must go and awake Mr. Rose. I don't happen to have the key to-night." And so saying, he shut the door.

"Phew! Here's a go!" said Wildney, recovering immediately. "It'll never do to awake old Rose. He'd smell a rat in no time."

"I have it," said Pietrie. "I've got an old nail, with which I believe I can open the lock quite simply. Let's try."

"Quietly and quick, then," said Eric.

In ten minutes he had silently shot back the lock with the old nail, and the boys were on the landing. They carried their shoes in their hands, ran noiselessly down stairs, and went to the same window at which Eric and Wildney had got out before. Wildney had taken care beforehand to break the pane and move away the glass, so they had only to loosen the bar and slip through one by one.

It was cold and very dark, and as on the March morning they stood out in the playground, all four would rather have been safely and harmlessly in bed. But the novelty and the excitement of the enterprise bore them up, and they started off quickly for the house at which Mr. Gordon and his pupils lived, which was about half a mile from the school. They went arm in arm to assure each other a little, for at first in their fright they were inclined to take every post and tree for a man in ambush, and to hear a recalling voice in every sound of wind and wave.

Not far from Mr. Gordon's was a carpenter's shop, and outside of this there was generally a ladder standing. They had arranged to carry this ladder with them (as it was only a short one), climb the low garden wall with it, and then place it against the house, immediately under the dovecot which hung by the first storey-windows. Wildney, as the lightest of the four, was to take the birds, while the others held the ladder.

Slanting it so that it should be as far from the side of the window as possible, Wildney ascended and thrust both hands into the cot. He succeeded in seizing a pigeon with each hand, but in doing so threw the other birds into a state of such alarm that they fluttered about in the wildest manner, and the moment his hands were withdrawn, flew out with a great flapping of hurried wings.

The noise they made alarmed the plunderer, and he hurried down the ladder as fast as he could. He handed the pigeons to the others, who instantly wrung their necks.

"I'm nearly sure I heard somebody stir," said Wildney; "we haven't been half quiet enough. Here! let's crouch down in this corner."

All four shrank up as close to the wall as they could, and held their breath. Some one was certainly stirring, and at last they heard the window open.

A head was thrust out, and Mr. Gordon's voice asked sternly—"Who's there?"

He seemed at once to have caught sight of the ladder, and made an endeavour to reach it; but though he stretched out his arm at full length, he could not manage to do so.

"We must cut for it," said Eric; "it's quite too dark for him to see who we are, or even to notice that we are boys."

They moved the ladder to the wall, and sprang over, one after the other, as fast as they could. Eric was last, and just as he got to the top of the wall he heard the back door open, and some one run out into the yard.

"Run for your lives," said Eric hurriedly; "it's Gordon, and he's raising the alarm."

They heard footsteps following them, and an occasional shout of "thieves! thieves!"

"We must separate and run different ways, or

o

we've no chance of escape.   We'd better turn towards
the town to put them off the right scent," said Eric again.

" Don't leave me," pleaded Wildney ; " you know
I can't run very fast."

" No, Charlie, I won't ;" and grasping his hand, Eric
hurried him over the stile and through the fields as
fast as he could, while Pietrie and Graham took the
opposite direction.

Some one (they did not know who it was, but suspected it to be Mr. Gordon's servant-man) was running
after them, and they could distinctly hear his footsteps,
which seemed to be half a field distant.   He carried a
light, and they heard him panting.   They were themselves tired, and in the utmost trepidation ; the usually
courageous Wildney was trembling all over, and his
fear communicated itself to Eric.   Horrible visions of
a trial for burglary, imprisonment in the castle jail, and
perhaps transportation, presented themselves to their
excited imaginations, as the sound of the footsteps came
nearer and nearer.

" I can't run any farther, Eric," said Wildney.
" What shall we do ? don't leave me for heaven's sake."

" Not I, Charlie.   We must hide the minute we
get t'other side of this hedge."

They scrambled over the gate, and plunged into
the thickest part of a plantation close by, lying down
on the ground behind some bushes, and keeping as still
as they possibly could, taking care to cover over their
white collars.

The pursuer reached the gate, and no longer hearing footsteps in front of him, he paused. He went a little distance up the hedge on both sides and held up his light, but did not detect the cowering boys, and at last giving up the search in despair, went slowly home. They heard him plodding back over the field, and it was not until the sound of his footsteps had died away, that Eric cautiously broke cover, and looked over the hedge. He saw the man's light gradually getting more distant, and said, "All right now, Charlie. We must make the best of our way home."

"Are you sure he's gone?" said Wildney, who had not yet recovered from his fright.

"Quite; come along. I only hope Pietrie and Graham ain't caught."

They got back about half-past four, and climbed in unheard and undetected through the window pane. They then stole up stairs with beating hearts, and sate in Eric's room to wait for the other two. To their great relief they heard them enter the lavatory about ten minutes after.

"Were you twigged?" asked Wildney eagerly.

"No," said Graham; "precious near it though. Old Gordon and some men were after us, but at last we doubled rather neatly, and escaped them. It's all serene, and we shan't be caught. But it's a precious long time before I run such a risk again for a brace of rubbishing pigeons."

"Well, we'd best to bed now," said Eric; "and,

to my thinking, we should be wise to keep a quiet tongue in our heads about this affair."

" Yes, we had better tell *no one.*"   They agreed, and went off to bed again.   So, next morning, they all four got up quite as if nothing had happened, and made no allusion to the preceding night, although they could not help chuckling inwardly a little when the Gordonites came to morning school, brimful of a story about their house having been attacked in the night by thieves, who, after bagging some pigeons, had been chevied by Gordon and the servants.   Wildney professed immense interest in the incident, and asked many questions, which shewed that there was not a shadow of suspicion in any one's mind as to the real culprits.

Carter, the school servant, didn't seem to have noticed that the lavatory door was unlocked, and Mr. Harley never alluded again to his disturbance in the night.   So the theft of the pigeons remained undiscovered, and remains so till this day.   If any old Roslyn boy reads this veracious history, he will doubtless be astounded to hear that the burglars on that memorable night were Eric, Pietrie, Graham, and Wildney.

CHAPTER VIII.

SOWING THE WIND.

" Præpediuntur
Crura vacillanti, tardescit lingua, madet mens,
Nant oculi." Lucr. iii. 417.

EXT evening, when preparation began, Pietrie and Graham got everything ready for the carouse in their class-room. Wildney, relying on the chance of names not being called over (which was only done in case any one's absence was observed), had absented himself altogether from the boarders' room, and helped busily to spread the table for the banquet. The cook had roasted for them the fowls and pigeons, and Billy had brought an ample supply of beer and some brandy for the occasion. A little before eight o'clock everything was ready, and Eric, Attlay, and Llewellyn were summoned to join the rest.

The fowls, pigeons, and beer had soon vanished, and the boys were in the highest spirits. Eric's reckless gaiety was kindled by Wildney's frolicsome vivacity, and Graham's sparkling wit; they were all six in a roar of perpetual laughter at some fresh sally of fun elicited by the more phlegmatic natures of Attlay or Llewellyn, and the dainties of Wildney's parcel were accompanied by draughts of brandy and water, which were sometimes exchanged for potations of the raw liquor. It was not the first time, be it remembered, that the members of that young party had been present at similar scenes, and even the scoundrel Billy was astonished, and occasionally alarmed at the quantities of spirits and other inebriating drinks that of late had found their way to the studies. The disgraceful and deadly habit of tippling had already told physically on both Eric and Wildney. The former felt painfully that he was losing his clear-headedness, and that his intellectual tastes were getting not only blunted but destroyed; and while he perceived in himself the terrible effects of his sinful indulgence, he saw them still more indisputably in the gradual coarseness which seemed to be spreading, like a grey lichen, over the countenance, the mind, and the manners of his younger companion. Sometimes the vision of a Nemesis breaking in fire out of his darkened future, terrified his guilty conscience in the watches of the night; and the conviction of some fearful Erynnis, some discovery dawning out of the night of his undetected sins, made his heart beat fast with agony and fear. But he fancied it too late to repent. He strangled the half-formed resolutions as they rose, and trusted to the time when, by leaving school, he should escape, as he idly supposed, the temptations to which he had yielded. Meanwhile, the friends who would have rescued him had been alienated by his follies, and the principles which might have preserved him had been eradicated by his guilt. He had long flung away the shield of prayer, and the helmet of holiness, and the sword of the Spirit, which is the word of God; and now, unarmed and helpless, Eric stood alone, a mark for the fiery arrows of his enemies, while, through the weakened inlet of every corrupted sense, temptation rushed in upon him perpetually and unawares.

As the class-room they had selected was in a remote part of the building, there was little immediate chance of detection. So the laughter of the party grew louder and sillier; the talk more foolish and random; the merriment more noisy and meaningless. But still most of them mingled some sense of caution with their enjoyment, and warned Eric and Wildney more than once that they must look out, and not take too much that night for fear of being caught. But it was Wildney's birth-day, and Eric's boyish mirth, suppressed by his recent troubles, was blazing out unrestrained. In the riot of their feasting, the caution had been utterly neglected, and the two boys were far from being sober when the sound of the prayer-bell ringing through the great hall, startled them into momentary consciousness.

" Good heavens! " shouted Graham, springing up;

"there's the prayer-bell; I'd no notion it was so late. Here, let's shove these brandy bottles and things into the cupboards and drawers, and then we must run down."

There was no time to lose. The least muddled of the party had cleared the room in a moment, and then addressed themselves to the more difficult task of trying to quiet Eric and Wildney, and conduct them steadily into the prayer-room.

Wildney's seat was near the door, so there was little difficulty in getting him to his place comparatively unobserved. Llewellyn took him by the arm, and after a little stumbling, helped him safely to his seat, where he assumed a look of preternatural gravity. But Eric sat near the head of the first table, not far from Dr. Rowlands' desk, and none of the others had to go to that part of the room. Graham grasped his arm tight, led him carefully down stairs, and, as they were reaching the door, said to him, in a most earnest and imploring tone,

"Do try and walk sensibly to your place, Eric, or we shall all be caught."

It was rather late when they got down. Everybody was quietly seated, and most of the Bibles were already open, although the Doctor had not yet come in. Consequently, the room was still, and the entrance of Graham and Eric after the rest attracted general notice. Eric had just sense enough to try and assume his ordinary manner; but he was too giddy with the fumes of drink to walk straight, or act naturally.

Vernon was sitting next to Wright, and stared at his brother with great eyes and open lips. He was not the only observer.

" Wright," whispered he, in a timid voice ; " just see how Eric walks. What can be the matter with him ? Good gracious, he must be ill!" he said, starting up, as Eric suddenly made a great stagger to one side, and nearly fell in the attempt to recover himself.

Wright pulled the little boy down with a firm hand.

" Hush!" he whispered ; " take no notice ; he 's been drinking, Verny, and I fear he 'll be caught."

Vernon instantly sat down, and turned deadly pale. He thought, and he had hoped, that since the day at the " Jolly Herring," his brother had abandoned all such practices, for Eric had been most careful to conceal from him the worst of his failings. And now he trembled violently with fear for his discovery, and horror at his disgraceful condition.

The sound of Eric's unsteady footsteps had made Mr. Rose quickly raise his head ; but at the same moment Duncan hastily made room for the boy on the seat beside him, and held out his hand to assist him. It was not Eric's proper place ; but Mr. Rose, after one long glance of astonishment, looked down at his book again, and said nothing.

It made other hearts besides Vernon's ache to see the unhappy boy roll to his place in that helpless way.

Dr. Rowlands came in, and prayers commenced.

When they were finished, the names were called, and Eric, instead of quietly answering his " adsum," as he should have done, stood up, with a foolish look, and said, " Yes, Sir." The head master looked at him for a minute ; the boy's glassy eyes, and jocosely stupid appearance, told an unmistakeable tale ; but Dr. Rowlands only remarked, " Williams, you don't look well. You had better go at once to bed."

It was hopeless for Eric to attempt getting along without help, so Duncan at once got up, took him by the arm, and with much difficulty (for Eric staggered at every step) conducted him to his bed-room, where he left him without a word.

Wildney's condition was also too evident ; and Mr. Rose, while walking up and down the dormitories, had no doubt left on his mind that both Eric and Wildney had been drinking. But he made no remarks to them, and merely went to the Doctor to talk over the steps which were to be taken.

" I shall summon the school," said Dr. Rowlands, " on Monday, and by that time we will decide on the punishment. Expulsion, I fear, is the only course open to us."

" Is not that a *very* severe line to take ?"

" Perhaps ; but the offence is of the worst character. I must consider the matter."

" Poor Williams ! " sighed Mr. Rose, as he left the room.

The whole of the miserable Sunday that followed

was spent by Eric and his companions in vain inquiries and futile restlessness. It seemed clear that two of them at least were detected, and they were inexpressibly wretched with anxiety and suspense. Wildney, who had to stay in bed, was even more depressed; his head ached violently, and he was alone with his own terrified thoughts. He longed for the morrow, that at least he might have the poor consolation of knowing his fate. No one came near him all day. Eric wished to do so, but as he could not have visited the room without express leave, the rest dissuaded him from asking, lest he should excite further suspicion. His apparent neglect made poor Wildney even more unhappy, for Wildney loved Eric as much as it was possible for his volatile mind to love any one; and it seemed hard to be deserted in the moment of disgrace and sorrow by so close a friend.

At school the next morning the various masters read out to their forms a notice from Dr. Rowlands, that the whole school were to meet at ten in the great school-room. The object of the summons was pretty clearly understood; and few boys had any doubt that it had reference to the drinking on Saturday night. Still nothing had been *said* on the subject as yet; and every guilty heart among those 250 boys beat fast lest *his* sin too should have been discovered, and he should be called out for some public and heavy punishment.

The hour arrived. The boys thronging into the great school-room, took their places according to their respective forms. The masters in their caps and gowns were all seated on a small semicircular bench at the upper end of the room, and in the centre of them, before a small table, sate Dr. Rowlands.

The sound of whispering voices sank to a dead and painful hush. The blood was tingling consciously in many cheeks, and not even a breath could be heard in the deep expectation of that anxious and solemn moment.

Dr. Rowlands spread before him the list of the school, and said, "I shall first read out the names of the boys in the first-fifth, and upper-fourth forms."

This was done to ascertain formally whether the boys were present on whose account the meeting was convened; and it at once told Eric and Wildney that *they* were the boys to be punished, and that the others had escaped.

The names were called over, and an attentive observer might have told, from the sound of the boys' voices as they answered, which of them were afflicted with a troubled conscience.

Another slight pause, and breathless hush.

"Eric Williams and Charles Wildney, stand forward."

The boys obeyed. From his place in the fifth, where he was sitting with his head propped on his hand, Eric rose and advanced; and Wildney, from the other end of the room, where the younger boys sat, getting up, came and stood by his side.

Both of them fixed their eyes on the ground, whence

they never once raised them; and in the deadly pallor
of their haggard faces, you could scarcely have recognised the joyous high-spirited friends, whose laugh and
shout had often rung so merrily through the playground,
and woke the echos of the rocks along the shore.
Every eye was on them, and they were conscious of it,
though they could not see it—painfully conscious of it,
so that they wished the very ground to yawn beneath
their feet for the moment, and swallow up their shame.
Companionship in disgrace increased the suffering; had
either of them been alone, he would have been less
acutely sensible to the trying nature of his position;
but that they, so different in their ages and position in
the school, should thus have their friendship and the
results of it blazoned, or rather branded, before their
friends and enemies, added keenly to the misery they
felt. So, with eyes bent on the floor, Eric and Charlie
awaited their sentence.

"Williams and Wildney," said Dr. Rowlands in a
solemn voice, of which every articulation thrilled to the
heart of every hearer, "you have been detected in a
sin most disgraceful and most dangerous. On Saturday
night you were both drinking, and you were guilty of
such gross excess, that you were neither of you in a fit
state to appear among your companions—least of all to
appear among them at the hour of prayer. I shall not
waste many words on an occasion like this; only I
trust that those of your schoolfellows who saw you
staggering and rolling into the room on Saturday evening

in a manner so unspeakably shameful and degrading, will learn from that melancholy sight the lesson which the Spartans taught their children by exhibiting a drunkard before them—the lesson of the brutalising and fearful character of this most ruinous vice. Eric Williams and Charles Wildney, your punishment will be public expulsion, for which you will prepare this very evening. I am unwilling that for a single day either of you—especially the elder of you—should linger, so as possibly to contaminate others with the danger of so pernicious an example."

Such a sentence was wholly unexpected; it took boys and masters equally by surprise. The announcement of it caused an uneasy sensation, which was evident to all present, though no one spoke a word; but Dr. Rowlands took no notice of it, and only said to the culprits—

" You may return to your seats."

The two boys found their way back instinctively, they hardly knew how. They seemed confounded and thunderstruck by their sentence, and the painful accessories of its publicity. Eric leaned over the desk with his head resting on a book, too stunned even to think; and Wildney looked straight before him with his eyes fixed in a stupid and unobservant stare.

Form by form the school dispersed, and the moment he was liberated Eric sprang away from the boys, who would have spoken to him, and rushed wildly to his study, where he locked the door. In a moment, however, he re-opened it, for he heard Wildney's step, and, after admitting him, locked it once more.

Without a word Wildney, who looked very pale, flung his arms round Eric's neck, and, unable to bear up any longer, burst into a flood of tears. Both of them felt relief in giving the reins to their sorrow, and silently satiating the anguish of their hearts.

" O, my father! my father!" sobbed Wildney at length, " What will he say? He will disown me, I know; he is so stern always with me when he thinks I bring disgrace on him."

Eric thought of Fairholm, and of his own far-distant parents, and of the pang which *his* disgrace would cause their loving hearts; but he could say nothing, and only stroked Wildney's dark hair again and again with a soothing hand.

They sat there long, hardly knowing how the time passed; Eric could not help thinking how very very different their relative positions might have been; how, while he might have been aiding and ennobling the young boy beside him, he had alternately led and followed him into wickedness and disgrace. His heart was full of misery and bitterness, and he felt almost indifferent to all the future, and weary of his life.

A loud knocking at the door disturbed them. It was Carter, the school servant.

" You must pack up to go this evening, young gentlemen."

" O no! no! no!" exclaimed Wildney; "I *cannot* be

sent away like this. It would break my father's heart. Eric, *do* come and entreat Dr. Rowlands to forgive us only this once."

"Yes," said Eric, starting up with sudden energy; "he *shall* forgive us—*you* at any rate. I will not leave him till he does. Cheer up, Charlie, cheer up, and come along."

Filled with an irresistible impulse, he pushed Carter aside, and sprang down stairs three steps at a time, with Wildney following him. They went straight for the Doctor's study, and without waiting for the answer to their knock at the door, Eric walked up to Dr. Rowlands, who sate thinking in his arm-chair by the fire, and burst out passionately, "O sir, forgive us, forgive us this once."

The Doctor was completely taken by surprise, so sudden was the intrusion, and so intense was the boy's manner. He remained silent a moment from astonishment, and then said with asperity—

"Your offence is one of the most dangerous possible. There could be no more perilous example for the school, than the one you have been setting, Williams. Leave the room," he added, with an authoritative gesture, "my mind is made up."

But Eric was too excited to be overawed by the master's manner; an imperious passion blinded him to all ordinary considerations, and, heedless of the command he broke out again,

"O sir, try me but once, *only* try me. I promise

you most faithfully that I will never again commit the sin. O sir, do, do trust me, and I will be responsible for Wildney too."

Dr. Rowlands, seeing that in Eric's present mood he must and would be heard, unless he were ejected by actual force, began to pace silently up and down the room in perplexed and anxious thought ; at last he stopped and turned over the pages of a thick school register, and found Eric's name.

" It is not your first offence, Williams, even of this very kind. That most seriously aggravates your fault."

" O sir ! give us one more chance to mend. O, I feel that I *could* do such great things, if you will but be merciful, and give me time to change. O, I entreat you, sir, to forgive us only this once, and I will never ask again. Let us bear *any* other punishment but this. O sir," he said, approaching the doctor in an imploring attitude, " spare us this one time for the sake of our friends."

The head master made no reply for a time, but again paced the room in silence. He was touched, and seemed hardly able to restrain his emotion.

" It was my deliberate conclusion to expel you, Williams. I must not weakly yield to entreaty. You must go."

Eric wrung his hands in agony. " O sir, then if you must do so, expel me only, and not Charlie. *I* can bear it, but do not let me ruin him also. O I implore you, sir, for the love of God do, do forgive him. It is I who have misled him ;" and he flung himself on his knees, and lifted his hands entreatingly towards the Doctor.

Dr. Rowlands looked at him — at his blue eyes drowned with tears, his agitated gesture, his pale, expressive face, full of passionate supplication. He looked at Wildney too, who stood trembling with a look of painful and miserable suspense, and occasionally added his wild word of entreaty, or uttered sobs more powerful still, that seemed to come from the depth of his heart. He was shaken in his resolve, wavered for a moment, and then once more looked at the register.

" Yes," he said, after a long pause, " here is an entry which shall save you this time. I find written here against your name, ' April 3. Risked his life in the endeavour to save Edwin Russell at the Stack.' That one good and noble deed shall be the proof that you are capable of better things. It may be weak perhaps—I know that it will be called weak—and I do not feel certain that I am doing right; but if I err it shall be on the side of mercy. I shall change expulsion into some other punishment. You may go."

Wildney's face lighted up as suddenly and joyously as when a ray of sun-light gleams for an instant out of a dark cloud.

" O thank you, thank you, sir," he exclaimed, drying his eyes, and pouring into the words a world of expression, which it was no light pleasure to have heard.

But Eric spoke less impulsively, and while the two boys were stammering out their deep gratitude, a timid hand knocked at the door, and Vernon entered.

" I have come, sir, to speak for poor Eric," he said in a voice low and trembling with emotion, as, with downcast eyes, he modestly approached towards Dr. Rowlands, not even observing the presence of the others in the complete absorption of his feelings. He stood in a sorrowful attitude, not venturing to look up, and his hand played nervously with the ribbon of his straw hat.

" I have just forgiven him, my little boy," said the Doctor kindly, patting his stooping head ; " there he is, and he has been speaking for himself."

" O, Eric, I am so, so glad, I don't know what to say for joy. O Eric, thank God that you are not to be expelled ;" and Vernon went to his brother, and embraced him with the deepest affection.

Dr. Rowlands watched the scene with moist eyes. He was generally a man of prompt decision, and he well knew that he would incur by this act the charge of vacillation. It was a noble self-denial in him to be willing to do so, but it would have required an iron heart to resist such earnest supplications, and he was more than repaid when he saw how much anguish he had removed by yielding to their entreaties.

Once more humbly expressing their gratitude, the boys retired.

They did not know that other influences had been

also exerted in their favour, which, although ineffectual at the time, had tended to alter the Doctor's intention. Immediately after school Mr. Rose had been strongly endeavouring to change the Doctor's mind, and had dwelt forcibly on all the good points in Eric's character, and the promise of his earlier career. And Montagu had gone with Owen and Duncan to beg that the expulsion might be commuted into some other punishment. They had failed to convince him ; but, perhaps, had they not thus exerted themselves, Dr. Rowlands might have been unshaken, though he could not be unmoved, by Vernon's gentle intercession and Eric's passionate prayers.

Wildney, full of joy, and excited by the sudden revulsion of feeling, only shook Eric's hands with all his might, and then darted out into the playground to announce the happy news. The boys all flocked round him, and received the intelligence with unmitigated pleasure. Among them all there was not one who did not rejoice that Eric and Wildney were yet to continue of their number.

But the two brothers returned to the study, and there, sorrowful in his penitence, with his heart still aching with remorse, Eric sat down on a chair facing the window, and drew Vernon to his side. The sun was setting behind the purple hills, flooding the green fields and silver sea with the crimson of his parting rays. The air was full of peace and coolness, and the merry sounds of the cricket-field blended joyously with the whisper of the evening breeze. Eric was fond of beauty in every shape, and his father had early taught him a keen appreciation of the glories of nature. He had often gazed before on that splendid scene, as he was now gazing on it thoughtfully with his brother by his side. He looked long and wistfully at the gorgeous pageantry of quiet clouds, and passed his arm more fondly round Vernon's shoulder.

"What are you thinking of, Eric? Why, I declare you are crying still," said Vernon playfully, as he wiped a tear which had overflowed on his brother's cheek; "aren't you glad that the Doctor has forgiven you?"

"Gladder, far gladder than I can say, Verny. O Verny, Verny, I hope your school-life may be happier than mine has been. I would give up all I have, Verny, to have kept free from the sins I have learnt. God grant that I may yet have time and space to do better."

"Let us pray together, Eric," whispered his brother reverently, and they knelt down and prayed; they prayed for their distant parents and friends; they prayed for their schoolfellows and for each other, and for Wildney, and they thanked God for all his goodness to them; and then Eric poured out his heart in a fervent prayer that a holier and happier future might atone for his desecrated past, and that his sins might be forgiven for his Saviour's sake.

The brothers rose from their knees calmer and more light-hearted, and gave each other a solemn affectionate kiss, before they went down again to the play-ground. But they avoided the rest of the boys, and took a stroll together along the sands, talking quietly and happily, and hoping bright hopes for future days.

CHAPTER IX.

WHOM THE GODS LOVE DIE YOUNG.

"Oh is it weed, or fish, or floating hair ?
  A tress of maiden's hair,
  Of drownèd maiden's hair,
  Above the nets at sea?—KINGSLEY.

RIC and Wildney were flogged and confined to gates for a time instead of being expelled, and they both bore the punishment in a manly and penitent way, and set themselves with all their might to repair the injury which their characters had received. Eric, especially, seemed to be devoting himself with every energy to regain, if possible, his long lost position, and by the altered complexion of his remaining school-life, to atone in some poor measure for its earlier sins. And he carried Wildney with him, influencing others also of his late companions in a greater or less degree. It was not Eric's nature to do things by halves, and it became obvious to all that his exertions to resist and abandon his old temptations were strenuous and un-wavering. He could no longer hope for the school distinctions, which would have once lain so easily within his reach, for the ground lost during weeks of idleness cannot be recovered by a wish ; but he succeeded sufficiently, by dint of desperately hard work, to acquit himself with considerable credit, and in the Easter examination came out sufficiently high in the upper fifth to secure his remove into the sixth form after the holidays.

He felt far happier in the endeavour to do his duty, than he had ever done during the last years of recklessness and neglect, and the change for the better in his character tended to restore unanimity and good-will to the school. Eric no longer headed the party which made a point of ridiculing and preventing industry ; and, sharing as he did the sympathy of nearly all the boys, he was able quietly and unobtrusively to calm down the jealousies and allay the heartburnings which had for so long a time brought discord and disunion into the school society. Cheerfulness and unanimity began to prevail once more at Roslyn, and Eric had the intense happiness of seeing how much good lay still within his power.

So the Easter holidays commenced with promise, and the few first days glided away in innocent enjoyments. Eric was now reconciled again to Owen and Duncan, and, therefore, had a wider choice of companions more truly congenial to his higher nature than the narrow circle of his late associates.

"What do you say to a boat excursion to-morrow?"

asked Duncan, as they chatted together one evening.

"I won't go without leave;" said Eric, "I should only get caught, and get into another mess. Besides, I feel myself pledged now to strict obedience."

"Ay, you're quite right. We'll get leave easily enough though, provided we agree to take Jim the boatman with us; so I vote we make up a party."

"By the bye, I forgot; I'm engaged to Wildney to-morrow."

"Never mind. Bring him with you, and Graham too, if you like."

"Most gladly," said Eric, really pleased; for he saw by this that Duncan observed the improvement in his old friends, and was falling in with the endeavour to make all the boys really cordial to each other, and destroy all traces of the late factions.

"Do you mind my bringing Montagu?"

"Not at all. Why should I?" answered Eric, with a slight blush. Montagu and he had never been formally reconciled, nor had they, as yet, spoken to each other. Indeed Duncan had purposely planned the excursion to give them an opportunity of becoming friends once more, by being thrown together. He knew well that they both earnestly wished it, although, with the natural shyness of boys, they hardly knew how to set about effecting it. Montagu hung back lest he should seem to be patronising a fallen enemy, and Eric lest he should have sinned too deeply to be forgiven.

The next morning dawned gloriously, and it was agreed that they should meet at Starhaven, the point where they were to get the boat, at ten o'clock. As they had supposed, Dr. Rowlands gave a ready consent to the row, on condition of their being accompanied by the experienced sailor whom the boys called Jim. The precaution was by no means unnecessary, for the various currents which ran round the island were violent at certain stages of the tide, and extremely dangerous for any who were not aware of their general course.

Feeling that the day would pass off very unpleasantly if any feeling of restraint remained between him and Montagu, Eric, by a strong effort, determined to "make up with him" before starting, and went into his study for that purpose after breakfast. Directly he came in, Montagu jumped up and welcomed him cordially, and when, without any allusion to the past, the two shook hands with all warmth, and looked the old proud look into each other's faces, they felt once more that their former affection was unimpaired, and that in heart they were real and loving friends. Most keenly did they both enjoy the renewed intercourse, and they found endless subjects to talk about on their way to Starhaven, where the others were already assembled when they came.

With Jim's assistance they shoved a boat into the water, and sprang into it in the highest spirits. Just as they were pushing off they saw Wright and Vernon running down to the shore towards them, and they waited to see what they wanted.

"Couldn't you take us with you?" asked Vernon, breathless with his run.

"I'm afraid not, Verny," said Montagu; "the boat won't hold more than six, will it, Jim?"

"No, sir, not safely."

"Never mind, you shall have my place, Verny," said Eric, as he saw his brother's disappointed look.

"Then Wright shall take mine," said Wildney.

"O, dear no," said Wright, "we wouldn't turn you out for the world. Vernon and I will take an immense walk down the coast instead, and will meet you here as we come back."

"Well, good bye, then; off we go;" and with light hearts the boaters and the pedestrians parted.

Eric, Graham, Duncan, and Montagu took the first turn at the oars, while Wildney steered. Graham's "crabs," and Wildney's rather crooked steering, gave plenty of opportunity for chaff, and they were full of fun, as the oar-blades splashed and sparkled in the waves. Then they made Jim sing them some of his old sailor-songs as they rowed, and joined vigorously in the choruses. They had arranged to make straight for St. Catherine's Head, and land somewhere near it to choose a place for their pic-nic. It took them nearly two hours to get there, as they rowed leisurely, and enjoyed the luxury of the vernal air. It was one of the sunniest days of early spring; the air was pure and delicious, and the calm sea breeze, just strong enough to make the sea flame and glister in the warm sunlight, was exhilarating as new wine.   Underneath them the water was transparent as crystal, and far below they could see the green and purple sea-weeds rising like a many-coloured wood, through which occasionally they saw a fish, startled by their oars, dart like an arrow.   The sky overhead was a cloudless blue, and as they kept not far from shore, the clearly cut outline of the coast, with its rocks and hills standing out in the vivid atmosphere, made a glowing picture, to which the golden green of the spring herbage, bathed in its morning sunlight, lent the magic of enchantment.   Who could have been otherwise than happy in such a scene and at such a time ? but these were boys with the long bright holiday before them, and happiness is almost too quiet a word to express the bounding exultation of heart, the royal and tingling sense of vigorous life, which made them shout and sing, as their boat rustled through the ripples, from a mere instinct of inexpressible enjoyment.

They had each contributed some luxury to the pic-nic, and it made a very tempting display as they spread it out, under a sunny pebbled cave, by St. Catherine's Head ; although, instead of anything more objectionable, they had thought it best to content them-selves with a very moderate quantity of beer.   When they had done eating, they amused themselves on the shore ; and had magnificent games among the rocks, and in every fantastic nook of the romantic promontory

And then Eric suggested a bathe to wind up with, as it was the first day when it had been quite warm enough to make bathing pleasant.

"But we've got no towels."

"Oh! chance the towels. We can run about till we're dry." So they bathed, and then getting in the boat to row back again, they all agreed that it was the very jolliest day they'd ever had at Roslyn, and voted to renew the experiment before the holidays were over, and take Wright and Vernon with them in a larger boat.

It was afternoon,—an afternoon still warm and beautiful,—when they began to row home; so they took it quietly, and kept near the land for variety's sake, laughing, joking, and talking as merrily as ever.

"I declare I think this is the prettiest or anyhow the grandest bit of the whole coast," said Eric, as they neared a glen through whose narrow gorge a green and garrulous little river gambolled down with noisy turbulence into the sea. He might well admire that glen; its steep and rugged sides were veiled with lichens, moss, and wild-flowers, and the sea-birds found safe refuge in its lonely windings, which were coloured with topaz and emerald by the pencillings of nature and the rich stains of time.

"Yes," answered Montagu, "*I* always stick up for Avon Glen as the finest scene we've got about here. But, I say, who's that gesticulating on the rock there to the right of it? I verily believe its Wright, apos-

trophising the ocean for Vernon's benefit. I only see
one of them though."

"I bet you he's spouting

> 'Roll on, thou deep and dark blue ocean—roll !
> Ten thousand fleets, etc.'"

said Graham laughing.

"What do you say to putting in to shore there ?" said
Duncan; "its only two miles to Starhaven, and I dare
say we could make shift to take them in for that distance.
If Jim says anything we'll chuck him overboard."

They rowed towards Avon Glen, and to their
surprise Wright, who stood there alone, (for with a
pocket telescope they clearly made out that it *was*
Wright), still continued to wave his arms and beckon
them in a manner which they at first thought ridiculous,
but which soon made them feel rather uneasy.

Jim took an oar, and they soon got within two
hundred yards of the beach. Wright had ceased to
make signals, but appeared to be shouting to them, and
pointing towards one corner of the glen; but though
they caught the sound of his voice they could not hear
what he said.

"I wonder why Vernon isn't with him," said Eric
anxiously; "I hope——why, what *are* you looking at,
Charlie ?"

"What's that in the water there ?" said Wildney,
pointing in the direction to which Wright was also
looking.

Montagu snatched the telescope out of his hand and

looked. "Good God!" he exclaimed, turning pale; "what can be the matter?"

"O *do* let me look" said Eric.

"No! stop, stop Eric, you'd better not, I think; pray don't, it may be all a mistake. You'd better not—but it looked——nay, you really *mustn't* Eric," he said, and, as if accidentally, he let the telescope fall into the water, and they saw it sink down among the seaweeds at the bottom.

Eric looked at him reproachfully. "What's the fun of that, Monty? you let it drop on purpose."

"O never mind; I'll get Wildney another. I really daren't let you look, for fear you should *fancy* the same as I did, for it must be fancy. O *don't* let us put in there—at least not all of us."

What *was* that thing in the water?—

When Wright and Vernon left the others, they walked along the coast, following the direction of the boat, and agreed to amuse themselves in collecting eggs. They were very successful, and, to their great delight, managed to secure some rather rare specimens. When they had tired themselves with this pursuit, they lay on the summit of one of the cliffs which formed the sides of Avon Glen, and Wright, who was very fond of poetry, read Vernon a canto of Marmion with great enthusiasm.

So they wiled away the morning, and when the canto was over, Vernon took a great stone and rolled it for amusement over the cliff's edge. It thundered over

the side, bounding down till it reached the strand, and
a large black cormorant, startled by the reverberating
echoes, rose up suddenly, and flapped its way with pro-
truded neck to a rock on the further side of the little
bay.

"I bet you that animal's got a nest somewhere
near here," said Vernon eagerly. "Come, let's have a
look for it; a cormorant's egg would be a jolly addition
to our collection."

They got up, and looking down the face of the cliff,
saw, some eight feet below them, a projection half hidden
by the branch of a tree, on which the scattered pieces
of stick clearly shewed the existence of a rude nest.
They could not, however, see whether it contained eggs
or no.

"I must bag that nest; it's pretty sure to have eggs
in it," said Vernon, "and I can get at it easy enough."

He immediately began to descend towards the place
where the nest was built, but he found it harder than
he expected.

"Hallo," he said, "this is a failure. I must climb
up again to reconnoitre if there isn't a better dodge for
getting at it."

He reached the top, and, looking down, saw a plan
of reaching the ledge which promised more hope of
success.

"You'd better give it up, Verny," said Wright.
"I'm sure its harder than we fancied. I couldn't
manage it, I know."

"O no, Wright, never say die. Look; if I get down more toward the right the way's plain enough, and I shall have reached the nest in no time."

Again he descended in a different direction, but again he failed. The nest could only be seen from the top, and he lost the right route.

"You must keep more to the right."

"I know," answered Vernon; "but, bother take it, I can't manage it, now I'm so far down. I must climb up *again*."

"*Do* give it up, Verny, there's a good fellow. You *can't* reach it, and really it's dangerous."

"O no, not a bit of it. My head's very steady, and I feel as cool as possible. We mustn't give up; I've only to get at the tree, and then I shall be able to reach the nest from it quite easily."

"Well, do take care, that's a dear fellow."

"Never fear," said Vernon, who was already commencing his third attempt.

This time he got to the tree, and placed his foot on a part of the root, while with his hands he clung on to a clump of heather.

"Hurrah!" he cried, "it's got two eggs in it, Wright;" and he stretched downwards to take them. Just as he was doing so, he heard the root on which his foot rested give a great crack, and with a violent start he made a spring for one of the lower branches. The motion caused his whole weight to rest for an instant on his arms;——unable to sustain the wrench, the heather gave way, and with a wild shriek he fell headlong down the surface of the cliff.

With a wild shriek!——but silence followed it.

"Vernon! Vernon!" shouted the terrified Wright, creeping close up to the edge of the precipice. "O Vernon! for heaven's sake speak!"

There was no answer, and leaning over, Wright saw the young boy outstretched on the stones three hundred feet below. For some minutes he was horror-struck beyond expression, and made wild attempts to descend the cliff and reach him. But he soon gave up the attempt in despair. There was a tradition in the school that the feat had once been accomplished by an adventurous and active boy, but Wright at any rate found it hopeless for himself. The only other way to reach the glen was by a circuitous route which led to the entrance of the narrow gorge, along the sides of which it was possible to make way, with difficulty down the bank of the river to the place where it met the sea. But this would have taken him an hour and a half, and was far from easy when the river was swollen with high tide. Nor was there any house within some distance at which assistance could be procured, and Wright, in a tumult of conflicting emotions, determined to wait where he was, on the chance of seeing the boat as it returned from St. Catherine's Head. It was already three o'clock, and he knew that they could not now be longer than an hour at most; so with eager eyes he sat watching the headland, round which he knew they would first come in sight. He watched with wild eager eyes, absorbed in the one longing desire to catch sight of them ; but the leaden-footed moments crawled on like hours, and he could not help shivering with agony and fear. At last he caught a glimpse of them, and springing up, began to shout at the top of his voice, and wave his handkerchief and his arms in the hope of attracting their attention. Little thought those blithe merry-hearted boys, in the midst of the happy laughter which they sent ringing over the waters, little they thought how terrible a tragedy awaited them.

At last Wright saw that they had perceived him, and were putting inland, and now, in his fright, he hardly knew what to do ; but feeling sure that they could not fail to see Vernon, he ran off as fast as he could to Starhaven, where he rapidly told the people at a farmhouse what had happened, and asked them to get a cart ready to convey the wounded boy to Roslyn school.

Meanwhile the tide rolled in calmly and quietly in the rosy evening, radiant with the diamond and gold of reflected sunlight and transparent wave. Gradually, gently it crept up to the place where Vernon lay ; and the little ripples fell over him wonderingly, with the low murmur of their musical laughter, and blurred and dimmed the vivid splashes and crimson streaks upon the white stone on which his head had fallen, and washed away some of the purple bells and green sprigs of heather round which his fingers were closed in the grasp of death, and played softly with his fair hair as it rose, and fell, and floated on their undulations like a leaf of golden-coloured weed, until they themselves were faintly discoloured by his blood. And then, tired with their new plaything, they passed on, until the swelling of the water was just strong enough to move rudely the boy's light weight, and in a few moments more would have tossed it up and down with every careless wave among the boulders of the glen. And then it was that Montagu's horror-stricken gaze had identified the object at which they had been gazing. In strange foreboding silence they urged on the boat, while Eric at the prow seemed wild with the one intense impulse to verify his horrible suspicion. The suspicion grew and grew :—it *was* a boy lying in the water;—it was Vernon;—he was motionless;—he must have fallen there from the cliff.

Eric could endure the suspense no longer. The instant that the boat grated on the shingle, he sprang into the water, and rushed to the spot where his brother's body lay. With a burst of passionate affection, he flung himself on his knees beside it, and took the cold hand in his own—the little rigid hand in which the green blades of grass, and fern, and heath, so tightly clutched, were unconscious of the tale they told.

"Oh Verny, Verny, darling Verny, speak to me!" he cried in anguish, as he tenderly lifted up the body, and marked how little blood had flowed. But the child's head fell back heavily, and his arms hung motionlessly beside him, and with a shriek, Eric suddenly caught the look of dead fixity in his blue open eyes.

The others had come up. " O God, save my brother, save him, save him from death," cried Eric, " I cannot live without him. Oh God! Oh God! Look! look!" he continued, " he has fallen from the cliff with his head on this cursed stone," pointing to the block of quartz, still red with blood-stained hair; but we must get a doctor. He is not dead! no, no, no, he *cannot* be dead. Take him quickly, and let us row home. Oh God! why did I ever leave him?"

The boys drew round in a frightened circle, and lifted Vernon's corpse into the boat; and then, while Eric still supported the body, and moaned, and called to him in anguish, and chafed his cold pale brow and white hands, and kept saying that he had fainted and was not dead, the others rowed home with all speed, while a feeling of terrified anxiety lay like frost upon their hearts.

They reached Starhaven, and got into the cart with the lifeless boy, and heard from Wright how the accident had taken place. Few boys were about the playground, so they got unnoticed to Roslyn, and Dr. Underhay, who had been summoned, was instantly in attendance. He looked at Vernon for a moment, and then shook his head in a way that could not be mistaken.

Eric saw it, and flung himself with uncontrollable agony on his brother's corpse. " O Vernon, Vernon, my own dear brother! oh God, then he is dead." And, unable to endure the blow, he fainted away.

I cannot dwell on the miserable days that followed,

when the very sun in heaven seemed dark to poor
Eric's wounded and crushed spirit.   He hardly knew
how they went by.   And when they buried Vernon in
the little green churchyard by Russell's side, and the
patter of the earth upon the coffin—that most terrible
of all sounds—struck his ear, the iron entered into his
soul, and he had but one wish as he turned away from
the open grave, and that was, soon to lie beside his
beloved little brother, and to be at rest.

CHAPTER X.

THE LAST TEMPTATION.

'Η δ' "Ατη σθεναρή τε καὶ ἄρτιπος· οὕνεκα πάσας
Πολλὸν ὑπεκπροθέει, φθανέει δ' δέ τε πᾶσαν ἐπ' αἶαν
Βλάπτους' ἀνθρώπους.   Hom. Il. ix. 505.

TIME, the great good angel, Time, the merciful
healer, assuaged the violence of Eric's grief,
which seemed likely to settle down into a sober
sadness.   At first his letters to his parents and
to Fairholm were almost unintelligible in their
fierce abandonment of sorrow; but they grew
calmer in time,—and while none of his schoolfellows ever ventured in his presence to allude to
Vernon, because of the emotion which the slightest
mention of him excited, yet he rarely wrote any letters
to his relations in which he did not refer to his brother's
death, in language which grew at length both manly
and resigned.

A month after, in the summer term, he was sitting
alone in his study in the afternoon (for he could not
summon up spirit enough to play regularly at cricket),

writing a long letter to his aunt. He spoke freely and un-
reservedly of his past errors,—more freely than he had
ever done before,—and expressed not only deep penitence,
but even strong hatred of his previous unworthy courses.
" I can hardly even yet realize," he added, " that I am
alone here, and that I am writing to my aunt Trevor
about the death of my brother, my noble, only brother,
Vernon. Oh how my whole soul yearns towards him.
I *must* be a better boy, I *will* be better than I have
been, in the hopes of meeting him again. Indeed, indeed,
dear aunt, though I have been so guilty, I am laying
aside, with all my might, idleness and all bad habits,
and doing my very best to redeem the lost years. I
do hope that the rest of my time at Roslyn will be
more worthily than any of it has been as yet."

He finished the sentence, and laid his pen down to
think, gazing quietly on the blue hills and sunlit sea.
A feeling of hope and repose stole over him ;—when
suddenly he saw at the door, which was ajar, the leering
eyes and villainously cunning countenance of Billy.

" What do you want ? " he said angrily, casting at
the intruder a look of intense disgust.

" Beg pardon, sir," said the man, pulling his hair.
" Anything in my line, sir, to-day ? "

" No ! " answered Eric, rising up in a gust of indignation. " What business have you here ? Get away
instantly."

" Not had much custom from you lately, sir," said
the man.

" What do you mean by having the insolence to begin talking to me? If you don't make yourself scarce at once, Ill——"

" O well," said the man; " if it comes to that, I've business enough. Perhaps you'll just pay me this debt," he continued, changing his fawning manner into a bullying swagger. " I've waited long enough."

Eric, greatly discomfited, took the dirty bit of paper. It purported to be a bill for various items of drink, all of which Eric *knew* to have been paid for, and among other things, a charge of £6 for the dinner at the " Jolly Herring."

" Why, you villain, these have all been paid. What! six pounds for the dinner! Why Brigson collected the subscriptions to pay for it before it took place."

" That's now't to me, sir. He never paid me; and as you was the young gen'lman in the cheer, I comes to you."

Now Eric knew for the first time what Brigson had meant by his threatened revenge. He saw at once that the man had been put up to act in this way by some one, and had little doubt that Brigson was the instigator. Perhaps it might be even true, as the man said, that he had never received the money. Brigson was quite wicked enough to have embezzled it for his own purposes.

" Go," he said to the man; " you shall have the money in a week."

"And mind it bean't more nor a week. I don't chuse to wait for my money no more," said Billy, impudently, as he retired with an undisguised chuckle, which very nearly made Eric kick him down stairs.

What was to be done? To mention the subject to Owen or Montagu, who were best capable of advising him, would have been to renew the memory of unpleasant incidents, which he was most anxious to obliterate from the memory of all. He had not the moral courage to face the natural consequences of his past misconduct, and was now ashamed to speak of what he had not then been ashamed to do. He told Graham and Wildney, who were the best of his old associates, and they at once agreed that *they* ought to be responsible for at least a share of the debt. Still, between them they could only muster three pounds out of the six which were required, and the week had half elapsed before there seemed any prospect of extrication from the difficulty; so Eric daily grew more miserable and dejected.

A happy thought struck him. He would go and explain the source of his trouble to Mr. Rose, his oldest, his kindest, his wisest friend. To him he could speak without scruple and without reserve, and from him he knew that he would receive nothing but the noblest advice and the warmest sympathy.

He went to him after prayers that night, and told his story.

"Ah, Eric, Eric!" said Mr. Rose; "you see, my boy, that sin and punishment are twins."

"O but, sir, I was just striving so hard to amend, and it seems cruel that I should receive at once so sad a check."

"There is only one way that I see, Eric. You must write home for the money, and confess the truth to them honestly, as you have to me."

It was a hard course for Eric's proud and loving heart to write and tell his aunt the full extent of his guilt. But he did it faithfully, extenuating nothing, and entreating her, as she loved him, to send the money by return of post.

It came, and with it a letter full of deep and gentle affection. Mrs. Trevor knew her nephew's character, and did not add by reproaches to the bitterness which she perceived he had endured; she simply sent him the money, and told him, that in spite of his many failures, "she still had perfect confidence in the true heart of her dear boy."

Touched by the affection which all seemed to be showing him, it became more and more the passionate craving of Eric's soul to be worthy of that love. But it is far, far harder to recover a lost path than to keep in the right one all along; and by one more terrible fall, the poor erring boy was to be taught for the last time the fearful strength of temptation, and the only source in earth and heaven from which deliverance can come. Theoretically he knew it, but as yet not practically. Great as his trials had been, and deeply as he had suffered, it was God's will that he should pass through

a yet fiercer flame ere he could be purified from pride
and passion and self-confidence, and led to the cross of
a suffering Saviour, there to fling himself down in
heart-rending humility, and cast his great load of cares
and sins upon Him who cared for him through all his
wanderings, and was leading him back through thorny
places to the green pastures and still waters, where at
last he might have rest.

The money came, and walking off straight to the
Jolly Herring, he dashed it down on the table before
Billy, and imperiously bade him write a receipt.

The man did so, but with so unmistakeable an air of
cunning and triumph that Eric was both astonished and
dismayed.   Could the miscreant have any further plot
against him ?   At first he fancied that Billy might
attempt to extort money by a threat of telling Dr.
Rowlands ; but this supposition he banished as unlikely,
since it might expose Billy himself to very unpleasant
consequences.

Eric snatched the receipt, and said contemptuously,
" Never come near me again ; next time you come up
to the studies I'll tell Carter to turn you out."

" Ho, ho, ho !" sneered Billy.   " How mighty we
young gents are all of a sudden.   Unless you buy of
me sometimes, you shall hear of me again ; never fear,
young gen'lman."   He shouted out the latter words,
for Eric had turned scornfully on his heel, and was
already in the street.

Obviously more danger was to be apprehended from

this quarter. At first the thought of it was disquieting, but three weeks glided away, and Eric, now absorbed heart and soul in school work, began to remember it as a mere vague and idle threat.

But one afternoon, to his horror, he again heard Billy's step on the stairs, and again saw the hateful iniquitous face at the door.

" Not much custom from you lately, sir," said Billy, mockingly. " Anything in my line to-day."

" Didn't I tell you never to come near me again, you foul villain? Go this instant, or I'll call Carter;" and, opening the window, he prepared to put his threat into execution.

" Ho, ho, ho! Better look at summat I've got first." It was a printed notice to the following effect—

" FIVE POUNDS REWARD.

" WHEREAS some evil-disposed persons stole some pigeons on the evening of April 6th from the Rev. H. Gordon's premises; the above reward will be given for any such information as may lead to the apprehension of the offenders."

Soon after the seizure of the pigeons there had been a rumour that Gordon had offered a reward of this kind, but the matter had been forgotten, and the boys had long fancied their secret secure, though at first they had been terribly alarmed.

" What do you show me that for?" he asked, reddening and then growing pale again.

Billy's only answer was to pass his finger slowly along the words " Five pounds reward ! "

" Well ? "

" I thinks I knows who took they pigeons."

" What's that to me ? "

" Ho, ho, ho ! that's a good un," was Billy's reply; and he continued to cackle as though enjoying a great joke.

" Unless you gives me five pound, anyhow, I knows where to get 'em. I know who them evil-disposed persons be ! So I'll give ye another week to decide."

Billy shambled off in high spirits; but Eric sank back into his chair. Five pounds ! The idea haunted him. How could he ever get them ? To write home again was out of the question. The Trevors, though liberal, were not rich, and after just sending him so large a sum, it was impossible, he thought, that they should send him five pounds more at his mere request. Besides, how could he be sure that Billy would not play upon his fears to extort further sums ? And to explain the matter to them fully was more than he could endure. He remembered now how easily his want of caution might have put Billy in possession of the secret, and he knew enough of the fellow's character to feel quite sure of the use he would be inclined to make of it. Oh how he cursed that hour of folly !

Five pounds ! He began to think of what money he could procure. He thought again and again, but.it was no use; only one thing was clear—he *had* not the money, and could not get it. Miserable boy! It was too late then? for him repentance was to be made impossible; every time he attempted it he was to be thwarted by some fresh discovery. And, leaning his head on his open palms, poor Eric sobbed like a child.

Five pounds! And all this misery was to come upon him for the want of five pounds! Expulsion was *certain,* was *inevitable* now, and perhaps for Wildney too as well as for himself. After all his fine promises in his letters home,—yes, that reminded him of Vernon. The grave had not closed for a month over one brother, and the other would be *expelled.* Oh misery, misery! He was sure it would break his mother's heart. Oh how cruel everything was to him!

Five pounds—he wondered whether Montagu would lend it him, or any other boy? But then it was late in the quarter, and all the boys would have spent the money they brought with them from home. There was no chance of any one having five pounds, and to a master he *dare* not apply, not even to Mr. Rose. The offence was too serious to be overlooked, and if noticed at all, he fancied that, after his other delinquencies, it *must,* as a matter of notoriety, be visited with expulsion. He could not face that bitter thought; he could not thus bring open disgrace upon his father's and his brother's name; this was the fear which kept recurring to him with dreadful iteration.

. By the bye, he remembered that if he had continued captain of the school eleven, he would have had easy command of the money by being treasurer of the cricket subscriptions.   But at Vernon's death he lost all interest in cricket for a time, and had thrown up his office, to which Montagu had been elected by the general suffrage.

He wondered whether there was as much as five pounds of the cricketing-money left?   He knew that the box which contained it was in Montagu's study, and he also knew where the key was kept.   It was merely a feeling of curiosity—he would go and look.

All this passed through Eric's mind as he sat in his study after Billy had gone.   It was a sultry summer day; all the study-doors were open, and all their occupants were absent in the cricket-field, or bathing.   He stole into Montagu's study, hastily got the key, and took down the box.

"O put it down, put it down, Eric," said Conscience; " what business have you with it?"

"Pooh! it is merely curiosity; as if I couldn't trust myself!"

"Put it down," repeated Conscience authoritatively, deigning no longer to argue or entreat.

Eric hesitated, and did put down the box; but he did not instantly leave the room.   He began to look at Montagu's books, and then out of the window.   The gravel play-ground was deserted, he noticed, for the cricket-field.   Nobody was near, therefore.   Well, what of that?   he was doing no harm.

"Nonsense!   I *will* just look and see if there's five

pounds in the cricket-box." Slowly at first he put out his hand, and then, hastily turning the key, opened the box. It contained three pounds in gold, and a quantity of silver. He began to count the silver, putting it on the table, and found that it made up three pounds ten more. " So that, altogether, there's six pounds ten; that's thirty shillings more than . . . . and it won't be wanted till next summer term, because all the bats and balls are bought now. I daresay Montagu won't even open the box again. I know he keeps it stowed away in a corner, and hardly ever looks at it, and I can put back the five pounds the very first day of next term, and it will save me from expulsion."

Very slowly Eric took the three sovereigns and put them in his pocket, and then he took up one of the heaps of shillings and sixpences which he had counted, and dropped them also into his trousers; they fell into the pocket with a great jingle . . . .

" Eric, you are a thief! " He thought he heard his brother Vernon's voice utter the words thrillingly distinct; but it was conscience who had borrowed the voice, and, sick with horror, he began to shake the money out of his pockets again into the box. He was only just in time; he had barely locked the box, and put it in its place, when he heard the sound of voices and footsteps on the stairs. He had no time to take out the key and put it back where he found it, and hardly time to slip into his own study again, when the boys had reached the landing.

They were Duncan and Montagu, and as they passed the door, Eric pretended to be plunged in books.

" Hallo, Eric ! grinding as usual," said Duncan, good-humouredly ; but he only got a sickly smile in reply.

" What ! are you the only fellow in the studies ? " asked Montagu. " I was nearly sure I heard some one moving about as we came up stairs."

" I do n't think there 's any one here but me," said Eric, " and I 'm going a walk now."

He closed his books with a bang, flew down stairs, and away through the play-ground towards the shore. But he could not so escape his thoughts. " Eric, you are a thief ! Eric, you are a thief ! " rang in his ear. " Yes," he thought ; " I am even a thief. Oh, good God, yes, *even* a *thief*, for I *had* actually stolen the money, until I changed my mind. What if they should discover the key in the box, knowing that I was the only fellow up stairs? Oh, mercy, mercy, mercy ! "

It was a lonely place, and he flung himself, with his face hid in the coarse grass, trying to cool the wild burning of his brow. And as he lay, he thrust his hand into the guilty pocket. Good heavens ! there was something still there. He pulled it out ; it was a sovereign ! Then he WAS a thief, even actually. Oh, everything was against him ; and, starting to his feet, he flung the accursed gold over the rocks far into the sea.

When he got home, he felt so inconceivably wretched, that, unable to work, he begged leave to go to bed at once. It was long before he fell asleep; but when he did, the sleep was more terrible than the haunted wakefulness. For he had no rest from tormenting and horrid dreams. Brigson and Billy, their bodies grown to gigantic proportions, and their faces fierce with demoniacal wickedness, seemed to be standing over him, and demanding five pounds on pain of death. Flights of pigeons darkening the air, settled on him, and flapped about him. He fled from them madly through the dark midnight, but many steps pursued him. He saw Mr. Rose, and running up, seized him by the hand, and implored protection. But in his dream Mr. Rose turned from him with a cold look of sorrowful reproach. And then he saw Wildney, and cried out to him, " O Charlie, save me ;" but Charlie ran away, saying, " Williams, you are a thief!" and then a chorus of voices took up that awful cry, voices of expostulation, voices of contempt, voices of indignation, voices of menace ; they took up the cry, and repeated and re-echoed it ; but, most unendurable of all, there were voices of wailing and voices of gentleness among them, and his soul died within him as he caught, amid the confusion of condemning sounds, the voices of Russell and Vernon, and they, too, were saying to him, in tender pity and agonized astonishment, " Eric, Eric, you are a thief!"

CHAPTER XI.

REAPING THE WHIRLWIND.

"For alas! alas! with me
  The light of life is o'er;
  No more—no more—no more!
(Such language holds the solemn sea
  To the sands upon the shore)
Shall bloom the thunder-blasted tree,
  Or the stricken eagle soar!"

EDGAR POE.

HE landlord of the Jolly Herring had observed, during his visits to Eric, that at mid-day the studies were usually deserted, and the doors for the most part left unlocked. He very soon determined to make use of this knowledge for his own purposes, and as he was well acquainted with the building (in which for a short time he had been a servant), he laid his plans without the least dread of discovery.

There was a back entrance into Roslyn school behind the chapel, and it could be reached by a path through the fields without any chance of being seen, if a person set warily to work and watched his opportunity. By this path Billy came, two days after his last visit, and walked straight up the great staircase, armed with the excuse of business with Eric in case any one met or questioned him. But no one was about, since between twelve and one the boys were pretty sure to be amusing themselves out of doors; and after glancing into each of the studies, Billy finally settled on searching Montagu's (which was the neatest and best furnished), to see what he could get.

The very first thing which caught his experienced eye was the cricket-fund box, with the key temptingly in the lock, just where Eric had left it when the sounds of some one coming had startled him. In a moment Billy had made a descent on the promising-looking booty, and opening his treasure, saw, with lively feelings of gratification, the unexpected store of silver and gold. This he instantly transferred to his own pocket, and then replacing the box where he had found it, decamped with the spoil unseen, leaving the study in all other respects exactly as he had found it.

Meanwhile the unhappy Eric was tossed and agitated with apprehension and suspense. Unable to endure his misery in loneliness, he had made several boys to a greater or less degree participators in the knowledge of his difficult position, and in the sympathy which his danger excited, the general nature of his dilemma with Billy (though not its special circumstances) was soon known through the school.

At the very time when the money was being stolen,

Eric was sitting with Wildney and Graham under the ruin by the shore, and the sorrow which lay at his heart was sadly visible in the anxious expression of his face, and the deep dejection of his attitude and manner.

The other two were trying to console him. They suggested every possible topic of hope; but it was too plain that there was nothing to be said, and that Eric had real cause to fear the worst. Yet though their arguments were futile, he keenly felt the genuineness of their affection, and it brought a little alleviation to his heavy mood.

" Well, well ; at least *do* hope the best, Eric," said Graham.

" Yes !" urged Wildney ; " only think, dear old fellow, what lots of worse scrapes we've been in before, and how we've always managed to get out of them somehow."

" No, my boy ; not worse scrapes," answered Eric. " Depend upon it this is the last for me; I shall not have the chance of getting into another at *Roslyn*, any-how."

" Poor Eric ! what shall I do if you leave?" said Wildney, putting his arm round Eric's neck. " Besides it's all my fault, hang it, that you got into this cursed row."

> " 'The curse is come upon me, cried
> The Lady of Shallott,'

" those words keep ringing in my ears," murmured Eric.

"Well, Eric, if *you* are sent away, I know I shall get my father to take me too, and then we'll join each other somewhere. Come, cheer up, old boy—being sent isn't such a very frightful thing after all."

"No," said Graham; "and besides, the bagging of the pigeons was only a lark, when one comes to think of it. It wasn't like stealing, you know; *that*'d be quite a different thing."

Eric winced visibly at this remark, but his companions did not notice it. "Ah," thought he, "there's *one* passage of my life which I never shall be able to reveal to any human soul."

"Come now, Eric," said Wildney, "I've got something to propose. You shall play cricket to-day; you haven't played for an age, and it's high time you should. If you don't you'll go mooning about the shore all day, and that'll never do, for you'll come back glummer than ever."

"No!" said Eric, with a heavy sigh, as the image of Vernon instantly passed through his mind; "no more cricket for me."

"Nay, but you *must* play to-day. Come, you shan't say no. You won't say no to me, will you, dear old fellow?" And Wildney looked up to him with that pleasant smile, and the merry light in his dark eyes, which had always been so charming to Eric's fancy.

"There's no refusing you," said Eric, with the ghost of a laugh, as he boxed Wildney's ears. "O you dear little rogue, Charlie, I wish I were you."

"Pooh! pooh! now you shan't get sentimental again. As if you weren't fifty times better than me every way. I'm sure I don't know how I shall ever love you enough, Eric," he added more seriously, "for all your kindness to me."

"I'm so glad you're going to play, though," said Graham; "and so will everybody be; and I'm certain it'll be good for you. The game will divert your thoughts."

So that afternoon Eric, for the first time since Verny's death, played with the first eleven, of which he had been captain. The school cheered him vigorously as he appeared again on the field, and the sound lighted up his countenance with some gleam of its old joyousness. When one looked at him that day with his straw hat on and its neat light-blue ribbon, and the cricket dress (a pink jersey and leather belt, with a silver clasp in front), showing off his well-built and graceful figure, one little thought what an agony was gnawing like a serpent at his heart. But that day, poor boy, in the excitement of the game he half forgot it himself, and more and more as the game went on.

The other side, headed by Montagu, went in first, and Eric caught out two, and bowled several. Montagu was the only one who stayed in long, and when at last Eric sent his middle wicket flying with a magnificent ball, the shouts of "Well bowled! well bowled *indeed*," were universal.

"Just listen to that, Eric," said Montagu; "why,

you're outdoing every body to-day, yourself included, and taking us by storm."

" Wait till you see me come out for a duck," said Eric laughing.

" Not you.   You're too much in luck to come out with a duck," answered Montagu.   " You see I've already become the Homer of your triumphs, and vaticinate in rhyme."

And now it was Eric's turn to go in.   It was long since he had stood before the wicket, but now he was there, looking like a beautiful picture as the sunlight streamed over him, and made his fair hair shine like gold. In the triumph of success his sorrows were flung to the winds, and his blue eyes sparkled with interest and joy.

He contented himself with blocking Duncan's balls until his eye was in ; but then, acquiring confidence, he sent them flying right and left.   His score rapidly mounted, and there seemed no chance of getting him out, so that there was every probability of his carrying out his bat.

" Oh, *well* hit ! *well* hit !   A three'r for Eric," cried Wildney to the scorer ; and he began to clap his hands and dance about with excitement at his friend's success.

" Oh, well hit ! well hit in—deed ! " shouted all the lookers on, as Eric caught the next ball half-volley, and sent it whizzing over the hedge, getting a sixer by the hit.

At the next ball they heard a great crack, and he got no run, for the handle of his bat broke right off.

"How unlucky!" he said, flinging down the handle with vexation. "I believe this was our best bat."

"Oh, never mind," said Montagu; "we can soon get another; we've got lots of money in the box."

What had come over Eric? if there had been a sudden breath of poison in the atmosphere he could hardly have been more affected than he was by Montagu's simple remark. Montagu could not help noticing it, but at the time merely attributed it to some unknown gust of feeling, and made no comment. But Eric, hastily borrowing another bat, took his place again quite tamely; he was trembling, and at the very next ball, he spooned a miserable catch into Graham's hand, and the shout of triumph from the other side proclaimed that his innings was over.

He walked dejectedly to the pavilion for his coat, and the boys, who were seated in crowds about it, received him, of course, after his brilliant score, with loud and continued plaudits. But the light had died away from his face and figure, and he never raised his eyes from the ground.

"Modest Eric!" said Wildney chaffingly, "you don't acknowledge your honours."

Eric dropped his bat in the corner, put his coat across his arm, and walked away. As he passed Wildney, he stooped down and whispered again in a low voice—

> "'The curse has come upon me, cried,
>   The Lady of Shallott.'"

"Hush, Eric, nonsense," whispered Wildney; "you're not going away," he continued aloud, as Eric turned towards the school. "Why, there are only two more to go in!"

"Yes, thank you, I must go."

"Oh, then, I'll come too."

Wildney at once joined his friend. "There's nothing more the matter, is there?" he asked anxiously, when they were out of hearing of the rest.

"God only knows."

"Well, let's change the subject. You've being playing brilliantly, old fellow."

"Have I?"

"I should just think so, only you got out in rather a stupid way."

"Ah well! it matters very little."

Just at this moment one of the servants handed Eric a kind note from Mrs. Rowlands, with whom he was a very great favourite, asking him to tea that night. He was not very surprised, for he had been several times lately, and the sweet womanly kindness which she always showed him caused him the greatest pleasure. Besides, she had known his mother.

"Upon my word, honours *are* being showered on you!" said Wildney. "First to get *the* score of the season at cricket, and bowl out about half the other side, and then go to tea with the head-master. Upon my word! Why any of us poor wretches would give our two ears for such distinctions. Talk of curse indeed! Fiddlestick end!"

But Eric's sorrow lay too deep for chaff, and only answering with a sigh, he went to dress for tea.

Just before tea-time Duncan and Montagu strolled in together. "How splendidly Eric played," said Duncan.

"Yes, indeed. I'm so glad. By the bye I must see about getting a new bat. I don't know exactly how much money we've got, but I know there's plenty. Let's come and see."

They entered his study, and he looked about everywhere for the key. "Hallo," he said, "I'm nearly sure I left it in the corner of this drawer, under some other things; but it isn't there now. What can have become of it"?

"Where's the box?" said Duncan; "let's see if any of my keys will fit it. Hallo! why *you're* a nice treasurer, Monty! here's the key *in* the box!"

"No, is it though?" asked Montagu, looking serious. "Here, give it me; I hope nobody's been meddling with it."

He opened it quickly, and stood in dumb and blank amazement to see it empty.

"Phew-w-w-w!" Montagu gave a long whistle.

"By Jove!" was Duncan's only comment.

The boys looked at each other, but neither dared to express what was in his thoughts.

"A bad, bad, business! what's to be done, Monty?"

"I'll rush straight down to tea, and ask the fellows

about it.   Would you mind requesting Rose not to
come in for five minutes?   Tell him there's a row.

He ran down stairs hastily and entered the tea-
room, where the boys were talking in high spirits about
the match, and liberally praising Eric's play.

"I've got something unpleasant to say," he announced, raising his voice.

"Hush! hush! hush! what's the row?" asked
half a dozen at once.

"The whole of the cricket money, some six pounds
at least, has vanished from the box in my study!"

For an instant the whole room was silent; Wildney
and Graham interchanged anxious glances.

"Does any fellow know anything about this?"

All, or most, had a vague suspicion, but no one
spoke.

"Where is Williams?" asked one of the sixth form
casually.

"He's taking tea with the Doctor," said Wildney.

Mr. Rose came in, and there was no opportunity
for more to be said, except in confidential whispers.

Duncan went up with Owen and Montagu to their
study.   "What's to be done?" was the general
question.

"I think we've all had a lesson once before not to
suspect too hastily.   Still, in a matter like this," said
Montagu, "one *must* take notice of apparent cues."

"I know what you're thinking of, Monty," said
Duncan.

" Well, then, did you hear anything when you and I surprised Eric suddenly two days ago?"

" I heard some one moving about in your study, as I thought."

" I heard more—though at the time it didn't strike me particularly. I distinctly heard the jingle of money."

" Well, it's no good counting up suspicious circumstances; we must *ask* him about it, and act accordingly."

" Will he come up to the studies again to night?"

" I think not," said Owen; " I notice he generally goes straight to bed after he has been out to tea; that's to say, directly after prayers."

The three sat there till prayer-time taciturn and thoughtful. Their books were open, but they did little work, and it was evident that Montagu was filled with the most touching grief. During the evening he drew out a little likeness which Eric had given him, and looked at it long and earnestly. " Is it possible?" he thought. " Oh Eric! can that face be the face of a thief?"

The prayer-bell dispelled his reverie. Eric entered with the Rowlands', and sat in his accustomed place. He had spent a pleasant, quiet evening, and, little knowing what had happened, felt far more cheerful and hopeful than he had done before, although he was still ignorant how to escape the difficulty which threatened him.

He couldn't help observing that as he entered he was the object of general attention; but he attributed it either to his playing that day, or to the circumstances in which he was placed by Billy's treachery, of which he knew that many boys were now aware. But when prayers were over, and he saw that every one shunned him, or looked and spoke in the coldest manner, his most terrible fears revived.

He went off to his dormitory, and began to undress. As he sat half abstracted on his bed doing nothing, Montagu and Duncan entered, and he started to see them, for they were evidently the bearers of some serious intelligence.

"Eric," said Duncan, "do you know that some one has stolen all the cricket money?"

"Stolen—what—*all?*" he cried, leaping up as if he had been shot. "Oh, what new retribution is this?" and he hid his face, which had turned ashy pale, in his hands.

"To cut matters short, Eric, do you know anything about it?"

"If it is all gone, it is not I who stole it," he said, not lifting his head.

"Do you know anything about it?"

"No!" he sobbed convulsively. "No, no, no! Yet stop; don't let me add a lie. . . . Let me think. No, Duncan!" he said, looking up, "I do *not* know who stole it."

They stood silent, and the tears were stealing down Montagu's averted face.

"O Duncan, Monty, be merciful, be merciful," said Eric. "Don't *yet* condemn me. I am guilty, not of

this, but of something as bad.   I admit I was tempted;
but if the money really is all gone, it is *not* I who am
the thief."

"You must know, Eric, that the suspicion against
you is very strong, and rests on some definite facts."

"Yes, I know it must.   Yet, oh, do be merciful,
and don't yet condemn me.   I have denied it.   Am I
a liar, Monty?   Oh Monty, Monty, believe me in this!"

But the boys still stood silent.

"Well then," he said, "I will tell you all.   But I
can only tell it to you, Monty.   Duncan, indeed you
mustn't be angry; you are my friend, but not so much
as Monty.   I can tell him, and him only."

Duncan left the room, and Montagu sat down beside
Eric on the bed, and put his arm round him to support
him, for he shook violently.   There, with deep and wild
emotion, and many interruptions of passionate silence,
Eric told to Montagu his miserable tale.   "I am the
most wretched fellow living," he said; "there must be
some fiend that hates me, and drives me to ruin.   But
let it all come; I care nothing, nothing, what happens
to me now.   Only, dear, dear Monty, forgive me, and
love me still."

"O Eric, it is not for one like me to talk of forgiveness; you were sorely tempted.   Yet God will
forgive you if you ask him.   Won't you pray to him
to-night?   I love you, Eric, still, with all my heart,
and do you think God can be less kind than man?
And *I,* too, will pray for you, Eric.   Good night, and

God bless you." He gently disengaged himself—for Eric clung to him, and seemed unwilling to lose sight of him—and a moment after he was gone.

Eric felt terribly alone. He knelt down and tried to pray, but somehow it didn't seem as if the prayer came from his heart, and his thoughts began instantly to wander far away. Still he knelt—knelt even until his candle had gone out, and he had nearly fallen asleep, thought-wearied, on his knees. And then he got into bed still dressed. He had been making up his mind that he could bear it no longer, and would run away to sea that night.

He waited till eleven, when Dr. Rowlands took his rounds. The Doctor had been told all the circumstances of suspicion, and they amounted in his mind to certainty. It made him very sad, and he stopped to look at the boy from whom he had parted on such friendly terms so short a time before. Eric did not pretend to be asleep, but opened his eyes, and looked at the head-master. Very sorrowfully Dr. Rowlands shook his head, and went away. Eric never saw him again.

The moment he was gone Eric got up. He meant to go to his study, collect the few presents, which were his dearest mementos of Russell, Wildney, and his other friends—above all, Vernon's likeness—and then make his escape from the building, using for the last time the broken pane and loosened bar in the corridor, with which past temptations had made him so familiar.

He turned the handle of the door and pushed, but
it did not yield. Half contemplating the possibility of
such an intention on Eric's part, Dr. Rowlands had
locked it behind him when he went out.

" Ha !" thought the boy, "then he too knows and
suspects. Never mind. I must give up my treasures
—yes, even poor Verny's picture ; perhaps it is best I
should, for I'm only disgracing his noble memory. But
they shan't prevent me from running away."

Once more he deliberated. Yes, there could be
no doubt about the decision. He *could* not endure
another public expulsion, or even another birching ;
he *could* not endure the cold faces of even his best
friends. No, no ! he *could* not face the horrible phan-
tom of detection, and exposure, and shame. Escape he
must.

After using all his strength in long-continued efforts,
he succeeded in loosening the bar of his bed-room window. He then took his two sheets, tied them together
in a firm knot, wound one end tightly round the remaining
bar, and let the other fall down the side of the building.
He took one more glance round his little room, and
then let himself down by the sheet, hand under hand,
until he could drop to the ground. Once safe, he ran
towards Starhaven as fast as he could, and felt as if he
were flying for his life. But when he got to the end
of the playground he could not help stopping to take
one more longing, lingering look at the scenes he was
leaving for ever. It was a chilly and overclouded

night, and by the gleams of struggling moonlight, he saw the whole buildings standing out black in the night air. The past lay behind him like a painting. Many and many unhappy or guilty hours had he spent in that home, and yet those last four years had not gone by without their own wealth of life and joy. He remembered how he had first walked across that playground, hand in hand with his father, a little boy of twelve. He remembered his first troubles with Barker, and how his father had at last delivered him from the annoyances of his old enemy. He remembered how often he and Russell had sat there, looking at the sea, in pleasant talk, especially the evening when he had got his first prize and head-remove in the lower fourth; and how, on the night of Russell's death, he had gazed over that playground from the sick-room window. He remembered how often he had got cheered there for his feats at cricket and football, and how often he and Upton in old days, and he and Wildney afterwards, had walked there on Sundays, arm in arm. Then the stroll to Fort Island, and Barker's plot against him, and the evening at the Stack, passed through his mind; and the dinner at the Jolly Herring and, above all, Vernon's death. Oh! how awful it seemed to him now, as he looked through the darkness at the very road along which they had brought Verny's dead body. Then his thoughts turned to the theft of the pigeons, his own drunkenness, and then his last cruel, cruel experiences, and this dreadful end of the day which, for an hour or two, had seemed so bright on that very spot where he stood. Could it be that this (oh, how little he had ever dreamed of it)—that this was to be the conclusion of his school days?

Yes, in those rooms, of which the windows fronted him, there they lay, all his schoolfellows—Montagu, and Wildney, and Duncan, and all whom he cared for best. And there was Mr. Rose's light still burning in the library window; and he was leaving the school and those who had been with him there so long, in the dark night, by stealth, penniless and broken-hearted, with the shameful character of a thief.

Suddenly Mr. Rose's light moved, and, fearing discovery or interception, he roused himself from the bitter reverie and fled to Starhaven through the darkness. There was still a light in the little sailor's tavern; and, entering, he asked the woman who kept it, "if she knew of any ship which was going to sail next morning?"

"Why, your'n is, bean't it, Maister Davey?" she asked, turning to a rough-looking sailor, who sat smoking in the bar.

"Ees," grunted the man.

"Will you take me on board?" said Eric.

"You be a runaway, I'm thinking?"

"Never mind. I'll come as cabin-boy—anything."

The sailor glanced at his striking appearance and neat dress. "Hardly in the cabun-buoy line I should say."

"Will you take me?" said Eric. "You'll find me strong and willing enough."

"Well—if the skipper don't say no. Come along."

They went down to a boat, and "Maister Davey" rowed to a schooner in the harbour, and took Eric on board.

"There," he said, "you may sleep there for to-night," and he pointed to a great heap of sailcloth beside the mast.

Weary to death, Eric flung himself down, and slept deep and sound till the morning, on board the "Stormy Petrel."

CHAPTER XII.

THE STORMY PETREL.

" They hadna sailed a league, a league,
　　A league, but barely three,
　　When the lift grew dark, and the wind grew high,
　　And gurly grew the sea."
　　　　　　　　　　SIR PATRICK SPENS.

ILLOA!" exclaimed the skipper with a sudden start, next morning, as he saw Eric's recumbent figure on the ratlin-stuff, " Who be this young varmint ? "

" Oh, I brought him aboord last night," said Davey; " he wanted to be cabun-buoy."

" Precious like un *he* looks.　Never mind, we've got him and we'll use him."

The vessel was under way when Eric woke, and collected his scattered thoughts to a remembrance of his new position.　At first, as the Stormy Petrel dashed its way gallantly through the blue sea, he felt one absorbing sense of joy to have escaped from Roslyn. But before he had been three hours on board, his eyes were opened to the trying nature of his circumstances, which were, indeed, *so* trying that *anything* in the world seemed preferable to enduring them. He had not been three hours on board when he would have given everything in his power to be back again; but such regrets were useless, for the vessel was now fairly on her way for Corunna, where she was to take in a cargo of cattle.

There were eight men belonging to the crew; and as the ship was only a little trading schooner, these were sailors of the lowest and coarsest grade. They all seemed to take their cue from the captain, who was a drunken, blaspheming, and cruel vagabond.

This man from the first took a savage hatred to Eric, partly because he was annoyed with Davey for bringing him on board. The first words he addressed to him were—

"I say, you young lubber, you must pay your footing."

"I've got nothing to pay with. I brought no money with me."

"Well, then, you shall give us your gran' clothes. Them things isn't fit for a cabin-boy."

Eric saw no remedy, and making a virtue of necessity, exchanged his good cloth suit for a rough sailor's shirt and trousers, not over clean, which the captain gave him. His own clothes were at once appropriated by that functionary, who carried them into his cabin. But it was lucky for Eric that, seeing how matters were likely to go, he had succeeded in secreting his watch.

The day grew misty and comfortless, and towards evening the wind rose to a storm. Eric soon began to feel very sick, and, to make his case worse, could not endure either the taste, smell, or sight of such coarse food as was contemptuously flung to him.

"Where am I to sleep?" he asked, "I feel very sick."

"Babby," said one of the sailors, "what's your name?"

"Williams."

"Well, Bill, you'll have to get over your sickness pretty soon, *I* can tell ye. Here," he added, relenting a little, "Davey's slung ye a hammock in the forecastle."

He showed the way, but poor Eric in the dark, and amid the lurches of the vessel, could hardly steady himself down the companion-ladder, much less get into his hammock. The man saw his condition, and, sulkily enough, hove him into his place.

And there, in that swinging bed, where sleep seemed impossible, and out of which he was often thrown, when the ship rolled and pitched through the dark, heaving, discoloured waves, and with dirty men sleeping round him at night, until the atmosphere of the forecastle became like poison, hopelessly and helplessly sick, and half-starved, the boy lay for two days. The crew neglected him shamefully. It was nobody's business to wait on him, and he could procure neither sufficient food, nor any water; they only brought him

some grog to drink, which in his weakness and sickness
was nauseous to him as medicine.

"I say, you young cub down there," shouted the
skipper to him from the hatchway, "come up and swab
this deck."

He got up, and after bruising himself severely, as
he stumbled about to find the ladder, made an effort to
obey the command. But he staggered from feebleness
when he reached the deck, and had to grasp for some
fresh support at every step.

"None of that 'ere slobbering and shamming, Bill.
Why, d—— you, what d'ye think you're here for, eh?
You swab this deck, and in five minutes, or I'll teach
you, and be d——d."

Sick as death, Eric slowly obeyed, but did not get
through his task without many blows and curses. He
felt very ill—he had no means of washing or cleaning
himself; no brush, or comb, or soap, or clean linen; and
even his sleep seemed unrefreshful when the waking
brought no change in his condition. And then the
whole life of the ship was odious to him. His sense of
refinement was exquisitely keen, and now to be called
Bill, and kicked and cuffed about by these gross-minded
men, and to hear their rough, coarse, drunken talk, and
sometimes endure their still more intolerable familiarities,
filled him with deeply-seated loathing. His whole
soul rebelled and revolted from them all, and, seeing
his fastidious pride, not one of them showed him the

least glimpse of open kindness, though he observed
that one of them did seem to pity him in heart.

Things grew worse and worse.. The perils which he
had to endure at first, when ordered about the rigging,
were what affected him least; he longed for death,
and often contemplated flinging himself into those cold
deep waves which he gazed on daily over the vessel's
side. Hope was the only thing which supported him.
He had heard from one of the crew that the vessel
would be back in not more than six weeks, and he
made a deeply-seated resolve to escape the very first
day that they again anchored in an English harbour.

The homeward voyage was even more intolerable,
for the cattle on board greatly increased the amount of
necessary menial and disgusting work which fell to his
share, as well as made the atmosphere of the close little
schooner twice as poisonous as before. And to add
to his miseries, his relations with the crew got more
and more unfavourable, and began to reach their
climax.

One night the sailor who occupied the hammock
next to his heard him winding up his watch. This he
always did in the dark, as secretly and silently as he
could, and never looked at it, except when no one could
observe him; while, during the day, he kept both watch
and chain concealed in his trousers.

Next morning the man made proposals to him to
sell the watch, and tried by every species of threat and
promise to extort it from him. But the watch had

been his mother's gift, and he was resolute never to part with it into such hands.

"Very well, you young shaver, I shall tell the skipper, and he'll soon get it out of you as your footing, depend on it."

The fellow was as good as his word, and the skipper demanded the watch as pay for Eric's feed, for he maintained that he'd done no work, and was perfectly useless. Eric, grown desperate, still refused, and the man struck him brutally on the face, and at the same time aimed a kick at him, which he vainly tried to avoid. It caught him on the knee-cap, and put it out, causing him the most excruciating agony.

He now could do no work whatever, not even swab the deck. It was only with difficulty that he could limp along, and every move caused him violent pain. He grew listless and dejected, and sat all day on the vessel's side, eagerly straining his eyes to catch any sight of land, or gazing vacantly into the weary sameness of sea and sky.

Once, when it was rather gusty weather, all hands were wanted, and the skipper ordered him to furl a sail.

"I can't," said Eric, in an accent of despair, barely stirring, and not lifting his eyes to the man's unfeeling face.

"Can't, d—— you. Can't. We'll soon see whether you can or no! You do it, or I shall have to mend your leg for you;" and he showered down a storm of oaths.

Eric rose, and resolutely tried to mount the rigging, determined at least to give no ground he could help to their wilful cruelty. But the effort was vain, and with a sharp cry of suffering he dropped once more on deck.

"Cursed young brat! I suppose you think we're going to bother ourselves with you, and yer impudence, and get victuals for nothing. It's all sham. Here, Jim, tie him up."

A stout sailor seized the unresisting boy, tied his hands together, and then drew them up above his head, and strung them to the rigging.

"Why didn't ye strip him first, d—— you?" roared the skipper.

"He's only got that blue shirt on, and that's soon mended," said the man, taking hold of the collar of the shirt on both sides, and tearing it open with a great rip.—

Eric's white back was bare, his hands tied up, his head hanging, and his injured leg slightly lifted from the ground. "And now for some rope-pie for the stubborn young lubber," said the skipper, lifting a bit of rope as he spoke.

Eric, with a shudder, heard it whistle through the air, and the next instant it had descended on his back with a dull thump, rasping away a red line of flesh. Now Eric knew for the first time the awful reality of intense pain; he had determined to utter no sound, to give no sign; but when the horrible rope fell on him, griding across his back, and making his body literally creak under the blow, he quivered like an aspen-leaf in every limb, and could not suppress the harrowing murmur, "O God, help me, help me."

Again the rope whistled in the air, again it grided across the boy's naked back, and once more the crimson furrow bore witness to the violent laceration. A sharp shriek of inexpressible agony rang from his lips, so shrill, so heart-rending, that it sounded long in the memory of all who heard it. But the brute who administered the torture was untouched. Once more, and again, the rope rose and fell, and under its marks the blood first dribbled, and then streamed from the white and tender skin.

But Eric felt no more; that scream had been the last effort of nature; his head had dropped on his bosom, and though his limbs still seemed to creep at the unnatural infliction, he had fainted away.

"Stop, master, stop, if you don't want to kill the boy outright," said Roberts, one of the crew, stepping forward, while the hot flush of indignation burned through his tanned and weather-beaten cheek. The sailors called him "Softy Bob," from that half-gentleness of disposition which had made him, alone of all the men, speak one kind or consoling word for the proud and lonely cabin-boy.

"Undo him then, and be ——," growled the skipper, and rolled off to drink himself drunk.

"I doubt he's well-nigh done for him already," said Roberts, quickly untying Eric's hands, round which the cords had been pulled so tight as to leave two blue rings round his wrists. "Poor fellow, poor fellow! it's all over now," he murmured soothingly, as the boy's body fell motionless into his arms, which he hastily stretched to prevent him from tumbling on the deck.

But Eric heard not; and the man, touched with the deepest pity, carried him down tenderly into his hammock, and wrapped him up in a clean blanket, and sat by him till the swoon should be over.

It lasted very long, and the sailor began to fear that his words had been prophetic.

" How is the young varmint?" shouted the skipper, looking into the forecastle.

" You've killed him, I think."

The only answer was a volley of oaths; but the fellow was sufficiently frightened to order Roberts to do all he could for his patient.

At last Eric woke with a moan. To think was too painful, but the raw state of his back, ulcerated with the cruelty he had undergone, reminded him too bitterly of his situation. Roberts did for him all that could be done, but for a week Eric lay in that dark and fetid place, in the languishing of absolute despair. Often and often the unbidden tears flowed from very weakness from his eyes, and in the sickness of his heart, and the torment of his wounded body, he thought that he should die.

But youth is very strong, and it wrestled with despair, and agony, and death, and, after a time, Eric could rise from his comfortless hammock. The news that land was in sight first roused him, and with the help of Roberts, he was carried on deck, thankful, with childlike gratitude, that God suffered him to breathe once more the pure air of heaven, and sit under the canopy of its gold-pervaded blue. The breeze and the sunlight refreshed him, as they might a broken flower; and, with eyes upraised, he poured from his heart a prayer of deep unspeakable thankfulness to a Father in Heaven.

Yes! at last he had remembered his Father's home. There, in the dark berth, where every move caused irritation, and the unclean atmosphere brooded over his senses like lead; when his forehead burned, and his heart melted within him, and he had felt almost inclined to curse his life, or even to end it by crawling up and committing himself to the deep cold water which he heard rippling on the vessel's side; then, even then, in that valley of the shadow of death, a Voice had come to him— a still small Voice—at whose holy and healing utterance Eric had bowed his head, and had listened to the messages of God, and learnt his will; and now, in humble resignation, in touching penitence, with solemn self-devotion, he had cast himself at the feet of Jesus, and prayed to be helped, and guided, and forgiven. One little star of hope rose in the darkness of his solitude, and its rays grew brighter and brighter, till they were glorious now. Yes, for Jesus' sake he was washed, he was cleansed, he was sanctified, he was justified; he would fear no evil, for God was with him, and underneath were the everlasting arms.

And while he sat there, undisturbed at last, and unmolested by harsh word or savage blow, recovering health with every breath of the sea wind, the skipper came up to him, and muttered something half-like an apology.

The sight of him, and the sound of his voice, made Eric shudder again, but he listened meekly, and, with no flash of scorn or horror, put out his hand to the man to shake. There was something touching and noble in the gesture, and, thoroughly ashamed of himself for once, the fellow shook the proffered hand, and slunk away.

They entered the broad river at Southpool.

" I must leave the ship when we get to port, Roberts," said Eric.

" I doubt whether yon'll let you," answered Roberts, jerking his finger towards the skipper's cabin.

" Why ? "

" He'll be afeard you might take the law on him."

" He needn't fear."

Roberts only shook his head.

" Then I must run away somehow. Will you help me ? "

" Yes, that I will."

That very evening Eric escaped from the Stormy Petrel, unknown to all but Roberts. They were in the dock, and he dropped into the water in the evening, and swam to the pier, which was only a yard or two distant ; but the effort almost exhausted his strength, for his knee was still painful, and he was very weak.

Wet and penniless, he knew not where to go, but spent the sleepless night under an arch. Early the next morning he went to a pawnbroker's, and raised £2 : 10s. on his watch, with which money he walked straight to the railway station.

It was July, and the Roslyn summer holidays had commenced. As Eric dragged his slow way to the station, he suddenly saw Wildney on the other side of the street. His first impulse was to spring to meet him, as he would have done in old times. His whole heart yearned towards him. It was six weeks now since Eric had seen one loving face, and during all that time he had hardly heard one kindly word. And now he saw before him the boy whom he loved so fondly, with whom he had spent so many happy hours of school-boy friendship, with whom he had gone through so many school-boy adventures, and who, he believed, loved him fondly still.

Forgetful for the moment of his condition, Eric moved across the street. Wildney was walking with his cousin, a beautiful girl, some four years older than himself, whom he was evidently patronising immensely. They were talking very merrily, and Eric overheard the word Roslyn. Like a lightning-flash the memory of the theft, the memory of his ruin came upon him; he looked down at his dress—it was a coarse blue shirt, which Roberts had given him in place of his old one, and the back of it was stained and saturated with blood from his unhealed wounds; his trousers were dirty,

tarred, and ragged, and his shoes, full of holes, barely
covered his feet.   He remembered too that for weeks
he had not been able to wash, and that very morning,
as he saw himself in a looking-glass at a shop-window,
he had been deeply shocked at his own appearance.
His face was white as a sheet, the fair hair matted and
tangled, the eyes sunken and surrounded with a dark
colour, and dead and lustreless.   No! he could not
meet Wildney as a sick and ragged sailor-boy; perhaps
even he might not be recognised if he did.   He drew
back, and hid himself till the merry-hearted pair had
passed, and it was almost with a pang of jealousy that
he saw how happy Wildney could be, while *he* was
thus; but he cast aside the unworthy thought at once.
"After all, how is poor Charlie to know what has
happened to me?"

CHAPTER XIII.

HOME AT LAST.

" I will arise and go to my Father."

———

" Ach! ein Schicksal droht,
Und es droht nicht lange!
Auf der holden Wange
Brennt ein böses Roth!"—TIEDGE.

ERIC Williams pursued his disconsolate way to the station, and found that his money only just sufficed to get him something to eat during the day, and carry him third class by the parliamentary train to Charlesbury, the little station where he had to take the branch line to Ayrton.

He got into the carriage, and sat in the far corner, hiding himself from notice as well as he could. The weary train—(it carried poor people for the most part, so, of course it could matter but little how tedious or slow it was!)—the weary train, stopping at every station, and often waiting on the rail until it had been passed by trains that started four or five hours after it,—dragged its slow course through the fair counties of England. Many people got in and out of the carriage,

which was generally full, and some of them tried occasionally to enter into conversation with him.   But poor
Eric was too sick, and tired, and his heart was too full
to talk much, and he contented himself with civil
answers to the questions put to him, dropping the
conversation as soon as he could.

At six in the evening the train stopped at Charlesbury, and he got down.

"Ticket," said the station-man.

Eric gave it, turning his head away, for the man
knew him well from having often seen him there.   It
was no use; the man looked hard at him, and then,
opening his eyes wide, exclaimed,

"Well, I never! what, Master Williams of Fairholm, can that be you?"

"Hush John, hush! yes, I am Eric Williams.
But don't say a word, that's a good fellow; I'm going
on to Ayrton this evening."

"Well sir, I *am* hurt like to see you looking so
ragged and poorly.   Let me give you a bed to-night,
and send you on by first train to-morrow."

"O no, thank you, John.   I've got no money,
and——"

"Tut, tut sir; I thought you'd know me better nor
that.   Proud I'd be any day to do anything for Mrs.
Trevor's nephew, let alone a young gentleman like you.
Well, then, let me drive you, sir, in my little cart this
evening."

"No, thank you, John, never mind; you are very,

very good, but," he said, and the tears were in his eyes, "I want to walk in alone to-night."

"Well, God keep and bless you, sir," said the man, "for you look to need it;" and touching his cap, he watched the boy's painful walk across some fields to the main road.

"Who'd ha' thought it, Jenny?" he said to his wife. "There's that young Master Williams, whom we've always thought so noble like, just been here as ragged as ragged, and with a face the colour o' my white signal flag."

"Lawks!" said the woman; "well well! poor young gentleman, I'm afeard he's been doing something bad."

Balmily and beautiful the evening fell, as Eric, not without toil, made his way along the road towards Ayrton, which was ten miles off. The road wound through the valley, across the low hills that encircled it, sometimes spanning or running parallel to the bright stream that had been the delight of Eric's innocent childhood. There was something enjoyable at first to the poor boy's eyes, so long accustomed to the barren sea, in resting once more on the soft undulating green of the summer fields, which were intertissued with white and yellow flowers, like a broidery of pearls and gold. The whole scene was bathed in the exquisite light, and rich with the delicate perfumes of a glorious evening, which filled the sky over his head with every perfect gradation of rose and amber and amethyst, and breathed over the quiet landscape a sensation of unbroken peace. But peace did not remain long in Eric's heart; each well-remembered landmark filled his soul with recollections of the days when he had returned from school, oh! how differently; and of the last time when he had come home with Vernon by his side. "Oh Verny, Verny, noble little Verny, would to God that I were with you now. But you are resting, Verny, in the green grave by Russell's side, and I—oh God be merciful to me now!"

It was evening, and the stars came out and shone by hundreds, and Eric walked on by the moonlight. But the exertion had brought on the pain in his knee, and he had to sit down a long time by the road-side to rest. He reached Ayrton at ten o'clock, but even then he could not summon up courage to pass through the town where he was so well known, lest any straggler should recognise him,—and he took a detour in order to get to Fairholm. He did not arrive there till eleven o'clock; and then he could not venture into the grounds, for he saw through the trees of the shrubbery that there was no light in any of the windows, and it was clear that they were all gone to bed.

What was he to do? He durst not disturb them so late at night. He remembered that they would not have heard a syllable of or from him since he had run away from Roslyn, and he feared the effect of so sudden an emotion as his appearance at that hour might excite.

So under the star-light he lay down to sleep on a

cold bank beside the gate, determining to enter early in the morning. It was long before he slept, but at last weary nature demanded her privilege with importunity, and gentle sleep floated over him like a dark dewy cloud, and the sun was high in heaven before he woke.

It was about half-past nine in the morning, and Mrs. Trevor, with Fanny, was starting to visit some of her poor neighbours, an occupation full of holy pleasure to her kind heart, and in which she had found more than usual consolation during the heavy trials which she had recently suffered; for she had loved Eric and Vernon as a mother does her own children, and now Vernon, the little cherished jewel of her heart, was dead—Vernon was dead, and Eric, she feared, not dead but worse than dead, guilty, stained, dishonoured. Often had she thought to herself, in deep anguish of heart, "Our darling little Vernon dead—and Eric fallen and ruined!"

"Look at that poor fellow asleep on the grass," said Fanny, pointing to a sailor boy, who lay coiled up on the bank beside the gate. "He has had a rough bed, mother, if he has spent the night there, as I fear."

Mrs. Trevor had grasped her arm. "What is Flo' doing?" she said, stopping, as the pretty little spaniel trotted up to the boy's reclining figure, and began snuffing about it, and then broke into a quick short bark of pleasure, and fawned and frisked about him, and leapt upon him, joyously wagging his tail.

The boy rose with the dew wet from the flowers

upon his hair;—he saw the dog, and at once began
playfully to fondle it, and hold its little silken head
between his hands; but as yet he had not caught sight
of the Trevors.

"It is—oh, good heavens! it is Eric," cried Mrs.
Trevor, as she flew towards him. Another moment
and he was in her arms, silent, speechless, with long
arrears of pent-up emotion.

"O my Eric, our poor, lost, wandering Eric—come
home; you are forgiven, more than forgiven, my own
darling boy. Yes, I knew that my prayers would be
answered; this is as though we received you from the
dead." And the noble lady wept upon his neck, and
Eric, his heart shaken with accumulated feelings, clung
to her and wept.

Deeply did that loving household rejoice to receive
back their lost child. At once they procured him a
proper dress, and a warm bath, and tended him with
every gentle office of female ministering hands. And
in the evening, when he told them his story in a broken
voice of penitence and remorse, their love came to him
like a sweet balsam, and he rested by them, " seated,
and clothed, and in his right mind."

The pretty little room, fragrant with sweet flowers
from the greenhouse, was decorated with all the refinement of womanly taste, and its glass doors opened on
the pleasant garden. It was long, long since Eric had
ever seen anything like it, and he had never hoped to
see it again. " Oh dearest aunty," he murmured, as he

rested his weary head upon her lap, while he sate on a low stool at her feet, " O aunty, you will never know how different this is from the foul horrible hold of the ' Stormy Petrel,' and its detestable inmates."

When Eric was dressed once more as a gentleman, and once more fed on nourishing and wholesome food, and was able to move once more about the garden by Fanny's side, he began to recover his old appearance, and the soft bloom came back to his cheek again, and the light to his blue eye. But still his health gave most serious cause for apprehension; weeks of semi-starvation, bad air, sickness, and neglect, followed by two nights of exposure and wet, had at last undermined the remarkable strength of his constitution, and the Trevors soon became aware of the painful fact that he was sinking to the grave, and had come home only to die.

Above all, there seemed to be some great load at his heart which he could not remove; a sense of shame, the memory of his disgrace at Roslyn, and of the dark suspicion that rested on his name. He avoided the subject, and they were too kind to force it on him, especially as he had taken away the bitterest part of their trial in remembering it, by explaining to them that he was far from being so wicked in the matter of the theft as they had at first been (how slowly and reluctantly!) almost forced to believe.

" Have you ever heard—oh, how shall I put it?— have you ever heard, aunty, how things went on at

Roslyn after I ran away?" he asked one evening, with evident effort.

"No, love, I have not. After they had sent home your things, I heard no more; only two most kind and excellent letters—one from Dr. Rowlands, and one from your friend Mr. Rose—informed me of what had happened about you."

"O, have they sent home my things?" he asked eagerly. "There are very few among them that I care about, but there is just one ——"

"I guessed it, my Eric, and, but that I feared to agitate you, should have given it you before;" and she drew out of a drawer the little likeness of Vernon's sweet childish face.

Eric gazed at it till the sobs shook him, and tears blinded his eyes.

"Do not weep, my boy," said Mrs. Trevor, kissing his forehead. "Dear little Verny, remember, is in a land where God himself wipes away all tears from off all eyes."

"Is there anything else you would like?" asked Fanny, to divert his painful thoughts. "I will get you anything in a moment."

"Yes, Fanny dear, there is the medal I got for saving Russell's life, and one or two things which he gave me;—ah, poor Edwin, you never knew him!"

He told her what to fetch, and when she brought them it seemed to give him great pleasure to recal his friends to mind by name, and speak of them—especially of Montagu and Wildney.

"I have a plan to please you, Eric," said Mrs. Trevor. " Shall I ask Montagu and Wildney here? we have plenty of room for them."

" O, thank you," he said, with the utmost eagerness. " Thank you, dearest aunt." Then suddenly his countenance fell. " Stop—shall we?—yes, yes, I am going to die soon, I know; let me see them before I die."

The Trevors did not know that he was aware of the precarious tenure of his life, but they listened to him in silence, and did not contradict him; and Mrs. Trevor wrote to both the boys (whose directions Eric knew), telling them what had happened, and begging them, simply for his sake, to come and stay with her for a time. She hinted clearly that it might be the last opportunity they would ever have of seeing him.

Wildney and Montagu accepted the invitation; and they arrived together at Fairholm on one of the early autumn evenings. They both greeted Eric with the utmost affection; and he seemed never tired of pressing their hands, and looking at them again. Yet every now and then a memory of sadness would pass over his face, like a dark ripple on the clear surface of a lake.

" Tell me, Monty," he said one evening, " all about what happened after I left Roslyn."

" Gladly, Eric; now that your name is cleared, there is ——"

" My name cleared!" said Eric, leaning forward eagerly. " Did you say that?"

"Yes, Eric.   Didn't you know, then, that the thief had been discovered?"

"No," he murmured faintly, leaning back again; "O, thank God, thank God!   Do tell me all about it, Monty."

"Well, Eric, I will tell you all from the beginning. You may guess how utterly astonished we were in the morning, when we heard that you had run away. Wildney here was the first to discover it, for he went early to your bed-room ——"

"Dear little Sunbeam," interrupted Eric, resting his hand against Wildney's cheek; but Wildney shook his fist at him when he heard the forbidden name.

"He found the door locked," continued Montagu, "and called to you, but there came no answer; this made us suspect the truth, and we were certain of it when some one caught sight of the pendent sheet.   The masters soon heard the report, and sent Carter to make inquiries, but they did not succeed in discovering anything definite about you.   Then, of course, everybody assumed as a certainty that you were guilty, and I fear that my bare assertion on the other side had little weight."

Eric's eyes glistened as he drank in his friend's story.

"But, about a fortnight after, *more* money ·and several other articles disappeared from the studies, and all suspicion as to the perpetrator was baffled; only now the boys began to admit that, after all, they had been premature in condemning you.   It was a miserable time; for every one was full of distrust, and the more nervous boys were always afraid lest any one should on some slight grounds suspect *them*. *Still*, things kept disappearing.

"We found out at length that the time when the robberies were effected must be between twelve and one, and it was secretly agreed that some one should be concealed in the studies for a day or two during those hours. Carter undertook the office, and was ensconced in one of the big cupboards in a study which had not yet been touched. On the third day he heard some one stealthily mount the stairs. The fellows were more careful now, and used to keep their doors shut, but the person was provided with keys, and opened the study in which Carter was. He moved about for a little time—Carter watching him through the key-hole, and prepared to spring on him before he could make his escape. Not getting much, the man at last opened the cupboard door, where Carter had just time to conceal himself behind a great-coat. The great-coat took the plunderer's fancy; he took it down off the peg, and —there stood Carter before him! Billy—for it was he —stood absolutely confounded, as though a ghost had suddenly appeared; and Carter, after enjoying his unconcealed terror, collared him, and hauled him off to the police station. He was tried soon after, and finally confessed that it was he who had taken the cricket-money too; for which offences he was sentenced to transportation. So Eric, dear Eric, at last your name was cleared."

" As I always knew it would be, dear old boy,"
said Wildney.

Montagu and Wildney found plenty to make them
happy at Fairholm, and were never tired of Eric's
society, and of his stories about all that befel him on
board the " Stormy Petrel." They perceived a marvellous change in him. Every trace of recklessness and
arrogance had passed away; every stain of passion had
been removed; every particle of hardness had been
calcined in the flame of trial. All was gentleness, love,
and dependence, in the once bright, impetuous, self-willed
boy; it seemed as though the lightning of God's anger
had shattered and swept away all that was evil in his
heart and life, and left all his true excellence, all the
royal prerogatives of his character, pure and unscathed.
Eric, even in his worst days, was, as I well remember,
a loveable and noble boy; but at this period there must
have been something about him for which to thank
God, something unspeakably winning, and irresistibly
attractive. During the day, as Eric was too weak to
walk with them, Montagu and Wildney used to take
boating and fishing excursions by themselves, but in
the evening the whole party would sit out reading and
talking in the garden till twilight fell. The two visitors
began to hope that Mrs. Trevor had been mistaken, and
that Eric's health would still recover; but Mrs. Trevor
would not deceive herself with a vain hope, and the
boy himself shook his head when they called him con-
valescent.

Their hopes were never higher than one evening about a week after their arrival, when they were all seated, as usual, in the open air, under a lime-tree on the lawn. The sun was beginning to set, and the rain of golden sunlight fell over them through the green ambrosial foliage of the tree, whose pale blossoms were still murmurous with bees. Eric was leaning back in an easy chair, with Wildney sitting on the grass, cross-legged at his feet, while Montagu, resting on one of the mossy roots, read to them the "Midsummer Night's Dream," and the ladies were busy with their work.

"There—stop now," said Eric, "and let's sit out and talk until we see some of 'the fiery a'es and o'es of light' which he talks of."

"I'd no idea Shakspeare was such immensely jolly reading," remarked Wildney naïvely. "I shall take to reading him through when I get home."

"Do you remember, Eric," said Montagu, "how Rose used to chaff us in old days for our ignorance of literature, and how indignant we used to be when he asked if we'd ever heard of an obscure person called William Shakspeare?"

"Yes, very well," answered Eric, laughing heartily. And in this strain they continued to chat merrily, while the ladies enjoyed listening to their school-boy mirth.

"What a perfectly delicious evening. It's almost enough to make me wish to live," said Eric.

He did not often speak thus; and it made them sad. But Eric half sang, half murmured to himself, a hymn with which his mother's sweet voice had made him familiar in their cottage-home at Ellan :—

> " There is a calm for those who weep,
>   A rest for weary pilgrims found ;
> They softly lie, and sweetly sleep,
>   Low in the ground.
>
> " The storm that wrecks the winter sky,
>   No more disturbs their deep repose,
> Than summer evening's latest sigh
>   That shuts the rose."

The last two lines lingered pleasantly in his fancy, and he murmured to himself again, in low tones—

> " Than summer evening's latest sigh
>   That shuts the rose."

" Oh hush, hush, Eric !" said Wildney, laying his hand upon his friend's lips ; " don't let's spoil to-night by forebodings."

It seemed, indeed, a shame to do so, for it was almost an awful thing to be breathing the splendour of the transparent air, as the sun broadened and fell, and a faint violet glow floated over soft meadow and silver stream.   One might have fancied that the last rays of sunshine loved to linger over Eric's face, now flushed with a hectic tinge of pleasure, and to light up sudden glories in his bright hair, which the wind just fanned off his forehead as he leaned back and inhaled the luxury of evening perfume, which the flowers of the garden poured on the gentle breeze.   Ah, how sad that such scenes should be so rare and so short-lived !

" Hark—tirra-la-lirra-lirra!" said Wildney; "there goes the postman's horn! Shall I run and get the letter-bag as he passes the gate?"

" Yes, do," they all cried; and the boy bounded off full of fun, greeting the postman with such a burst of merry apostrophe, that the man shook with laughing at him.

" Here it is at last," said Wildney. " Now, then, for the key. Here's a letter for me, hurrah!—two for you, Miss Trevor—*what* people you young ladies are for writing to each other! None for you, Monty— Oh, yes! I'm wrong, here's one; but none for Eric."

" I expected none," said Eric, sighing; but his eye was fixed earnestly on one of Mrs. Trevor's letters. He saw that it was from India, and directed in his father's hand.

Mrs. Trevor caught his look. " Shall I read it aloud to you, dear? Do you think you can stand it? Remember it will be in answer to ours, telling them of ——"

" Oh, yes, yes," he said eagerly, "do let me hear it."

With instinctive delicacy Montagu and Wildney rose, but Eric pressed them to stay. " It will help me to bear what mother says, if I see you by me," he pleaded.

God forbid that I should transcribe that letter. It was written from the depths of such sorrow as He only can fully sympathize with, who for thirty years pitched his tent in the valley of human misery. By the former

S

mail Mrs. Williams had heard of Verny's melancholy death; by the next she had been told that her only other child, Eric, was, not dead indeed, but a wandering outcast, marked with the brand of terrible suspicion. Let her agony be sacred; it was God who sent it, and he only enabled her to endure it. With bent head, and streaming eyes, and a breast that heaved involuntarily with fitful sobs, Eric listened as though to his mother's voice, and only now and then he murmured low to himself, " O mother, mother, mother—but I am forgiven now. O mother, God and man have forgiven me, and we shall be at peace again once more."

Mrs. Trevor's eyes grew too dim with weeping, to read it all, and Fanny finished it. " Here is a little note from your father, Eric, which dropped out when we opened dear aunt's letter. Shall I read it, too."

" Perhaps not now, love," said Mrs. Trevor. " Poor Eric is too tired and excited already."

" Well, then, let me glance it myself, aunty," he said. He opened it, read a line or two, and then, with a scream, fell back swooning, while it dropped out of his hands.

Terrified, they picked up the fallen paper; it told briefly, in a few heartrending words, that, after writing the letter, Mrs. Williams had been taken ill; that her life was absolutely despaired of, and that, before the letter reached England, she would, in all human probability, be dead. It conveyed the impression of a soul resigned indeed, and humble, but crushed down to the very earth with the load of mysterious bereavement and irretrievable sorrow.

"Oh, I have killed her, I have killed my mother!" said Eric, in a hollow voice, when he came to himself. "O God, forgive me, forgive me!"

They gathered round him; they soothed, and comforted, and prayed for him; but his soul refused comfort, and all his strength appeared to have been broken down at once like a feeble reed. At last a momentary energy returned; his eyes were lifted to the gloaming heaven where a few stars had already begun to shine, and a bright look illuminated his countenance. They listened deeply—"Yes, mother," he murmured, in broken tones, "forgiven now, for Christ's dear sake. O thou merciful God! Yes, there they are, and we shall meet again. Verny—oh, happy, happy at last—too happy!"

The sounds died away, and his head fell back; for a transient moment more the smile and the brightness played over his fair features like a lambent flame. It passed away, and Eric was with those he dearliest loved, in the land where there is no more curse.

"Yes, dearest Eric, forgiven and happy now," sobbed Mrs. Trevor; and her tears fell fast upon the dead boy's face, as she pressed upon it a long, last kiss.

But Montagu, as he consoled the poignancy of Wildney's grief, was reminded by Mrs. Trevor's words of that sweet German verse,

"Dach fonft an keinem orte
Wohnt die erfehute Ruh;
Nur durch die dunkle Pforte
Geht man der Heimath zu."

CHAPTER XIV.

CONCLUSION.

"And hath that early hope been blessed with truth?
  Hath he fulfilled the promise of his youth?
  And borne unscathed through danger's stormy field
  Honour's white wreath and virtue's stainless shield?"

HARROW. A Prize Poem.

THE other day I was staying with Montagu. He has succeeded to his father's estate, and is the best-loved landlord for miles around. He intends to stand for the county at the next general election, and I haven't the shadow of a doubt that he will succeed. If he does, Parliament will have gained a worthy addition. Montagu has the very soul of honour, and he can set off the conclusions of his vigorous judgment, and the treasures of his cultivated taste, with an eloquence that rises to extraordinary grandeur when he is fulminating his scorn at any species of tyranny or meanness.

It was very pleasant to talk with him about our old school days in his charming home. We sate by the open window (which looks over his grounds, and then across one of the richest plains in England) one long summer evening, recalling all the vanished scenes and figures of the past, until we almost felt ourselves boys again.

" I have just been staying at Trinity," said I, " and Owen, as I suppose you know, is doing brilliantly. He has taken a high first class, and they have already elected him fellow and assistant tutor."

" Is he liked ? "

" Yes, very much. He always used to strike me at school as one of those fellows who are much more likely to be happy and successful as men, than they had ever any chance of being as boys. I hope the *greatest* things of him ; but have you heard anything of Duncan lately ? "

" Yes, he 's just been gazetted as lieutenant. I had a letter from him the other day. He 's met two old Roslyn fellows, Wildney and Upton, the latter of whom in now Captain Upton ; he says that there are not two finer or manlier officers in the whole service, and Wildney, as you may easily guess, is the favourite of the mess-room. You know, I suppose, that Graham is making a great start at the bar."

" Is he ? I 'm delighted to hear it."

" Yes. He had a ' mauvais sujet ' to defend the other day, in the person of our old enemy Brigson, who, having been at last disowned by his relations, is at present a policeman in London."

" On the principle, I suppose, of ' Set a thief to catch a thief,'" said Montagu, with a smile.

" Yes ; but he exemplifies the truth ' chassez le naturel, il revient au galop ;' for he was charged with abetting a street fight between two boys, which very nearly ended fatally. However, he was penitent, and Graham got him off with wonderful cleverness."

" Ah !" said Montagu, sighing, " there was *one* who would have been the pride of Roslyn had he lived. Poor, poor Eric !"

We talked long of our loved friend ; his bright face, his winning words, his merry smile, came back to us with the memory of his melancholy fate, and a deep sadness fell over us.

" Poor boy, he is at peace now," said Montagu ; and he told me once more the sorrowful particulars of his death. " Shall I read you some verses," he asked, " which he must have composed, poor fellow, on board the ' Stormy Petrel,' though he probably wrote them at Fairholm afterwards."

" Yes, do."

And Montagu, in his pleasant musical voice, read me, with much feeling, these lines, written in Eric's boyish hand, and signed with his name.

ALONE, YET NOT ALONE.

Alone, alone ! ah, weary soul,
  In all the world alone I stand,
With none to wed their hearts to mine.
  Or link in mine a loving hand.

Ah ! tell me not that I have those
  Who own the ties of blood and name ;
Or pitying friends who love me well,
  And dear returns of friendship claim.

I have, I have ! but none can heal,
  And none shall see my inward woe,
And the deep thoughts within me veiled
  No other heart but mine shall know.

And yet amid my sins and shames
  The shield of God is o'er me thrown ;
And, 'neath its awful shade I feel
  Alone,—yet, ah, not all alone !

Not all alone ! and though my life
  Be dragged along the stained earth,
O God ! I feel thee near me still,
  And thank thee for my birth !
                    E. W.

Montagu gave me the paper, and I cherish it as my dearest memorial of my erring but noble schoolboy friend.

Knowing how strong an interest Mr. Rose always took in Eric, I gave him a copy of these verses when last I visited him at his pleasant vicarage of Seaford, to which he was presented a year or two ago by Dr. Rowlands, now Bishop of Roslyn, who has also appointed him examining chaplain. I sat and watched Mr. Rose while he read them. A mournful interest was depicted on his 'face, his hand trembled a little, and I fancied that he bent his grey hair over the paper to hide a tear. We always knew at school that Eric was one of his greatest favourites, as indeed he and Vernon were with all of us; and when the unhappy boy had run away without even having the opportunity for bidding any one farewell, Mr. Rose displayed such real grief, that for weeks he was like a man who went mourning for a son.   After those summer holidays, when we returned to school, Montagu and Wildney brought back with them the intelligence of Eric's return to Fairholm, and of his death.   The news plunged many of us in sorrow, and when, on the first Sunday in chapel, Mr. Rose alluded to this sad tale, there were few dry eyes among those who listened to him.   I shall never forget that Sunday afternoon.   A deep hush brooded over us, and before the sermon was over, many a face was hidden to conceal the emotion which could not be suppressed.

"I speak," said Mr. Rose, "to a congregation of mourners, for one who but a few weeks back was sitting among you as one of yourselves.   But, for myself, I do *not*-mourn over his death.   Many a time have I mourned for him in past days, when I marked how widely he went astray,—but I do not mourn now; for after his fiery trials he died penitent and happy, and at last his sorrows are over for ever, and the dreams of ambition have vanished, and the fires of passion have been quenched, and for all eternity the young soul is in the presence of its God.   Let none of you think that his life has been wasted.   Possibly, had it pleased heaven to spare him, he might have found great works to do among his fellow-men, and he would have done them as few else could. But do not let us fancy that our work must cease of necessity with our lives. Not so; far rather must we believe that it will continue for ever, seeing that we are all partakers of God's unspeakable blessing, the common mystery of immortality. Perhaps it may be the glorious destiny of very many here to recognise that truth more fully when we meet and converse with our dear departed brother in a holier and happier world."

I have preserved some faint echo of the words he used, but I can give no conception of the dignity and earnestness of his manner, or the intense pathos of his tones.

The scene passed before me again as I looked at him, while he lingered over Eric's verses, and seemed lost in a reverie of thought.

At last he looked up and sighed. "Poor Eric!— But no, I will not call him poor; after all he is happier now than we. You loved him well," he continued; "why do you not try and preserve some records of his life?"

The suggestion took me by surprise, but I thought over it, and at once began to accomplish it. My own reminiscences of Eric were numerous and vivid, and several of my old schoolfellows and friends gladly supplied me with other particulars, especially the Bishop of Roslyn, Mr. Rose, Montagu, and Wildney. So the story of Eric's ruin has been told, and told as he would have wished it done, with simple truth. Noble Eric!

I do not fear that I have wronged your memory, and you I know would rejoice to think how sorrowful hours have lost something of their sorrow, as I wrote the scenes in so many of which we were engaged together in our school-boy days.

I visited Roslyn a short time ago, and walked for hours along the sands, picturing in my memory the pleasant faces, and recalling the joyous tones of the many whom I had known and loved. Other boys were playing by the sea-side, who were strangers to me and I to them; and as I marked how wave after wave rolled up the shore, with its murmur and its foam, each sweeping farther than the other, each effacing the traces of the last, I saw an emblem of the passing generations, and was content to find that my place knew me no more.

> Ah me! the golden time!—
>   But its hours have passed away,
> With the pure and bracing clime,
>   And the bright and merry day.
> And the sea still laughs to the rosy shells ashore,
>   And the shore still shines in the lustre of the wave;
> But the joyaunce and the beauty of the boyish days is o'er,
>   And many of the beautiful lie quiet in the grave;—
>   And he who comes again
>   Wears a brow of toil and pain,
> And wanders sad and silent by the melancholy main.

FINIS.

ΤΩ ΘΕΩ ΔΟΞΑ.